The King Invites You To His Table

Revealing the Biblical festivals in your life

By

Dr. David E. Jones

The King Invites You To His Table

Revealing the Biblical festivals in your life

By Dr. David E. Jones

Cover by David Jones, Faith Jones and Parry Design

Published by Ruach Ministries Int'l.

P.O. Box 6370

Brandon, FL 33508

Dedication

This book is dedicated to my endearing, beloved wife Faith and our wonderful children, Yakira, Joshua and Hannah. I would not have been able to finish this book if it had not been for your sacrifices and support. I truly am blessed to have you all in my life.

<u>Special Thanks</u>

First, foremost and above all, I desire to thank my Savior, Messiah and Shield, Yeshua. I also would like to thank all in the congregation of Ruach Ministries International for your generous love, prayers and support. A pastor could not ask for a better congregation. I also desire to thank a man and woman of YHWH that is always an encouragement and strength to me continually, Pastor Curtis and Karen Taylor. I thank Alan and Eileen Westfall for their commitment to this work. May YHWH continue to bless you in your heart for His people. Last but not least, I want to thank all those who gave their prayer and support without which this book would not be possible.

Table of Contents

Introduction...ii

Glossary of Terms v

Chapter One

      Appointed Times 1

Chapter Two

      Passover...29

Chapter Three

      A Messianic Seder 63

Chapter Four

      Unleavened Bread 103

Chapter Five

      FirstFruits 115

Chapter Six

      Shavuot (Pentecost) 129

Chapter Seven

      Yom Teruah (Day of Trumpets) 173

Chapter Eight

      Yom Kippur (Day of Atonement)............202

Chapter Nine

      Sukkot (Feat of Tabernacles)..................259

Bibliography 291

Introduction

When you think of building a relationship with someone, what is the first thing that comes to mind? In the list of things that you thought of, I am sure that somewhere near the top of the list is "spending time with someone" and "getting to know someone." It is no different in the relationship we have with our heavenly Father.

Our heavenly Father desires to spend time with His people. We know that we can all have a personal close relationship with our Father in Yeshua, our Messiah. It is a necessity of our faith to pray continually and to study the living Word of YHWH. As we examine the Word we will see that not only can we come to the King any and every day, but there are times and seasons in our walk that have been fore-ordained by the Father to reveal certain things at specific times.

Have you ever read the Word and discovered something that you had never seen before? It was there all along. Why didn't we see it earlier? The answer is, we didn't see it because it was concealed. The things that are concealed belong to the LORD. The great thing is that as we search out the Word we walk in a progressive revelation of our heavenly Father. In other words, He reveals Himself to His people at the appropriate time.

Proverbs 25:2
It is the glory of God to conceal a thing: but the honour of kings is to search out a matter.

1 Corinthians 13:11-12

(11) When I was a child, I spake as a child, I understood as a child, I thought as a child: but when I became a man, I put away childish things.

(12) For now we see through a glass, darkly; but then face to face: now I know in part; but then shall I know even as also I am known.

As we grow in our faith, we are growing in our relationship with our Heavenly Father. In this process, we learn more about Him. We come to see Him for who He says He is, not what we have thought He was. First impressions are not always correct. Especially if someone else told you what your first impression was without ever meeting who they were talking about.

Our heavenly Father has chosen to lay out certain times and seasons with His people for the purpose of drawing them closer and empowering them to live an overcoming life here on Earth. These times in Scripture are called "Moedim" in Hebrew. The definition of the word moedim is, set appointed times.

We have been given appointments with the King of kings and LORD of Lords. These times throughout Scripture are prophetic in their nature. They reveal the work of the Messiah and show how the people of YHWH are equipped to walk in this life victoriously. If the King says that He wants to have an appointment with us, will we be faithful to prepare for the time appointed?

It is the prayer of this author that by the time you finish this book that you will have a deeper understanding of the work that Yeshua, our Messiah, has done in your life. That as you search out the Scriptures, you will see that the appointed times that were given to the people of YHWH were given as appointments with the creator of heaven and earth. In these appointments, we find strength in our LORD and grow in our faith.

May we continue to grow in the wisdom, knowledge and understanding that can only come from our heavenly Father, through Yeshua our Messiah, by His Ruach HaKodesh.

Amen.

Dr. David E. Jones

Glossary Of Terms

There is some terminology that will be used in this book that you may or may not be familiar with. I will list some of them here so that you will better understand what you are reading. When referring to the Name of God, I will use the names given in the Hebrew texts. I will use YHWH, Yahweh, LORD or Adonai in place of "God". I will also use Yeshua or Yahshua in place of Jesus.

The Scriptures used to quote from most often in this book is "The Hebrew Names Version". It will place a transliteration (the sounding out) of a word from the Hebrew text for certain names, words or customs. A definition of these words are as follows.

Hebrew	Definition	Hebrew	Definition
Echad	Unified one	Shabbat (Shabbatot)	Sabbath(s)
Elohim	A name for God	Shaul	The Apostle Paul
Kohen (cohen)	Priest	Tanakh	Old Testament
Kohen Gadol	High Priest	Torah	Teaching and Instruction
Matzah	Unleavened bread	Tzitzit (Tzitziyot)	Fringes
Mitzvah (Mitzvot)	Command(s)	Tziyon	Zion
Mikvah	Ritual baptism	Ya'akov	Jacob (Israel)
Moshe	Moses	Yehudah	Judah
Perushim	Pharisees	Yisrael	Israel
Ruach HaKodesh	Holy Spirit	Yitzchak	Isaac

Appointed times
of the LORD

Did God set aside certain days for specific purposes?

What are the Biblical Feasts in Scripture?

What is a mô'êd?

What did God call them?

Who did He give them to?

How are they observed?

Did Jesus (Yeshua in Hebrew) observe them?

Are they still relevant?

By the end of this reading these questions and more will be addressed.

Did God, the creator of Heaven and Earth, set aside certain days and times for specific purposes?

Of the Messiah Scripture says;

Galatians 4:4
> But when the fulness of the time was come, God sent forth his Son, made of a woman, made under the law,

Concerning the birth of Isaac:

Genesis 18:14
> Is any thing too hard for the LORD? At the time appointed I will return unto thee, according to the time of life, and Sarah shall have a son.

Job speaks of the time of man

Job 7:1
> *Is there* not an appointed time to man upon earth? *are not* his days also like the days of an hireling?

Job 14:13-14
> (13) O that thou wouldest hide me in the grave, that thou wouldest keep me secret, until thy wrath be past, that thou wouldest appoint me a set time, and remember me!
> (14) If a man die, shall he live *again?* all the days of my appointed time will I wait, till my change come.

Daniel testifies of an appointed time for the end

Daniel 8:19
> And he said, Behold, I will make thee know what shall be in the last end of the indignation: for at the time appointed the end *shall be.*

The feasts of YHWH are set appointed times for His people. These are times that were given to understand what the Father desires for His people. All of the Moedim (appointed times) speak prophetically and straight to the heart of a people set apart and called by His Name.

Let's start with a couple questions to help us lay a foundation to understanding these appointed times.

The feasts of YHWH
• What are they?
• Who do they belong to?
• Why were they given?

We will discuss this in more detail throughout this reading. For now we will give a short answer, broken down for emphasis, as found in Leviticus 23:1-2.
- And the LORD spake unto Moses, saying,
- (2) Speak unto the children of Israel, and say unto them,
- Concerning the feasts of the LORD,
- which ye shall proclaim
- to be holy convocations,
- even these are my feasts.

The feasts of the LORD are also called Moedim. Which leads to the next question, what is a Moed?

A moed is defined in the Strongs concordance as a Designated time. It is the Strongs word H4150.

מוֹעֵד   מעֵד   מוֹעֵדה
mô'âdâh   mô'êd   mô'êd
an appointment, a fixed time or season; a festival; an assembly (as convened for a definite purpose); appointed (sign, time), (set, solemn) feast, (appointed, due) season, set time appointed

The Hebrew language is rich. It is a verb oriented language, the emphasis is action. Each letter in the Hebrew Alef-Beit has a meaning all on its own. Ancient Paleo-Hebrew was originally pictographs. Each letter was a picture, each picture represented something. One was to take the pictures, put the actions together to form a function, thus a word was formed. The name of something was called after its function or action.

To find out more concerning ancient Hebrew, you can reference the "Ancient Hebrew Lexicon of the Bible" from the Ancient Hebrew Research Center. If we apply this thought to the word for the festivals of Yahweh we will see a little more insight into the meaning of the word.

4

The Paleo – Hebrew compared to the modern Hebrew looks like this;

<u>Paleo</u> <u>Modern</u>

𐤌 𐤅 𐤏 𐤃 מועד

If we break down the word "moed" in the Paleo Hebrew by the meaning of each letter would be-

- 𐤌- waves of water and sea, the sea was a feared and unknown place, for this reason this letter is used as a question word, in the sense of searching.
- 𐤅 - a peg or hook, which are used for securing something. The meaning of this letter is to add or secure.
- 𐤏 - seeing and watching as well as knowledge as the eye is the window of knowledge.
- 𐤃 - through the tent through the door

So, if we take the meaning of each letter and form the word "Moed" it would say-

𐤌 𐤅 𐤏 𐤃

- Water, searching...
- To secure and add to...
- To see and know...
- The way into the tent through the door

If one was to look at the meaning, one would see a picture given to reveal the Messiah.

- <u>Water, searching</u>... - Jesus (Yeshua in Hebrew) testified that He was the Living Water (John 4:10,11)
- <u>To secure and add to...</u> - in Him we are joined to the Father and are joint-heirs of the promises and covenants of Yahweh (Romans 8:17 & John 17:21)
- <u>To see and know...</u> to see and know Yeshua, is to see and know the Father (John 14:7-9)
- <u>The way into the tent through the door</u> - the tent represents family, through the door (Yeshua) we have access into the family of God (John 10:7-9)

So, a moed is a designated time that was set and appointed knowing that it would reveal messiah and a way in to the family of God.

Are the Moedim anything else? Lets look again into Leviticus 23 verses 1&2.
- (1) Adonai said to Moshe,
- (2) "Tell the people of Isra'el: 'The designated times of Adonai which you are to proclaim as <u>holy convocations</u> are my designated times. (CJB)

Not only do we see designated times, we also see holy convocations. A convocation is the Hebrew word Miqra. It is the Strongs concordance word H4744.

מקרא miqra'ˆ
<u>From H7121</u>; something called out, a public meeting; also a rehearsal: - assembly, calling, convocation, reading.

A Holy convocation, or Miqra, is from the word Qara.
Strongs H7121 קרא qara'ˆ
- to call out to (address by name)
- call (for, forth)
- Invite, preach,
- (make) proclamation

According to the definitions of these words, the moedim (plural of moed) are;
A designated time that was set and appointed knowing that it would reveal Messiah and a way in to the family of God, that would be a public calling forth to proclaim the word of Yahweh!

So the next question would be; Who do the moedim belong to? Again we will look at Leviticus 23.
- (1) Adonai said to Moshe,
- (2) "Tell the people of Isra'el: 'The designated times **of Adonai** which you are to proclaim as holy convocations are my designated times. (CJB)

The literal reading of Scripture says that the moedim belong to Yahweh (Adonai, the LORD), not a specific grouping of people, other than a people called out by His Name. This is consistent through the entire chapter of Leviticus 23, where all the Moedim (feasts, appointed times) are listed.

If they belong to God, Why were they given to people?
- To teach us to have faith in YHWH
- To set His people apart
- To have continual reminders of the provision of the Father

• To prophetically speak of what we are to look for

God gave His people many blessings. One thing He declares of His people is that He sets them apart. We are supposed to be a set apart people. As a people set apart we acknowledge the fact that at times it is very noticeable that you are set apart from the world. We do not act, think, talk, walk or look like the world, we have been changed in Messiah, we are a new creation, old things have passed away and all things have become new (2 Corinthians 5:17). When we are set apart, we are given a sign in order to testify of that fact.

Exodus 31:13
• Speak thou also unto the children of Israel, saying,
• Verily my sabbaths ye shall keep:
• for it is a sign between me and you
• throughout your generations;
• that ye may know that I am the LORD
• that doth sanctify you.

Ezekiel 20:12
Moreover also I gave them my sabbaths, to be a sign between me and them, that they might know that I am the LORD that sanctify them.

The Sabbath is the foundation for all of the other Moedim. It is the first appointed time listed in Leviticus 23. These things were established before we read about them in Leviticus 23. Which leads us to ask...

When were the Moedim established? The Moedim were already were planned and existed by the time they are first mentioned in Leviticus 23. The sun, moon and stars all testified of the Moedim, the set appointed times to come.

Psalms 104:19 tells us;
He appointed the moon <u>for seasons</u> (L'moedim in Hebrew), : the sun knoweth his going down.

If God appointed the moon for the Moedim, set apart appointed times, it was created with purpose. One of those purposes was to testify of the Moedim.

Genesis 1:14
And God said, Let there be lights in the firmament of the heaven to divide the day from
the night; and let them be for signs, and for seasons, and for days, and years:

The moon and the stars were given on the fourth day of creation in order to divide the day from the night; and then it is said let them be for (given to) signs (l'ohtot),
seasons (moedim),Days and years. If we look back at Genesis 1:14 we see that they were given for the purpose of <u>signs and seasons</u>. Let's look at these two words in Hebrew.

Signs is the Hebrew word H226 in the Strongs concordance;
אות
'ôth
a signal (literally or figuratively), a flag, beacon, monument, omen, prodigy, evidence, mark, miracle, (en)sign, token

The first reason(duty)mentioned of the moon, stars, and sun was to be a sign.
Signs in scripture were given ...
A. To be seen
B. To be a confirmation of something

Exodus 31 tells us that there will be a sign between YHWH and His people for all generations. Exodus 31:13-17 says;
(13) Speak thou also unto the children of Israel, saying, Verily my sabbaths ye shall keep: <u>for it is a sign between me and you throughout your generations;</u> **that ye may know that** I am the LORD that doth sanctify you.
(14) Ye shall keep the sabbath therefore; for it is holy unto you: every one that defileth it shall surely be put to death: for whosoever doeth any work therein, that soul shall be cut
off from among his people.
(15) Six days may work be done; but in the seventh is the sabbath of rest, holy to the LORD: whosoever doeth any work in the sabbath day, he shall surely be put to death.
(16) Wherefore the children of Israel shall keep the sabbath, to observe the sabbath throughout their generations, for a perpetual covenant.
(17) **It is a sign between me and the children of Israel for ever**: for in six days the LORD made heaven and earth, and on the seventh day he rested, and was refreshed.

Acts 2:19 (quoting Joel 2:30) confirms the giving of signs to testify of something.

And I will shew wonders in heaven above, and signs in the earth beneath; blood, and fire, and vapour of smoke:

This sign in Exodus 31 was to be given to state the fact that it is the LORD Himself that sanctifies us, sets us apart. Notice it says that it was given to the children of Israel forever. Which leads to a much deeper question that we do not have time to fully address here. However, we will very briefly cover it and give a few verses.

Who are the children of Israel? The first answer is, they are the sons of Jacob. Jacob descended from Isaac. Isaac descended from Abraham. Abraham was Jacob's great grandfather. In Hebrew and Hebraic thought, we would not say great grandfather. We would say Abraham is his father, or even he is the son (or seed) of Abraham. This is very clear in all of the genealogies that are given throughout scripture. So, we could safely say that Israel is Abrahams seed, as well as we could say that Israel is the twelve sons of Jacob (who was later renamed Israel in Genesis 32:28).

Are there any other sons of Abraham that we have heard of or can find in scripture? Judah (Yehudah) is where we get the name "Jew". This is only one of the sons of Israel, and while Judah is the seed of Abraham, He is not the only seed of Abraham. The book of Galatians testifies that if you are a believer in the Messiah, then YOU are the child (seed) of Abraham. That gives you equal right to be part of the covenant promises that God gave to Abraham because all of the promises were given to Abraham and his seed.

Galatians 3:6-9
(6) Even as Abraham believed God, and it was accounted to him for righteousness.
(7) Know ye therefore that they which are of faith, the same are the children of Abraham.
(8) And the scripture, foreseeing that God would justify the heathen through faith, preached before the gospel unto Abraham, *saying,* In thee shall all nations be blessed.

9

(9) So then they which be of faith are blessed with faithful Abraham.

So, it is by faith that you come to Messiah and are counted as part of the covenant and receive the blessing of the covenant that God gave to Abraham. That means you are now adopted or even "grafted in" to the family of Israel. You are not the whole family, nor did you push anyone aside to get there, you have become a **part of** and equal sharers in the family called Israel.

Romans 11:16-27
(16) For if the firstfruit *be* holy, the lump *is* also *holy:* and if the root *be* holy, so *are* the branches.
(17) And if some of the branches be broken off, and thou, being a wild olive tree, wert graffed in among them, and with them partakest of the root and fatness of the olive tree;
(18) Boast not against the branches. But if thou boast, thou bearest not the root, but the root thee.
(19) Thou wilt say then, The branches were broken off, that I might be graffed in.
(20) Well; because of unbelief they were broken off, and thou standest by faith. Be not highminded, but fear:
(21) For if God spared not the natural branches, *take heed* lest he also spare not thee.
(22) Behold therefore the goodness and severity of God: on them which fell, severity; but toward thee, goodness, if thou continue in *his* goodness: otherwise thou also shalt be cut off.
(23) And they also, if they abide not still in unbelief, shall be graffed in: for God is able to graff them in again.
(24) For if thou wert cut out of the olive tree which is wild by nature, and wert graffed contrary to nature into a good olive tree: how much more shall these, which be the natural *branches,* be graffed into their own olive tree?
(25) For I would not, brethren, that ye should be ignorant of this mystery, lest ye should be wise in your own conceits; that blindness in part is happened to Israel, until the fulness of the Gentiles be come in.
(26) And so all Israel shall be saved: as it is written, There shall come out of Sion the Deliverer, and shall turn away ungodliness from Jacob:
(27) For this *is* my covenant unto them, when I shall take away their sins.

Romans 8:14-17

(14) For as many as are led by the Spirit of God, they are the sons of God.

(15) For ye have not received the spirit of bondage again to fear; but ye have received the Spirit of adoption, whereby we cry, Abba, Father.

(16) The Spirit itself beareth witness with our spirit, that we are the children of God:

(17) And if children, then heirs; heirs of God, and joint-heirs with Christ; if so be that we suffer with *him*, that we may be also glorified together.

John 10:16

And other sheep I have, which are not of this fold: them also I must bring, and they shall hear my voice; and there shall be one fold, *and* one shepherd.

Matthew 10:6

But go rather to the lost sheep of the house of Israel.

Back to Genesis 1:14

And God said, Let there be lights in the firmament of the heaven to divide the day from the night; and let them be for signs, **and for seasons**, and for days, and years:

The word used in Genesis 1:14 for seasons is the word moed. Again, Moed is the Hebrew word 4150 in the Strong's concordance.

H4150 מועדה מעד מועד

מô'âdâh   mô'êd   mô'êd

an appointment, a fixed time or season; a festival; an assembly (as convened for a efinite purpose); appointed (sign, time), (set, solemn) feast, (appointed, due) season, set time appointed.

Let us understand that Seasons here is the Hebrew word Moed. In this word we can see a few definitions and relative words to help explain it.

מועד - Moed

Root of "moed" is the word "ed" עד

In the Hebrew prayers it is often said "L'olam va'ed" which means, forever and ever.

"Ed" עד is eternity, eternal

"Edut" עדות is formed from the word "ed" and is found in Exodus 31:18 –tablets of testimony (which ended up broken) the word for testimony is "Edut"

עדה 'êdâh – witness

עדי 'ădîy – ornament/jewelry

עדה 'êdâh – assembly, congregation
Based on what we know, Moed is from the word "ed or ad"
עד – ad= eternal / eternity
מ – "mem" is used as a prefix meaning "from"
מעד – Moed – from eternity
The moedim of YHWH are eternal !

The adversary will always try to distract you from the Moedim. He will set up copies of the pure word of YHWH (Yahweh) to draw attention and emphasis off of what YHWH wants us to look on. Do you remember the sin of the golden calf in Exodus 32?

Exodus 32:3-5
(3) And all the people brake off the golden earrings which were in their ears, and brought them unto Aaron.
(4) And he received them at their hand, and fashioned it with a graving tool, after he had made it a molten calf: and they said, These be thy gods, O Israel, which brought thee up out of the land of Egypt.
(5) And when Aaron saw it, he built an altar before it; and Aaron made proclamation and said, To morrow is a feast (Chag - חג) to the LORD.

Aharon and the people...
- Set up an idol
- Called it God
- Tied it in with their redemption
- Built an altar to it
- Made proclamation (what are they supposed to proclaim? Qara -Lev.23)

12

- And declared a festival (Chag חג) to YHWH that was not an appointed time (moed- מעד) of YHWH

Do we ever put God in a box? Do we approach the creator of heaven and earth with our own ideas and agendas and believe that He will conform to our ideals? Have you ever said or heard someone say "I would never serve a god that_____?"

Psalms 74:4 says
Thine enemies roar in the midst of thy congregations (Moedecha - מוֹעֲדֶךָ); they set up their ensigns [for] signs.

It is interesting to see that in Psalms 74 the word congregations, is the word Moed. Also, that the purpose of the adversary was to set up <u>their signs</u>, false or lying signs, in the moed.

Isaiah 14:12-13 says
(12) "How did you come to fall from the heavens, morning star, son of the dawn? How did you come to be cut to the ground, conqueror of nations?
(13) You thought to yourself, 'I will scale the heavens, I will raise my throne above God's stars. I will sit on the Mount of Assembly (behar moed- בְּהַר מוֹעֵד) far away in the north.

We see here that the adversary declared that he would sit on the mount of assembly. The word there for assembly is the word moed. He declares that he will rule over the moed, and the mount of the moed. So, where is the mount of the moed? It is Jerusalem! It was there that people were to gather three times a year for the moedim.

Deuteronomy 12:5& 11
(5) But unto the place which the LORD your God shall choose out of all your tribes to put his name there, *even* unto his habitation shall ye seek, and thither thou shalt come:
(11) Then there shall be a place which the LORD your God shall choose to cause his name to dwell there; thither shall ye bring all that I command you; your burnt offerings, and your sacrifices, your tithes, and the heave offering of your hand, and all your choice vows which ye vow unto the LORD:

The Father states that it is His desire for His people to keep His feasts. We could even say that these are prophetic because

13

we see that we will be keeping them in the new heavens and earth.

Nahum 1:15
Behold upon the mountains the feet of him that bringeth good tidings, that publisheth peace! O Judah, keep thy solemn feasts, perform thy vows: for the wicked shall no more pass through thee; he is utterly cut off.

Isaiah 66:22-23 says
(22) For as the new heavens and the new earth, which I will make, shall remain before me, saith the LORD, so shall your seed and your name remain.
(23) And it shall come to pass, that from one new moon to another, and from one sabbath to another, shall all flesh come to worship before me, saith the LORD.

Remember that this is prophetic, in a time to come.

Zephaniah 3:13-20
(13) The remnant of Israel shall not do iniquity, nor speak lies; neither shall a deceitful tongue be found in their mouth: for they shall feed and lie down, and none shall make them afraid.
(14) Sing, O daughter of Zion; shout, O Israel; be glad and rejoice with all the heart, O daughter of Jerusalem.
(15) The LORD hath taken away thy judgments, he hath cast out thine enemy: the king of Israel, even the LORD, is in the midst of thee: thou shalt not see evil any more.
(16) In that day it shall be said to Jerusalem, Fear thou not: and to Zion, Let not thine hands be slack.
(17) The LORD thy God in the midst of thee is mighty; he will save, he will rejoice over thee with joy; he will rest in his love, he will joy over thee with singing.
(18) I will gather them that are sorrowful for the solemn assembly (moed- מועד), who are of thee, to whom the reproach of it was a burden. [because they cannot keep them]
(19) Behold, at that time I will undo all that afflict thee: and I will save her that halteth, and gather her that was driven out; and I will get them praise and fame in every land where they have been put to shame.
(20) At that time will I bring you again, even in the time that I gather you: for I will make you a name and a praise among all

people of the earth, when I turn back your captivity before your eyes, saith the LORD.

All of these set appointed times were given to...
- Impart revelation from YHWH
- Reveal the work of the Messiah
- Show us how to draw close to the Father
- Teach us how to gather in unity
- Teach us how to come and worship with each other

By now we see that there is one question that needs to be asked. What are the Moedim & what do they mean to me? One of the best places to see the moedim together in a list so that they can be explained is found in the book of Leviticus. If we look to Leviticus 23 we will see a lot of information concerning the moedim. Throughout this reading we will continue to refer back to Leviticus 23 to help us to see and explain the moedim of the LORD.

Leviticus 23:1-44
(1) And the LORD spake unto Moses, saying,
(2) Speak unto the children of Israel, and say unto them, *Concerning* the feasts of the LORD, which ye shall proclaim *to be* holy convocations, *even* these *are* my feasts.
(3) Six days shall work be done: but the seventh day *is* the sabbath of rest, an holy convocation; ye shall do no work *therein:* it *is* the sabbath of the LORD in all your dwellings.
(4) These *are* the feasts of the LORD, *even* holy convocations, which ye shall proclaim in their seasons.
(5) In the fourteenth *day* of the first month at even *is* the LORD'S passover.
(6) And on the fifteenth day of the same month *is* the feast of unleavened bread unto the LORD: seven days ye must eat unleavened bread.
(7) In the first day ye shall have an holy convocation: ye shall do no servile work therein.
(8) But ye shall offer an offering made by fire unto the LORD seven days: in the seventh day *is* an holy convocation: ye shall do no servile work *therein.*
(9) And the LORD spake unto Moses, saying,
(10) Speak unto the children of Israel, and say unto them, When ye be come into the land which I give unto you, and shall

reap the harvest thereof, then ye shall bring a sheaf of the firstfruits of your harvest unto the priest:

(11) And he shall wave the sheaf before the LORD, to be accepted for you: on the morrow after the sabbath the priest shall wave it.

(12) And ye shall offer that day when ye wave the sheaf an he lamb without blemish of the first year for a burnt offering unto the LORD.

(13) And the meat offering thereof *shall be* two tenth deals of fine flour mingled with oil, an offering made by fire unto the LORD *for* a sweet savour: and the drink offering thereof *shall be* of wine, the fourth *part* of an hin.

(14) And ye shall eat neither bread, nor parched corn, nor green ears, until the selfsame day that ye have brought an offering unto your God: *it shall be* a statute for ever throughout your generations in all your dwellings.

(15) And ye shall count unto you from the morrow after the sabbath, from the day that ye brought the sheaf of the wave offering; seven sabbaths shall be complete:

(16) Even unto the morrow after the seventh sabbath shall ye number fifty days; and ye shall offer a new meat offering unto the LORD.

(17) Ye shall bring out of your habitations two wave loaves of two tenth deals: they shall be of fine flour; they shall be baken with leaven; *they are* the firstfruits unto the LORD.

(18) And ye shall offer with the bread seven lambs without blemish of the first year, and one young bullock, and two rams: they shall be *for* a burnt offering unto the LORD, with their meat offering, and their drink offerings, *even* an offering made by fire, of sweet savour unto the LORD.

(19) Then ye shall sacrifice one kid of the goats for a sin offering, and two lambs of the first year for a sacrifice of peace offerings.

(20) And the priest shall wave them with the bread of the firstfruits *for* a wave offering before the LORD, with the two lambs: they shall be holy to the LORD for the priest.

(21) And ye shall proclaim on the selfsame day, *that* it may be an holy convocation unto you: ye shall do no servile work *therein: it shall be* a statute for ever in all your dwellings throughout your generations.

(22) And when ye reap the harvest of your land, thou shalt not make clean riddance of the corners of thy field when thou reapest, neither shalt thou gather any gleaning of thy

harvest: thou shalt leave them unto the poor, and to the stranger: I *am* the LORD your God.

(23) And the LORD spake unto Moses, saying,

(24) Speak unto the children of Israel, saying, In the seventh month, in the first *day* of the month, shall ye have a sabbath, a memorial of blowing of trumpets, an holy convocation.

(25) Ye shall do no servile work *therein:* but ye shall offer an offering made by fire unto the LORD.

(26) And the LORD spake unto Moses, saying,

(27) Also on the tenth *day* of this seventh month *there shall be* a day of atonement: it shall be an holy convocation unto you; and ye shall afflict your souls, and offer an offering made by fire unto the LORD.

(28) And ye shall do no work in that same day: for it *is* a day of atonement, to make an atonement for you before the LORD your God.

(29) For whatsoever soul *it be* that shall not be afflicted in that same day, he shall be cut off from among his people.

(30) And whatsoever soul *it be* that doeth any work in that same day, the same soul will I destroy from among his people.

(31) Ye shall do no manner of work: *it shall be* a statute for ever throughout your generations in all your dwellings.

(32) It *shall be* unto you a sabbath of rest, and ye shall afflict your souls: in the ninth *day* of the month at even, from even unto even, shall ye celebrate your sabbath.

(33) And the LORD spake unto Moses, saying,

(34) Speak unto the children of Israel, saying, The fifteenth day of this seventh month *shall be* the feast of tabernacles *for* seven days unto the LORD.

(35) On the first day *shall be* an holy convocation: ye shall do no servile work *therein.*

(36) Seven days ye shall offer an offering made by fire unto the LORD: on the eighth day shall be an holy convocation unto you; and ye shall offer an offering made by fire unto the LORD: it *is* a solemn assembly; *and* ye shall do no servile work *therein.*

(37) These *are* the feasts of the LORD, which ye shall proclaim *to be* holy convocations, to offer an offering made by fire unto the LORD, a burnt offering, and a meat offering, a sacrifice, and drink offerings, every thing upon his day:

(38) Beside the sabbaths of the LORD, and beside your gifts, and beside all your vows, and beside all your freewill offerings, which ye give unto the LORD.

(39) Also in the fifteenth day of the seventh month, when ye have gathered in the fruit of the land, ye shall keep a feast unto the LORD seven days: on the first day *shall be* a sabbath, and on the eighth day *shall be* a sabbath.

(40) And ye shall take you on the first day the boughs of goodly trees, branches of palm trees, and the boughs of thick trees, and willows of the brook; and ye shall rejoice before the LORD your God seven days.

(41) And ye shall keep it a feast unto the LORD seven days in the year. *It shall be* a statute for ever in your generations: ye shall celebrate it in the seventh month.

(42) Ye shall dwell in booths seven days; all that are Israelites born shall dwell in booths:

(43) That your generations may know that I made the children of Israel to dwell in booths, when I brought them out of the land of Egypt: I *am* the LORD your God.

(44) And Moses declared unto the children of Israel the feasts of the LORD.

If we were to list the moedim as read in Leviticus 23 it would look like this;
Spring moedim
Passover
Unleavened bread
Firstfruits
Shavuot

Fall moedim
Yom Teruah
Yom Kippur
Sukkot

In order to understand the moedim, we should understand what they are built on. In other words, we must build the foundation first. There must be a foundation established if you are going to build something. The very first appointed time mentioned in Leviticus 23 is the Sabbath.

Leviticus 23:1-3
(1) And the LORD spake unto Moses, saying,
(2) Speak unto the children of Israel, and say unto them, Concerning the feasts of the LORD, which ye shall proclaim to be holy convocations, even these are my feasts.

(3) Six days shall work be done: but the seventh day is the sabbath of rest, an holy convocation; ye shall do no work therein: it is the sabbath of the LORD in all your dwellings.

According to the Strongs concordance, the word used for Sabbath is;
H7676
שַׁבָּת
shabbâth
Intensive from H7673; intermission, specifically the Sabbath: (+ every) sabbath.

H7673
שׁבת
shâbath
to repose, desist from exertion; cause to cease, celebrate, make to rest

The first question regarding our foundation is "When is the sabbath?" The Sabbath was referenced to the children of Israel while in the wilderness. They were to gather Manna in the desert on every day, but one. They were not to gather the Manna on the seventh day, which is the Sabbath.

Exodus 16:26
Six days ye shall gather it; but on the seventh day, which is the sabbath, in it there shall be none.

The word for seventh is the Hebrew word, Sheva from the Strongs it is;
H7651
שׁבע
sheba'
From H7650 seven (as the sacred full one); by implication a week; by extension an indefinite number: sevenfold

H7650
שׁבע
shâba'
properly to be complete, to seven oneself, that is, swear (as if by repeating a declaration seven times): charge (by an oath, with an oath), feed to the full, take an oath, cause to swear.

The first mention of the Sabbath is in the account of the creating at the beginning.

Genesis 2:2-3
(2) And on the seventh day God ended his work which he had made; and he rested on the seventh day from all his work which he had made.
(3) And <u>God blessed the seventh day</u>, <u>and sanctified it</u>: because that in it he had rested (שבת) from all his work which God created and made.

So how do we know which day is the seventh? Only recently did calendars not put Saturday as the seventh day. Further the days were given and assigned names. The days of the week that have been passed down for centuries, in Hebrew, are as follows.

יום ראשון yom reshon – first day
יום שני yom shnee – second day
יום שלישי yom shleshee – third day
יום רביעי yom rvee –fourth day
יום חמישי yom chameshe – fifth day
יום ששי yom shshee – sixth day
שבת Shabbat - Shabbat – not seventh day, but Shabbat. This is the only day <u>given the name</u> Shabbat, therefore we cannot call it by any other name.

Let's look at a few Scriptures regarding the Sabbath.

Exodus 20:10- But the seventh day is the sabbath of the LORD thy God: in it thou shalt not do any work, thou, nor thy son, nor thy daughter, thy manservant, nor thy maidservant, nor thy cattle, nor thy stranger that is within thy gates:

Exodus 31:14 - Ye shall keep the sabbath therefore; for it is holy unto you: every one that defileth it shall surely be put to death: for whosoever doeth any work therein, that soul shall be cut off from among his people.

Exodus 31:15 - Six days may work be done; but in the seventh is the sabbath of rest, holy to the LORD: whosoever doeth any work in the sabbath day, he shall surely be put to death.

Exodus 35:2 - Six days shall work be done, but on the seventh day there shall be to you an holy day, a sabbath of rest to the LORD: whosoever doeth work therein shall be put to death.

Leviticus 23:3 - Six days shall work be done: but the seventh day is the sabbath of rest, an holy convocation; ye shall do no work therein: it is the sabbath of the LORD in all your dwellings.

Deuteronomy 5:14 - But the seventh day is the sabbath of the LORD thy God: in it thou shalt not do any work, thou, nor thy son, nor thy daughter, nor thy manservant, nor thy maidservant, nor thine ox, nor thine ass, nor any of thy cattle, nor thy stranger that is within thy gates; that thy manservant and thy maidservant may rest as well as thou.

Jeremiah 17:22 - Neither carry forth a burden out of your houses on the sabbath day, neither do ye any work, but hallow ye the sabbath day, as I commanded your fathers.

Jeremiah 17:24 - And it shall come to pass, if ye diligently hearken unto me, saith the LORD, to bring in no burden through the gates of this city on the sabbath day, but hallow the sabbath day, to do no work therein;

Nehemiah 9:13-15
(13) Thou camest down also upon mount Sinai, and spakest with them from heaven, and gavest them right judgments, and true laws, good statutes and commandments:
(14) And madest known unto them thy holy sabbath, and commandedst them precepts, statutes, and laws, by the hand of Moses thy servant:
(15) And gavest them bread from heaven for their hunger, and broughtest forth water for them out of the rock for their thirst, and promisedst them that they should go in to possess the land which thou hadst sworn to give them.

Nehemiah 10:31
And if the people of the land bring ware or any victuals on the sabbath day to sell, that we would not buy it of them on the sabbath, or on the holy day: and that we would leave the seventh year (Sabbath year), and the exaction of every debt.

Nehemiah 13:15-22

(15) At that time I saw people in Judah pressing juice from grapes on the Sabbath. Others were loading grain, wine, grapes, figs, and other things on their donkeys and taking them into Jerusalem; I warned them not to sell anything on the Sabbath.

(16) Some people from the city of Tyre were living in Jerusalem, and they brought fish and all kinds of goods into the city to sell to our people on the Sabbath.

(17) I reprimanded the Jewish leaders and told them, "Look at the evil you're doing! You're making the Sabbath unholy.

(18) This is exactly why God punished your ancestors when he brought destruction on this city. And yet you insist on bringing more of God's anger down on Israel by profaning the Sabbath."

(19) So I gave orders for the city gates to be shut at the beginning of every Sabbath, as soon as evening began to fall, and not to be opened again until the Sabbath was over. I stationed some of my men at the gates to make sure that nothing was brought into the city on the Sabbath.

(20) Once or twice merchants who sold all kinds of goods spent Friday night outside the city walls.

(21) I warned them, "It's no use waiting out there for morning to come. If you try this again, I'll use force on you." From then on they did not come back on the Sabbath.

(22) I ordered the Levites to purify themselves and to go and guard the gates to make sure that the Sabbath was kept holy. Remember me, O God, for this also, and spare me because of your great love.

Isaiah 56:1-2

(1) Thus saith the LORD, Keep ye judgment, and do justice: for my salvation is near to come, and my righteousness to be revealed.

(2) Blessed is the man that doeth this, and the son of man that layeth hold on it; that keepeth the sabbath from polluting it, and keepeth his hand from doing any evil.

Isaiah 56:6-7

(6) Also the sons of the stranger, that join themselves to the LORD, to serve him, and to love the name of the LORD, to be his servants, every one that keepeth the sabbath from polluting it, and taketh hold of my covenant;

(7) Even them will I bring to my holy mountain, and make them joyful in my house of prayer: their burnt offerings and their

sacrifices shall be accepted upon mine altar; for mine house shall be called an house of prayer for all people.

Isaiah 58:13 If thou turn away thy foot from the sabbath, from doing thy pleasure on my holy day; and call the sabbath a delight, the holy of the LORD, honourable; and shalt honour him, not doing thine own ways, nor finding thine own pleasure, nor speaking thine own words:

Isaiah 58:13-14 (NLT)
(13) "Keep the Sabbath day holy. Don't pursue your own interests on that day, but enjoy the Sabbath and speak of it with delight as the LORD's holy day. Honor the Sabbath in everything you do on that day, and don't follow your own desires or talk idly.
(14) Then the LORD will be your delight. I will give you great honor and satisfy you with the inheritance I promised to your ancestor Jacob. I, the LORD, have spoken!"

Leviticus 19:3 - Ye shall fear every man his mother, and his father, and keep my sabbaths: I am the LORD your God.

Leviticus 19:30 - Ye shall keep my sabbaths, and reverence my sanctuary: I am the LORD.

Leviticus 26:2 - Ye shall keep my sabbaths, and reverence my sanctuary: I am the LORD.

Ezekiel 44:24 - And in controversy they shall stand in judgment; and they shall judge it according to my judgments: and they shall keep my laws and my statutes in all mine assemblies; and they shall hallow my sabbaths.

Exodus 20:8 - Remember the sabbath day, to keep it holy.

Exodus 31:14 - Ye shall keep the sabbath therefore; for it is holy unto you: every one that defileth it shall surely be put to death: for whosoever doeth any work therein, that soul shall be cut off from among his people.

Exodus 31:16 - Wherefore the children of Israel shall keep the sabbath, to observe the sabbath throughout their generations, for a perpetual covenant.

Deuteronomy 5:12 - Keep the sabbath day to sanctify it, as the LORD thy God hath commanded thee.

Deuteronomy 5:15 - And remember that thou wast a servant in the land of Egypt, and that the LORD thy God brought thee out thence through a mighty hand and by a stretched out arm: therefore the LORD thy God commanded thee to keep the sabbath day.

Exodus 20:6-11
(6) And shewing mercy unto thousands of them that love me, and keep my commandments.
(7) Thou shalt not take the name of the LORD thy God in vain; for the LORD will not hold him guiltless that taketh his name in vain.
(8) Remember the sabbath day, to keep it holy.
(9) Six days shalt thou labour, and do all thy work:
(10) But the seventh day is the sabbath of the LORD thy God: in it thou shalt not do any work, thou, nor thy son, nor thy daughter, thy manservant, nor thy maidservant, nor thy cattle, nor thy stranger that is within thy gates:
(11) For in six days the LORD made heaven and earth, the sea, and all that in them is, and rested the seventh day: wherefore the LORD blessed the sabbath day, and hallowed it.

Exodus 31:13 (separated for emphasis)
- Speak thou also unto the children of Israel, saying,
- Verily my sabbaths ye shall keep:
- for it is a sign between me and you
- throughout your generations;
- that ye may know
- that I am the LORD
- that doth sanctify you.

Remember the purpose of the Sabbath was to be a sign.
H226

נ ו א
'ôth
a signal, as a flag, beacon, monument, evidence, mark, miracle, sign, token.

נ ו א used 79 times in Tanakh (the Torah, the Prophets and the writings. What is commonly called the Old Testament.)

24

The first time this word is used is in Genesis 1:14;
And God said, Let there be lights in the firmament of the heaven to divide the day from the night; and let them be for signs, and for seasons, and for days, and years:

Ezekiel 20:10-13
(10) "And so I led them out of Egypt into the desert.
(11) I gave them my commands and taught them my laws, which bring life to anyone who obeys them.
(12) I made the keeping of the Sabbath a sign of the agreement between us, to remind them that I, the LORD, make them holy.
(13) But even in the desert they defied me. They broke my laws and rejected my commands, which bring life to anyone who obeys them. They completely profaned the Sabbath.

Ezekiel 20:18-20
(18) Instead, I warned the young people among them: Do not keep the laws your ancestors made; do not follow their customs or defile yourselves with their idols.
(19) I am the LORD your God. Obey my laws and my commands.
(20) Make the Sabbath a holy day, so that it will be a sign of the covenant we made, and will remind you that I am the LORD your God.

Mark 6:2 - And when the sabbath day was come, he began to teach in the synagogue: and many hearing him were astonished, saying, From whence hath this man these things? And what wisdom is this which is given unto him, that even such mighty works are wrought by his hands?

Luke 4:16 -And he (Jesus, Yeshua) came to Nazareth, where he had been brought up: and, as his custom was, he went into the synagogue on the sabbath day, and stood up for to read.

Luke 4:31- And came down to Capernaum, a city of Galilee, and taught them on the sabbath days.

Luke 6:6 - And it came to pass also on another sabbath, that he entered into the synagogue and taught: and there was a man whose right hand was withered.

Luke 13:10- And he was teaching in one of the synagogues on the sabbath.

Acts 13:14 - But when they departed from Perga, they came to Antioch in Pisidia, and went into the synagogue on the sabbath day, and sat down.

Acts 13:44- And the next sabbath day came almost the whole city together to hear the word of God.

Acts 15:21 -For Moses of old time hath in every city them that preach him, being read in the synagogues every sabbath day.

Acts 18:4 - And he reasoned in the synagogue every sabbath, and persuaded the Jews and the Greeks.

Colossians 2:16-17 - Then do not let anyone judge you in eating, or in drinking, or in part of a feast, or of a new moon, or of sabbaths, (17) which are a shadow of coming things, but the body is of Christ.

We know that all the feasts and Moedim point to Yeshua our Messiah. However, nowhere does it say that He changed them or stopped them.

Hebrews 4:1-11 says to us;
Therefore, let us fear lest perhaps a promise having been left to enter into His rest, that any of you may seem to come short.
(2) For, indeed, we have had the gospel preached to us, even as they also; but the Word did not profit those hearing it, not having been mixed with faith in the ones who heard.
(3) For we, the ones believing, enter into the rest, even as He said, "As I swore in My wrath, they shall not enter into My rest," though the works had come into being from the foundation of the world.
(4) For He has spoken somewhere about the seventh day this way, "And God rested from all His works in the seventh day."
(5) And in this again, "They shall not enter into My rest."- (Psalm 95:11)
(6) Therefore, since it remains for some to enter into it, and those who formerly had the gospel preached did not enter in on account of disobedience,
(7) He again marks out a certain day, saying in David, Today (after so long a time, according as He has said), "Today, if you hear His voice, do not harden your hearts." - (Psalm 95:7, 8)

(8) For if Joshua gave them rest, then He would not have afterwards spoken about another day.

(9) So, then, there remains a sabbath rest to the people of God.

(10) For he entering into His rest, he himself also rested from his works, as God had rested from His own.

(11) Therefore, let us exert ourselves to enter into that rest, that not anyone fall in the same example of disobedience.

Passover

פסח

(Pesach)

We have often heard that Jesus (Yeshua) was our Passover lamb. Do we truly understand what is meant by this statement? In order to say that He fulfilled the Passover, we should make sure we understand how. Is saying that Yeshua was our Passover only saying that the blood was applied? Is there more? If there is a need for the blood to be applied, what was it? If there is more here than at first glance meets the eye, what is it?

In order to build a solid understanding of the Moed Pesach (appointed time of Passover) we should first start with a couple definitions and then the background leading up to Passover.

What we call Passover, is the Hebrew word pesach. The term Passover refers specifically to the lamb that was slaughtered.

The Strongs concordance word H6453
פסח
pesach
From H6452; a pretermission, that is, exemption; used only technically of the Passover (the festival or the victim): - passover (offering).

Exodus 12:13 says "when I see the blood, I will pass over you" the word used there is pasach. This is the verb of the word.

The Strongs concordance word H6452
פסח
pâsach
A primitive root; to hop, that is, (figuratively) skip over (or spare); to hesitate; to limp, to dance: - halt, become lame, leap, pass over.

To start off, God knew how He was going to redeem His people. When God made a covenant with Abraham, He foretold that they would go into slavery and serve another nation. He told Abraham that they would come out of that nation with great wealth. There was a plan for the people of God from the beginning.

Genesis 15:13-14
(13) And he said unto Abram, Know of a surety that thy seed shall be a stranger in a land *that is* not theirs, and shall serve them; and they shall afflict them four hundred years;
(14) And also that nation, whom they shall serve, will I judge: and afterward shall they come out with great substance.

30

Exodus 12:40-41

(40) Now the sojourning of the children of Israel, who dwelt in Egypt, *was* four hundred and thirty years.

(41) And it came to pass at the end of the four hundred and thirty years, even the selfsame day it came to pass, that all the hosts of the LORD went out from the land of Egypt.

So, as the story unfolds, Jacob goes down to Egypt with all of his family to join his son Joseph. They grow to be a huge family and then "a king arose who did not know Joseph." The prophecy is in motion. Israel is taken captive in a land they occupy that is not their own.

God calls Moses to be a deliverer for Him. After trying this in his own strength, Moses is convinced that God has the wrong guy for this job. God tells Moses that He hasn't seen anything yet. He is about to reveal Himself in a way that Abraham, Isaac and Jacob never knew Him.

Exodus 6:2-3

(2) And God spake unto Moses, and said unto him, I *am* the LORD (יהוה):

(3) And I appeared unto Abraham, unto Isaac, and unto Jacob, by *the name of* God Almighty (El Shaddai), but by my name JEHOVAH (יהוה) was I not known to them.

God had revealed different aspects of His name and character to those who came before. Now, He is revealing Himself to His children and is doing it by His Name! To all others He revealed Himself as "the God that..." but now, He is revealing His Name! Right before God revealed Himself, He made a declaration of what He was about to do. It was then that He revealed Himself.

Exodus 6:1

Adonai said to Moshe, "Now you will see what I am going to do to Pharaoh. With a mighty hand he will send them off; with force he will drive them from the land!"

Amos 3:7

Surely the Lord GOD will do nothing, but he revealeth his secret unto his servants the prophets.

31

Now come the declarations from Moses and Aaron followed by judgments through signs and wonders. There have been nine judgments against the gods of Egypt so far. All of these led up to one last and great plague for Egypt. This is where we will pick up the Passover story.

Exodus 11:1-7
(1) And the LORD said unto Moses, Yet will I bring one plague more upon Pharaoh, and upon Egypt; afterwards he will let you go hence: when he shall let you go, he shall surely thrust you out hence altogether.
(2) Speak now in the ears of the people, and let every man borrow of his neighbour, and every woman of her neighbour, jewels of silver, and jewels of gold.
(3) And the LORD gave the people favour in the sight of the Egyptians. Moreover the man Moses was very great in the land of Egypt, in the sight of Pharaoh's servants, and in the sight of the people.
(4) And Moses said, Thus saith the LORD, About midnight will I go out into the midst of Egypt:
(5) And all the firstborn in the land of Egypt shall die, from the firstborn of Pharaoh that sitteth upon his throne, even unto the firstborn of the maidservant that is behind the mill; and all the firstborn of beasts.
(6) And there shall be a great cry throughout all the land of Egypt, such as there was none like it, nor shall be like it any more.
(7) But against any of the children of Israel shall not a dog move his tongue, against man or beast: **that ye may know how that the LORD doth put a difference between the Egyptians and Israel.**

The deliverance and redemption of the people of God was so tremendous that it truly was a day to "mark on your calendar". This was to be a day and time that the children of YHWH were to remember for the rest of their lives as well as pass it on to the following generations so that it is never forgotten. Such a tremendous sign this was to be, that it was counted as the head of the year.

We find the crux of the Passover story in Exodus chapter twelve. We will take much of this chapter and break it down a few verses at a time with some explanation and background given as we go.

Exodus 12:1-3

Adonai spoke to Moshe and Aharon in the land of Egypt; he said, (2) "You are to begin your calendar with this month; it will be the first month of the year for you.

(3) Speak to all the assembly of Isra'el and say, 'On the tenth day of this month, each man is to take a lamb or kid for his family, one per household —

We are told to begin our calendar with this month!

- This is called rosh chodesh (a new month, the new moon, literally new head)
- IF YOU WILL, ROSH HASHANNAH(head of the year) for the BIBLICAL CALENDAR
- The new moon when the crescent starts to be seen
- Each month begins with the sighting of the new moon
- This is the BIBLICAL CALENDAR

The calendar along with the concept of Rosh Chodesh was established on the fourth day of creation.

Genesis 1:14-19

God said, "Let there be lights in the dome of the sky to divide the day from the night; let them be for signs, seasons, days and years;

(15) and let them be for lights in the dome of the sky to give light to the earth"; and that is how it was.

(16) God made the two great lights — the larger light to rule the day and the smaller light to rule the night — and the stars.

(17) God put them in the dome of the sky to give light to the earth,

(18) to rule over the day and over the night, and to divide the light from the darkness; and God saw that it was good.

(19) So there was evening, and there was morning, a fourth day.

IN HEBREW THOUGHT, THERE ARE THREE CALENDARS: Biblical, Jewish Civil, Gregorian

BIBLICAL – ESTABLISHED HERE IN EXODUS 12

THIS IS THE CALENDAR YHWH SET IN PLACE TO DISCERN THE TIMES AND SEASONS

Psalms 104:19 says; You made the moon to mark the seasons - appointed times- מועדים and the sun knows when to set.

JEWISH CIVIL
- In the fourth century (359 C.E.), Hillel II established a fixed calendar based on mathematical and astronomical calculations.
- This calendar, still in use, standardized the length of months and the addition of months over the course of a 19 year cycle.
- THIS WAS IN PLACE OF THE NEW MOON MARKING THE BEGINNING OF EACH MONTH BY THE MOUTH OF THE SANHEIDRON AND TWO WITNESSES.

GREGORIAN (revised Julian)

This is the Calendar that we currently use every day.

The sun, moon and stars were put in place to mark the appointed times and seasons of YHWH. These are moedim מוֹעֲדִים.

The Strongs concordance moed is H4150
מועד
môʻêd
An appointment, a fixed time or season; specifically a festival; an assembly (as convened for a definite purpose); the congregation; by extension, the place of meeting; also a signal (as appointed beforehand): - appointed (sign, time), (place of, solemn), set solemn feast, (appointed, due) season, (set) time (appointed)

ALL THE BIBLICAL FESTIVALS
- ARE CALLED MOEDIM – APPOINTED TIMES FOR MEETING
- IF THE TIMES CAN BE CHANGED, IT WILL BE MAN CHANGING THEM, NOT YHWH
- HE WILL NOT CONTRADICT HIS WORD (Malachi 3:6)
- IF THE EMPHASIS OF A FESTIVAL CAN BE CHANGED, IT CHANGES YOUR FOCUS ON THAT FESTIVAL

Daniel 7:25 "This king will speak evil of God Most High, and he will be cruel to God's chosen ones. He will try to change God's Law and the sacred seasons. And he will be able to do this for a time, two times, and half a time.

IN ORDER TO OBSERVE PASSOVER, WE SHOULD KNOW AT WHAT TIME TO KEEP IT. WE ARE GIVEN THE REQUIREMENTS FOR THE FIRST MONTH

THE MONTH OF NISAN (AVIV - spring)

- IN ORDER TO GET THE DAY FOR THE PESACH RIGHT
- WE MUST KNOW WHAT THE FIRST DAY OF THE MONTH IS
- THIS WAS DONE IN YESHUA'S TIME WITH EYEWITNESSES FROM THE COURT AND WITH SIGNAL FIRES AND SHOFAR BLASTS
- WHEN THE TEMPLE WAS STANDING THE PEOPLE BROUGHT SACRIFICES AND HELD FEASTS TO HONOR A NEW TIME OF THE MERCY OF YHWH

ONCE THE MONTH WAS DETERMINED...
They had to select a lamb and bring it into their homes on the tenth day of the month.

Exodus 12:1-20
(3) Speak ye unto all the congregation of Israel, saying, In the tenth *day* of this month they shall take to them every man a lamb, according to the house of *their* fathers, a lamb for an house:
(4) And if the household be too little for the lamb, let him and his neighbour next unto his house take *it* according to the number of the souls; every man according to his eating shall make your count for the lamb.

The lamb was kept and inspected to make sure that it was a blameless offering. The slaughter of the lamb was performed at the same time throughout the whole community for the whole community.

Exodus 12:1-20
(5) Your animal must be without defect, a male in its first year, and you may choose it from either the sheep or the goats.
(6) " 'You are to keep it until the fourteenth day of the month, and then the entire assembly of the community of Isra'el will slaughter it at dusk. *(BETWEEN THE 14TH AND 15TH)*
(7) They are to take some of the blood and smear it on the two sides and top of the doorframe at the entrance of the house in which they eat it.
The blood was applied in observance of Passover. The blood went on the mezuzot (side posts) and the top post of the doors.

In Hebrew, the side post is called Mezuzah, both posts would be Mezuzot. This act of putting the blood on the side post was so important that there would be allusions to it through other scriptures. One of these other scriptures is recited as a prayer by Orthodox Jews three times a day. It is called the Shema. Because of the instructions in the Shema, it ties in very nicely to the redemption of Passover.

Deuteronomy 6:4-9 (CJB)"Sh'ma, Yisra'el! Adonai Eloheinu, Adonai echad [Hear, Isra'el! Adonai our God, Adonai is one]; (5) and you are to love Adonai your God with all your heart, all your being and all your resources. (6) These words, which I am ordering you today, are to be on your heart; (7) and you are to teach them carefully to your children. You are to talk about them when you sit at home, when you are traveling on the road, when you lie down and when you get up. (8) Tie them on your hand as a sign, put them at the front of a headband around your forehead, **(9) and write them** (the words of God) **on the door-frames** (mezuzot) **of your house and on your gates.**

In Biblical times, a servant was taken to the mezuzah and then the ear of the servant was pierced after making a declaration of loyalty. After this "ceremony" and a declaration of loyalty they were now called a bond servant, a servant for life.

Exodus 21:5-6
(5) Nevertheless, if the slave declares, 'I love my master, my wife and my children, so I don't want to go free,'
(6) then his master is to bring him before God; and there at the door or doorpost, his master is to pierce his ear with an awl; and the man will be his slave for life.

Deuteronomy 15:15-17
(15) And thou shalt remember that thou wast a bondman in the land of Egypt, and the LORD thy God redeemed thee: therefore I command thee this thing to day.
(16) And it shall be, if he say unto thee, I will not go away from thee; because he loveth thee and thine house, because he is well with thee;
(17) Then thou shalt take an aul, and thrust *it* through his ear unto the door, and he shall be thy servant for ever. And also unto thy maidservant thou shalt do likewise.

36

EXODUS 12:7

(7) They are to take some of the blood and smear it on the two sides and top of the doorframe at the entrance of the house in which they eat it. The two sides were called Ha'mzuzot in Hebrew. The singular form would be Mezuzah which is the Strongs concordance word H4201 מזוזה mezûzâh - a doorpost (as prominent): (door, side) post.

In modern day Israeli homes, a mezuzah is placed on the side of the door frames and on the gates. On the modern mezuzah used today, you will see the Hebrew letter "shin -ש" this is to stand for Shaddai, as in El Shaddai.

Exodus 6:3a

I appeared to Avraham, Yitz'chak and Ya`akov as El Shaddai (שׁדּי אֵל)

What does El Shaddai mean? Let's look in the Hebrew.

- H410 אל 'êl strength; mighty; especially the Almighty (but used also of any deity): - God (god), might (-y one), power, strong.
- H7706 שׁדּי shadday From H7703 שׁדד ; the Almighty: - Almighty. powerful; by implication to ravage: destroy (-er), spoil (-er), utterly (lay) waste.

Shaddai can also be seen as an acronym that explains something about YHWH. We know it as almighty God, but it is so much more!

שׁדּי - Shaddai

Hebrew reads right to left. As we look at this word the first letter would be "Shin- ש." Shin stands for the word Shamar- שׁמר – which is the Strongs concordance word; H8104.

A primitive root; properly to hedge about (as with thorns), that is, guard; generally to protect, attend to, etc.: - beware, be circumspect, take heed (to self), keep (-er, self), mark, look narrowly, observe, preserve, regard, reserve, save (self), sure, (that lay) wait (for), watch (-man).

שׁדּי - Shaddai

דלת – ד The second letter is "Dalet" or "Delet"
Which is the Strongs concordance word; H1817

37

From H1802; something swinging, that is, the valve of a door: - door (two-leaved), gate, leaf, lid

שַׁדַּי - Shaddai

יִשְׂרָאֵל – י the third is the letter "Yod" which stands for Israel

שַׁדַּי - Shaddai

שָׁמַר – שׁ

דֶּלֶת – דּ

י - יִשְׂרָאֵל

According to the acronym, El Shaddai (the Almighty God) is...

The watchman / guard
Over the doors / entryways
Of Israel

Psalms 141:3

Set a guard, Adonai, over my mouth; keep watch at the door of my lips.

The blood being applied to the mezuzah was to tell a story of rest, redemption and consolation to all Israel.

שַׁדַּי –- **Shaddai** guarded the homes by the word and blood being applied to it! Where else do we see the blood and the word working together to redeem the people of YHWH?

Revelation 12:11 And they overcame him by the blood of the Lamb, and by the word of their testimony; and they loved not their lives unto the death.

Revelation 19:13 And he [was] clothed with a vesture dipped in blood: and his name is called The Word of God.

YAHWEH HIMSELF SAW TO THE REDEMPTION OF HIS PEOPLE THROUGH THE JUDGMENT THAT HE EXECUTED! All the people had to do was to be obedient to the word that was given to them. Continuing on in Exodus chapter 12;

Exodus 12:8-14

(8) That night, they are to eat the meat,
- roasted in the fire;

- they are to eat it with matzah
- and maror.

(9) Don't eat it raw or boiled, but roasted in the fire, with its head, the lower parts of its legs and its inner organs.

(10) Let nothing of it remain till morning; if any of it does remain, burn it up completely.

(11) " 'Here is how you are to eat it: with your belt fastened, your shoes on your feet and your staff in your hand; and you are to eat it hurriedly. It is Adonai's Pesach [Passover].

(12) For that night, I will pass through the land of Egypt and kill all the firstborn in the land of Egypt, both men and animals; and I will execute judgment against all the gods of Egypt; I am Adonai.

(13) The blood will serve you as a sign marking the houses where you are; when I see the blood, I will pass over [pasach] you — when I strike the land of Egypt, the death blow will not strike you.

(14) " 'This will be a day for you to remember and celebrate as a festival to Adonai; from generation to generation you are to celebrate it by a perpetual regulation.

OBSERVATION OF PASSOVER

- ON THE TENTH CHOOSE A LAMB WITHOUT BLEMISH
- KEEP IT UNTIL THE FOURTEENTH AND SLAUGHTER IT AS EVENING OF THE 15TH APPROACHES (BETWEEN THE EVENINGS, ABOUT 3PM)
- PLACE THE BLOOD ON THE SIDEPOSTS AND TOP POST OF THE DOOR
- EAT THE LAMB –ALL OF IT
- WITH BITTER HERBS
- WITH MATZAH
- DON'T BOIL IT, BUT ROAST IT
- ANYTHING LEFT HAS TO BE BURNED – COMPLETELY CONSUMED
- EAT IT DRESSED READY TO LEAVE

The lamb that was slain is testified of from the beginning!

Revelation 13:8
And all that dwell upon the earth shall worship him (the beast), whose names are not written in the book of life of the Lamb slain from the foundation of the world.

Exodus 12:13-14
• (13) And the blood shall be to you for a token (SIGN) upon the houses where ye are: and when I see the blood, I will pass over you, and the plague shall not be upon you to destroy you, when I smite the land of Egypt.
• (14) And this day shall be unto you for a memorial; and ye shall keep it a feast to the LORD throughout your generations; ye shall keep it a feast by an ordinance for ever.

THE WORD IN VERSE 13 TRANSLATED TOKEN IS; OHT - SIGN
H226
אות
a signal (literally or figuratively), as a flag, beacon, monument, omen, prodigy, evidence, etc.: - mark, miracle, (en-) sign, token.

Remember, Messiah was to be a sign to the people and all the works of the Messiah were declared from the Beginning.

Isaiah 46:9-10
(9) Remember the former things of old: for I *am* God, and *there is* none else; *I am* God, and *there is* none like me,
(10) Declaring the end from the beginning, and from ancient times *the things* that are not *yet* done, saying, My counsel shall stand, and I will do all my pleasure:

Isaiah 44:6
     Thus saith the LORD the King of Israel, and his redeemer the LORD of hosts; I *am* the first, and I *am* the last; and beside me *there is* no God.

Isaiah 48:12
     Hearken unto me, O Jacob and Israel, my called; I *am* he; I *am* the first, I also *am* the last.

Rav Shaul (Apostle Paul) spoke Hebrew.
     ▪ Acts 21:40 ...Paul stood on the stairs, and beckoned with the hand unto the people. And when there was made a

great silence, *he spake unto them in the Hebrew tongue, saying,*

- Acts 22:2 (And when they heard that *he spake in the Hebrew tongue* to them, they kept the more silence: and he saith,)

On the road to Damascus, Paul made a point of saying that Jesus spoke to him, IN HEBREW.

Acts 26:12-15

(12) Whereupon as I went to Damascus with authority and commission from the chief priests,

(13) At midday, O king, I saw in the way a light from heaven, above the brightness of the sun, shining round about me and them which journeyed with me.

(14) And when we were all fallen to the earth, I heard a voice speaking unto me, and saying in the Hebrew tongue, Saul, Saul, why persecutest thou me? it is hard for thee to kick against the pricks.

(15) And I said, Who art thou, Lord? And he said, I am Jesus whom thou persecutest.

On the road to Emmaus after the crucifixion and resurrection, Yeshua encountered two men talking. He went with them on the road and joined in their conversation. They were talking about the One who they thought was the Messiah, was killed. We pick up the scripture here;

Luke 24:27

And beginning at Moses and all the prophets, he expounded unto them in all the scriptures the things concerning himself.

Yeshua, our Messiah did not decide to show some great miracle to show these two men who He was. He chose to reveal who the Messiah was starting with the writings of Moses and the writings of the prophets. He then revealed to them that He was the Messiah as He spoke a blessing and broke the Matzah.

After these events, He came to His disciples and revealed Himself to them by bringing reference to the writings of Moses and the prophets.

Luke 24:44-45

(44) And he said unto them, These *are* the words which I spake unto you, while I was yet with you, that all things must be fulfilled, which were written in the law of Moses, and *in* the prophets, and *in* the psalms, concerning me.

(45) Then opened he their understanding, that they might understand the scriptures,

The Apostle Paul used to go to the synagogues on the Sabbath and open the scriptures from the beginning and reveal the Messiah.

Acts 17:2-3

(2) And Paul, as his manner was, went in unto them, and three sabbath days reasoned with them out of the scriptures,

(3) Opening and alleging, that Christ must needs have suffered, and risen again from the dead; and that this Jesus, whom I preach unto you, is Christ.

YESHUA SAID: Revelation 1:8
I am Alpha and Omega, the beginning and the ending, saith the Lord, which is, and which was, and which is to come, the Almighty.

Genesis 1:1 –Messiah was declared in the beginning through The Aleph-Tav אֵת – the Aleph tav

בְּרֵאשִׁית בָּרָא אֱלֹהִים אֵת|הַשָּׁמַיִם וְאֵת הָאָרֶץ:

IN HEBREW, REVELATION 1:8 WOULD HAVE SAID:

אנ י ה א ל ף ו ה ת ו ר א ש ו ס ו ף
ani ha'alef v'hatav rosh v'suf
I AM THE "ET"
I AM THE ALEPH TAV

In the Hebrew language, this word "ET" has no translation. The only thing that we are told about it is that it points to something definite.

The Aleph-Tav worked with Yahweh for the creating of all things. That Aleph-Tav is Yeshua!

1Corinthians 8:6 yet for us there is one God, the Father, from whom all things come and for whom we exist; and one Lord,

42

Yeshua the Messiah, through whom were created all things and through whom we have our being.

Colossians 1:16-17 because in connection with him were created all things — in heaven and on earth, visible and invisible, whether thrones, lordships, rulers or authorities — they have all been created through him and for him. (17) He existed before all things, and he holds everything together.

WHAT WE SEE HERE IS; YESHUA THE "ET- aleph tav" BECAME THE "OHT- sign" - Messiah was to be a sign!

Luke 2:12
> And this *shall be* a sign unto you; Ye shall find the babe wrapped in swaddling clothes, lying in a manger.

Luke 2:25-35
(25) And, behold, there was a man in Jerusalem, whose name *was* Simeon; and the same man *was* just and devout, waiting for the consolation of Israel: and the Holy Ghost was upon him.
(26) And it was revealed unto him by the Holy Ghost, that he should not see death, before he had seen the Lord's Christ.
(27) And he came by the Spirit into the temple: and when the parents brought in the child Jesus, to do for him after the custom of the law,
(28) Then took he him up in his arms, and blessed God, and said,
(29) Lord, now lettest thou thy servant depart in peace, according to thy word:
(30) For mine eyes have seen thy salvation,
(31) Which thou hast prepared before the face of all people;
(32) A light to lighten the Gentiles, and the glory of thy people Israel.
(33) And Joseph and his mother marvelled at those things which were spoken of him.
(34) And Simeon blessed them, and said unto Mary his mother, Behold, this *child* is set for the fall and rising again of many in Israel; ***and for a sign*** which shall be spoken against;
(35) (Yea, a sword shall pierce through thy own soul also,) that the thoughts of many hearts may be revealed.

WHEN THE "VAV" PIERCES BETWEEN THE TWO LETTERS, THE "ET- את" BECAME THE "OHT- אות"

ו – VAV – 6th letter of the Hebrew Aleph Beit

6 – number of man

The "ET" "את" – Yeshua, becomes an "oht" "אות" the sign, when He takes on the sign of man.

By adding or "driving" in the "Vav" (ו or Y in paleo Hebrew) the word with no meaning, "ET" now becomes the word "sign."

The Paleo Hebrew Vav is a picture of a tent peg. The tent pegs were made of wood and may have been Y-shaped to prevent the rope from slipping off. This letter represents a peg or hook, which are used for securing something. The meaning of this letter is to add or secure. As in, our Salvation is secured by Messiah and the work of the cross. Yeshua, our Messiah was prophesied to be the lamb from God, even from Abraham.

Genesis 22:7-8

(7) And Isaac spake unto Abraham his father, and said, My father: and he said, Here am I, my son. And he said, Behold the fire and the wood: but where is the lamb for a burnt offering?

(8) And Abraham said, My son, God will provide himself a lamb for a burnt offering: so they went both of them together.

John declared Yeshua to be the lamb we see this in the book of John chapter 1.

John 1:29

The next day John seeth Jesus coming unto him, and saith, Behold the Lamb of God, which taketh away the sin of the world.

These scriptures refer back to Passover and Yom Kippur.

Passover was declared by God. He gave it as a sign of the redemption of His people. He asked His people to keep His word, for their own protection.

פסח – Passover

The message of Passover was heard by all of Israel. Hearing alone didn't matter. They had to hear the word and then keep it. In Hebrew that would be called "Shema". If they heard the word but did not obey it, they would have lost their firstborn. What the Father wanted from His people was to hear His instruction, keep it in faith and then they would be passed over from the plague.

This brings up the question of the blood. Did Yahweh know who belonged to Him? Yes! Then why did they have to apply the blood? Why couldn't they just make a declaration of faith? The blood was to be a sign! The blood being applied was to show not just Israel but the world that He would provide redemption and atonement through the blood.

Hebrews 4:1-3
(1) Therefore, let us be terrified of the possibility that, even though the promise of entering his rest remains, any one of you might be judged to have fallen short of it;
(2) for Good News has also been proclaimed to us, just as it was to them. But the message they heard didn't do them any good, because those who heard it did not combine it with trust (FAITH).
(3) For it is we who have trusted who enter the rest. It is just as he said, "And in my anger, I swore that they would not enter my rest." He swore this even though his works have been in existence since the founding of the universe.

We see in the Scriptures that all who believed obeyed what the Father said. The result was that all who believed were delivered!

Exodus 12:38-39
And a mixed multitude went up also with them; and flocks, and herds, even very much cattle.
(39) And they baked unleavened cakes of the dough which they brought forth out of Egypt, for it was not leavened; because they were thrust out of Egypt, and could not tarry, neither had they prepared for themselves any victual.

Matthew 11:28
Come unto me, <u>all</u> ye that labour and are heavy laden, and I will give you rest.

PASSOVER AND REDEMPTION ARE CONNECTED.

As we look back at Scripture we see that Pesach was a fulfillment of a promise that was given over 400 years earlier.

Genesis 15:13-14
• (13) And he said unto Abram, Know of a surety that thy seed shall be a stranger in a land that is not theirs, and shall serve them; and they shall afflict them four hundred years;
• (14) And also that nation, whom they shall serve, will I judge: and afterward shall they come out with great substance.

Yahweh had a plan for your redemption. It was revealed in the Passover, and the following wilderness experience:
• Their redemption did not come all at one time.
• Redemption came little by little,
• one step at a time until it was final

EXODUS 23:28-30
(28) And I will send hornets before thee, which shall drive out the Hivite, the Canaanite, and the Hittite, from before thee.
(29) I will not drive them out from before thee in one year; lest the land become desolate, and the beast of the field multiply against thee.
(30) By little and little I will drive them out from before thee, until thou be increased, and inherit the land.

Through the events leading up to and included in Passover, we see that the redemption of the people of God was declared four different ways. We see this listed in Exodus chapter six. We will now break down the few verses in chapter six in order to explain this.

FOUR WAYS OF REDEMPTION ACCORDING TO EXODUS 6:6-7
I will free you from the forced labor of the Egyptians,
- **rescue you** from their oppression, and
- **redeem you** with an outstretched arm and with great judgments.
- I will **take you** as my people, and I will be your God. Then you will know that I am Adonai your God, who freed you from the forced labor of the Egyptians.

1. **I will free you/bring you out**
H3318
א צ י
yâtsâ'
to go (causatively bring) out, break out, carry out, come (abroad, out, thereat, without), depart ,draw forth, escape, exact, get

46

away, grow, pluck out, proceed, pull out, put away, be risen, send with commandment, shoot forth, spread, spring out, stand out

Isaiah 55:11 So shall my word be that goeth forth out of my mouth: it shall not return unto me void, but it shall accomplish that which I please, and it shall prosper [in the thing] whereto I sent it.

Ezekiel 34:13 And I will bring them out from the people, and gather them from the countries, and will bring them to their own land, and feed them upon the mountains of Israel by the rivers, and in all the inhabited places of the country.

Ezekiel 33:30
Also, thou son of man, the children of thy people still are talking against thee by the walls and in the doors of the houses, and speak one to another, every one to his brother, saying, Come, I pray you, and hear what is the word that cometh forth from the LORD.

The word coming to you from YHWH is to bring you out

John 8:36
So if the Son frees you, you will really be free!

Ezekiel 33:30-33
(30) "Now you, human being, your people are gathering and talking about you by the walls and in the doorways of houses. They're saying to each other, each one telling his brother, 'Come, let's go and hear the latest word coming from Adonai.'
(31) So then they come to you, as people do, sit in front of you as my people, and hear your words; but they don't act on them. For with their mouths they flatter you, but their hearts are set on their own self-interest;
(32) so for them you are like a love-song sung by someone with a nice voice who can play an instrument well — they hear your words, but they don't act on them.
(33) So when all this comes true, then, at last, they will realize that a prophet has been there with them."

After you are drawn out...
- Then you are rescued
- defended
- and preserved

47

FOUR WAYS OF REDEMPTION ACCORDING TO EXODUS 6:6-7

- I will free you from the forced labor of the Egyptians,

rescue you from their oppression, and

- redeem you with an outstretched arm and with great judgments.
- I will take you as my people, and I will be your God. Then you will know that I am Adonai your God, who freed you from the forced labor of the Egyptians.

2. I will rescue you

H5337 נ צ ל nâtsal

to snatch away, defend, deliver , escape, without fail, preserve, recover, rescue, rid, save, take (out)

Psalms 34:17 [The righteous] cry, and the LORD heareth, and delivereth them out of all their troubles.

Psalms 97:10 Ye that love the LORD, hate evil: he preserveth the souls of his saints; he delivereth them out of the hand of the wicked.

Proverbs 11:4 Riches profit not in the day of wrath: but righteousness delivereth from death.

2 Timothy 4:18
The Lord will rescue me from every evil attack and bring me safely into his heavenly Kingdom. To him be the glory forever and ever. Amen.

After you are drawn out you are rescued, defended and preserved by the Father.

FOUR WAYS OF REDEMPTION ACCORDING TO EXODUS 6:6-7

- I will free you from the forced labor of the Egyptians,
- rescue you from their oppression, and

redeem you with an outstretched arm and with great judgments.

- I will take you as my people, and I will be your God. Then you will know that I am Adonai your God, who freed you from the forced labor of the Egyptians.

3. I will redeem you
H1350 גָּאַל gâ'al

to redeem, to be the next of kin (and as such to buy back a relative's property, marry his widow, etc.): avenger, deliver, purchase, ransom, redeem (-er), revenger.

Isaiah 54:5 For thy Maker [is] thine husband; the LORD of hosts [is] his name; and thy Redeemer the Holy One of Israel; The God of the whole earth shall he be called.

Isaiah 62:12 And they shall call them, The holy people, The redeemed of the LORD: and thou shalt be called, Sought out, A city not forsaken.

Isaiah 43:1 But now thus saith the LORD that created thee, O Jacob, and he that formed thee, O Israel, Fear not: for I have redeemed thee, I have called [thee] by thy name; thou [art] mine.

Revelation 5:9
And they sung a new song, saying, Thou art worthy to take the book, and to open the seals thereof: for thou wast slain, and hast redeemed us to God by thy blood out of every kindred, and tongue, and people, and nation;

FOUR WAYS OF REDEMPTION ACCORDING TO EXODUS 6:6-7
- I will free you from the forced labor of the Egyptians,
- rescue you from their oppression, and
- redeem you with an outstretched arm and with great judgments.

I will **take you** as my people, and I will be your God. Then you will know that I am Adonai your God, who freed you from the forced labor of the Egyptians.

4. I will take you as my people
H3947 לָקַח lâqach

to take,- accept, bring, buy, carry away, drawn, fetch, get, infold, place, receive (-ing), reserve, seize, send for

Ezekiel 36:24 For I will take you from among the heathen, and gather you out of all countries, and will bring you into your own land.

49

Deuteronomy 4:20 But the LORD hath taken you, and brought you forth out of the iron furnace, [even] out of Egypt, to be unto him a people of inheritance, as [ye are] this day.

Ephesians 2:10-13
(10) For we are his workmanship, created in Christ Jesus unto good works, which God hath before ordained that we should walk in them.
(11) Wherefore remember, that ye *being* in time past Gentiles in the flesh, who are called Uncircumcision by that which is called the Circumcision in the flesh made by hands;
(12) That at that time ye were without Christ, being aliens from the commonwealth of Israel, and strangers from the covenants of promise, having no hope, and without God in the world:
(13) But now in Christ Jesus ye who sometimes were far off are made nigh by the blood of Christ.

Hosea 14:1-2
(1) Return, Isra'el, to Adonai your God, for your guilt has made you stumble.
(2) Take words with you, and return to Adonai; say to him, "Forgive all guilt, and accept what is good; we will pay instead of bulls [the offerings of] our lips. (obedience)

Ephesians 1:6
To the praise of the glory of his grace, wherein he hath made us accepted in the beloved.

The redemption of the people of God, started with Him judging the nation that oppressed them. We see this in Exodus chapter 11.
EXODUS 11:1-5
(1) And the LORD said unto Moses, Yet will I bring one plague more upon Pharaoh, and upon Egypt; afterwards he will let you go hence: when he shall let you go, he shall surely thrust you out hence altogether.
(2) Speak now in the ears of the people, and let every man borrow of his neighbour, and every woman of her neighbour, jewels of silver, and jewels of gold.
(3) And the LORD gave the people favour in the sight of the Egyptians. Moreover the man Moses was very great in the land of

Egypt, in the sight of Pharaoh's servants, and in the sight of the people.
(4) And Moses said, Thus saith the LORD, About midnight will I go out into the midst of Egypt:
(5) And all the firstborn in the land of Egypt shall die, from the firstborn of Pharaoh that sitteth upon his throne, even unto the firstborn of the maidservant that is behind the mill; and all the firstborn of beasts.

This time of Passover had such an impact that it was to be a new beginning for Israel.

EXODUS 12:1-2
(1) And the LORD spake unto Moses and Aaron in the land of Egypt, saying,
(2) This month shall be unto you the beginning of months: it shall be the first month of the year to you.

In this new beginning, and in showing how He was to redeem His people, God explained that His desire was to bring the people to Him and into His family.

EXODUS 12:3
Speak to all the assembly of Isra'el and say, 'On the tenth day of this month, each man is to take a lamb or kid for his family, one _per household_'
- One lamb per household, not per son, emphasizing the saving of the household of Yahweh. Bringing us into His Family through the blood of the lamb.

So, let's continue in the book of Exodus chapter twelve. We've already addressed the observation of Passover. Now, we will read the Biblical account of the redemption of the people of YHWH through the Passover.

EXODUS 12:11-13
(11) And thus shall ye eat it; with your loins girded, your shoes on your feet, and your staff in your hand; and ye shall eat it in haste: it is the LORD'S passover. - not Jewish- YHWH's
(12) For I will pass through the land of Egypt this night, and will smite all the firstborn in the land of Egypt, both man and beast; and against all the gods of Egypt I will execute judgment: I am the LORD.

(13) _The blood will serve you as a sign_ marking the houses (note, not individual but collective) where you are; when I see the blood, I will pass over [pasach] you — when I strike the land of Egypt, the death blow will not strike you.

H226 ת ו א 'ôth a signal, a flag, beacon, monument, omen, prodigy, evidence, mark, miracle, (en-) sign, token.

ת א became ת ו א , by the blood that was shed (applied) to the house where you are

H1004 בית bayith - a house, especially family

WE REMEMBER AND OBSERVE PASSOVER & THE FEAST OF UNLEAVENED BREAD AS A MEMORIAL OF THE REDEMPTIONOF THE PEOPLE OF YHWH.

EXODUS 12:14-20
(14) And this day shall be unto you for a memorial; and ye shall keep it a feast to the LORD throughout your generations; ye shall keep it a feast by an ordinance for ever.
(15) Seven days shall ye eat unleavened bread; even the first day ye shall put away leaven out of your houses: for whosoever eateth leavened bread from the first day until the seventh day, that soul shall be cut off from Israel.
(16) And in the first day there shall be an holy convocation, and in the seventh day there shall be an holy convocation to you; no manner of work shall be done in them, save that which every man must eat, that only may be done of you.
(17) And ye shall observe the feast of unleavened bread; for in this selfsame day have I brought your armies out of the land of Egypt: therefore shall ye observe this day in your generations by an ordinance for ever.
(18) In the first month, on the fourteenth day of the month at even, ye shall eat unleavened bread, until the one and twentieth day of the month at even.
(19) Seven days shall there be no leaven found in your houses: for whosoever eateth that which is leavened, even that soul shall be cut off from the congregation of Israel, whether he be a stranger, or born in the land.
(20) Ye shall eat nothing leavened;
- in all your habitations
- shall ye eat unleavened bread.

In many places in Scripture leaven represents sin. It starts small but can grow quickly. Once it starts to grow and ferment the dough it is evidently seen that the whole batch of dough becomes fermented or "leavened." We could take the word to eat only unleavened things during this time to mean that we should be "eating" or taking into yourself, the Word of YHWH and living a sinless life.

James 1:14-15 KJV
(14) But every man is tempted, when he is drawn away of his own lust, and enticed.
(15) Then when lust hath conceived, it bringeth forth sin: and sin, when it is finished, bringeth forth death.

The Word of the LORD will teach you discernment as you continue in it. We are constantly faced with things in our life that need to be surrendered to the Father. We can call this "leaven." The time of Passover teaches us to look intently at ourselves and our lifestyle and if there is any "leaven" there, get rid of it. As we progress in our walk we look at ourselves as the Scripture tells us to. We can easily say what King David did in Psalms 26:2 "Examine me, O LORD, and prove me; try my reins and my heart."

Yeshua addressed this with His disciples in Matthew 16:11-12. "How is it that you do not understand that I did not speak to you about loaves of bread? But beware of the leaven of the Pharisees and Sadducees." (12) Then they understand that He did not tell them to beware of the leaven of loaves of bread, but of the teaching of the Pharisees and Sadducees.

We see again in Luke 12:1-3 *(italics added for clarification)*
(1) Meanwhile, as a crowd in the tens of thousands gathered so closely as to trample each other down, Yeshua began to say to his talmidim first, "Guard yourselves from the hametz *(Leaven)* of the P'rushim *(Pharisees)*, by which I mean their hypocrisy.
(Those who say they love the word, but do not do as it says)
(2) There is nothing covered up that will not be uncovered, or hidden that will not become known.
(3) What you have spoken in the dark will be heard in the light, and what you have whispered behind closed doors will be proclaimed on the housetops.

EXODUS 12:24-27

(24) And ye shall observe this thing for an ordinance to thee and to thy sons for ever.

(25) And it shall come to pass, when ye be come to the land which the LORD will give you, according as he hath promised, that ye shall keep this service.

(26) And it shall come to pass, when your children shall say unto you, What mean ye by this service?

(27) That ye shall say, It is the sacrifice of the LORD'S passover, who passed over the houses of the children of Israel in Egypt, when he smote the Egyptians, and delivered our houses. And the people bowed the head and worshipped.

Exodus 12:38 A mixed crowd also went up with them, as well as livestock in large numbers, both flocks and herds.

Exodus 12:43 Adonai said to Moshe and Aharon, "This is the regulation for the Pesach lamb: no foreigner is to eat it.

Exodus 12:46 It is to be eaten in one house. You are not to take any of the meat outside the house, and you are not to break any of its bones.

Exodus 12:47 The whole community of Isra'el is to keep it.

ROMANS 11:17

But if some of the branches were broken off,
-and you — a wild olive —
-were grafted in among them
-and have become equal sharers
-in the rich root of the olive tree,

A believer has been grafted in ***to be a part of*** Israel, by the covenant of Avraham, through the blood of Messiah. Yahweh gave one word to His people. He is completely unified as One, Father, Ruach (Spirit), and Son (Yeshua). He called out twelve tribes, and all those who decided to join with them, from Egypt. Together they were called His people, His nation, Israel. To one people (His) He gave One Word. The Torah, Writings, prophets (Old Testament, or Tanakh) goes perfectly with the New Testament. He gave One word which was from the beginning, for One people, His.

Exodus 12:49 One law (תורה Torah- teaching and instruction) shall be to him that is homeborn, and unto the stranger that sojourneth among you.

Exodus 12:49 (LITV) One law shall be to the native, and to the visitor, the one staying in your midst.

Numbers 15:16 One law and one manner shall be for you, and for the stranger that sojourneth with you.

When we were redeemed, we became servants to Yahweh! So, in truth we were never freed and released to our own volition. We continued our servitude, just to a different master!

ROMANS 1:1
From: Sha'ul, a slave of the Messiah Yeshua, an emissary because I was called and set apart for the Good News of God.

It was during this time of Passover that the firstborn was declared to be the ones given over to the service of Yahweh.

EXODUS 13:1-2 (CJB)
Adonai said to Moshe,
(2) "Set aside for me all the firstborn. Whatever is first from the womb among the people of Isra'el, both of humans and of animals, belongs to me."

The first born were to be the Priests and were to be in the service of YHWH.

1 PETER 2:5-12
(5) you yourselves, as living stones, are being built into a spiritual house to be cohanim set apart for God to offer spiritual sacrifices acceptable to him through Yeshua the Messiah.
(6) This is why the Tanakh says, "Look! I am laying in Tziyon a stone, a chosen and precious cornerstone; and whoever rests his trust on it will certainly not be humiliated."
(7) Now to you who keep trusting, he is precious. But to those who are not trusting, "The very stone that the builders rejected has become the cornerstone";

(8) also he is a stone that will make people stumble, a rock over which they will trip. They are stumbling at the Word, disobeying it — as had been planned.

(9) But you are a chosen people, the King's cohanim, a holy nation, a people for God to possess! Why? In order for you to declare the praises of the One who called you out of darkness into his wonderful light.

(10) Once you were not a people, but now you are God's people; before, you had not received mercy, but now you have received mercy.

(11) Dear friends, I urge you as aliens and temporary residents not to give in to the desires of your old nature, which keep warring against you;

(12) but to live such good lives among the pagans that even though they now speak against you as evil-doers, they will, as a result of seeing your good actions, give glory to God on the Day of his coming.

EXODUS 13:8-10

(8) On that day you are to tell your son, 'It is because of what Adonai did for me when I left Egypt.'

(9) "Moreover, it will serve you as a sign on your hand and as a reminder between your eyes, so that Adonai's Torah may be on your lips; because with a strong hand Adonai brought you out of Egypt.

(10) Therefore you are to observe this regulation at its proper time, year after year.

FULFILLMENT OF PASSOVER IN YESHUA THE MESSIAH

1. The feast marked a new year, a new beginning for Israel.

Exodus 12:1-2
(1) And the LORD spake unto Moses and Aaron in the land of Egypt, saying,
(2) This month *shall be* unto you the beginning of months: it *shall be* the first month of the year to you.

2 Corinthians 5:17
Therefore if any man *be* in Christ, *he is* a new creature: old things are passed away; behold, all things are become new.

2. The lamb was to be without blemish
   Yeshua was inspected by:
   a)   **Pilate (Matthew 27:11)**
   b)   **Herod (Luke 23:8–12)**
   c)   **Annas (John 18:12–13)**
   d)   **Caiaphas (Matthew 26:57)**
   They could find no fault in him. Yeshua truly is the "lamb without blemish or defect."

Exodus 12:5
   Your lamb shall be without blemish, a male of the first year: ye shall take *it* out from the sheep, or from the goats:

1 Peter 1:19
   But with the precious blood of Christ, as of a lamb without blemish and without spot:

3. Receiving the sacrifice through Yeshua will gather you in to be part of the Family of YHWH (Israel).

Exodus 12:6
   And ye shall keep it up until the fourteenth day of the same month: and the whole assembly of the congregation of Israel shall kill it in the evening.

Romans 3:21-26
   (21)   But now the righteousness of God without the law is manifested, being witnessed by the law and the prophets;
   (22)   Even the righteousness of God *which is* by faith of Jesus Christ unto all and upon all them that believe: for there is no difference:
   (23)   For all have sinned, and come short of the glory of God;
   (24)   Being justified freely by his grace through the redemption that is in Christ Jesus:
   (25)   Whom God hath set forth *to be* a propitiation through faith in his blood, to declare his righteousness for the remission of sins that are past, through the forbearance of God;
   (26)   To declare, *I say,* at this time his righteousness: that he might be just, and the justifier of him which believeth in Jesus.

4. The blood of the sacrificed lamb was applied to the doorframe—the lintel and side posts and because of the

covering of blood, _the house (the household)_ was spared from God's plague. Yeshua shed his blood to rescue and atone for his people. We need to be covered or justified by the blood of the Lamb to be rescued from condemnation. Yeshua is the Lamb that takes away the sins of the world.

Exodus 12:7, 12, 22

(7) And they shall take of the blood, and strike _it_ on the two side posts and on the upper door post of the houses, wherein they shall eat it.

(12) For I will pass through the land of Egypt this night, and will smite all the firstborn in the land of Egypt, both man and beast; and against all the gods of Egypt I will execute judgment: I _am_ the LORD.

(22) And ye shall take a bunch of hyssop, and dip _it_ in the blood that _is_ in the bason, and strike the lintel and the two side posts with the blood that _is_ in the bason; and none of you shall go out at the door of his house until the morning.

John 1:29

The next day John seeth Jesus coming unto him, and saith, Behold the Lamb of God, which taketh away the sin of the world.

5. During the Last Supper, Yeshua refers to the bread as "my body given for you; do this in remembrance of me." He only needed to do it once lasting forever.

Exodus 12:14

And this day shall be unto you for a memorial; and ye shall keep it a feast to the LORD throughout your generations; ye shall keep it a feast by an ordinance for ever.

Luke 22:19

And he took bread, and gave thanks, and brake _it,_ and gave unto them, saying, This is my body which is given for you: this do in remembrance of me.

6. YHWH commanded Israel not to break any bones of the sacrificed lamb.

Exodus 12:46

> In one house shall it be eaten; thou shalt not carry forth ought of the flesh abroad out of the house; neither shall ye break a bone thereof.

John 19:32-33

(32) Then came the soldiers, and brake the legs of the first, and of the other which was crucified with him.

(33) But when they came to Jesus, and saw that he was dead already, they brake not his legs:

Even in the Passover Haggadah, (the book that tells the Passover story- haggadah literally means "telling") that is used every year at the Passover Seder (the Passover dinner or the order of the telling) you can see many ways in which the Messiah is revealed.

At the Pesach telling, Yeshua revealed Himself and what was to be.

Matthew 26:27-29 *(italics added by author for emphasis)*

(27) And he took the cup, and gave thanks, and gave [it] to them, saying, Drink ye all of it;

(28) For this is my blood of the new testament, which is shed for many for the remission of sins. *(at the time He revealed Himself, He also made a vow that he would be set apart for His bride and that He would be waiting for her)*

(29) But I say unto you, I will not drink henceforth of this fruit of the vine, *(this was a vow made with witnesses and a timeframe was put on the vow)*

• until that day when I drink it new with you in my Father's kingdom.

Numbers 6:1-4

(1) Adonai said to Moshe, (2) "Tell the people of Isra'el, 'When either a man or a woman makes a special kind of vow, the vow of a nazir, consecrating himself to Adonai;

(3) he is to abstain from wine and other intoxicating liquor, he is not to drink vinegar from either source, he is not to drink grape juice, and he is not to eat grapes or raisins.

(4) As long as he remains a nazir he is to eat nothing derived from the grapevine, not even the grape-skins or the seeds.

59

Without an understanding of this vow, often called a Nazirite vow, we will misinterpret another scripture.

Matthew 27:34
they gave him wine mixed with bitter gall to drink; but after tasting it, he would not drink it. *(Yeshua had made the vow that He would not drink nor eat from the fruit of the vine until He rejoins His bride.)*

By making this declaration at the last supper, Yeshua was setting Himself apart with a Nazirite vow. The Hebrew word is Nazir.
H5139
נָזִיר
nâzîyr
From H5144; separate, consecrated, an unpruned vine (like an unshorn Nazirite). separate (-d), vine undressed.

H5144
נָזַר
nâzar
A primitive root; to hold aloof, abstain (from food and drink, from impurity), set apart (to sacred purposes), devote: consecrate, separate (-ing, self).

It was not necessary that a person would make this vow. A person who underwent a Nazirite vow was setting themselves apart as holy to the Father for a certain period of time. During this time there were certain things required of them. They would have spent a dedicated time to the sole pursuit of the Father and things that pertain to Him only. The Torah does not say you need to make a vow like this. It does however say that if you do make a vow of any kind, to KEEP IT. If you decide to set yourself apart there are requirements on you that may not be necessarily applicable to the "layman" of Israel. Many of the requirements for the Nazir were the same as the Levites.

It is my opinion that Yeshua was making this vow to allude to the fact that He is setting Himself aside as the High priest to go and serve in the Holy of Holies and to make intercession for us. When we partake of the cup with Him in the Kingdom, it will be great joy.

Yeshua further told us that every word we speak is held at a higher level of accountability. In other words, you will be held accountable to every word you say. Not just held accountable for vows alone. Say nothing unless you mean it.

Matthew 5:33-37

(33) "Again, you have heard that our fathers were told, 'Do not break your oath,' and 'Keep your vows to Adonai.'

(34) But I tell you not to swear at all — not 'by heaven,' because it is God's throne;

(35) not 'by the earth,' because it is his footstool; and not 'by Yerushalayim,' because it is the city of the Great King.

(36) And don't swear by your head, because you can't make a single hair white or black.

(37) Just let your 'Yes' be a simple 'Yes,' and your 'No' a simple 'No'; anything more than this has its origin in evil.

Our redemption was declared in the Spring feasts of Yahweh. They tell the story of the work of the Messiah when He came. To aid in further revealing the Messiah in the Passover, I have included in this writing a copy of a Messianic Seder. The difference between this Seder and a traditional one is that this Seder has included scriptures from the New Testament to help in bringing out the pictures and the shadows of Messiah Yeshua.

The order For a MESSIANIC PASSOVER SEDER

KADDESH - Kiddush blessing, setting apart this time

LEADER: We are gathered this evening to observe and remember Passover, God's deliverance of His people. God delivered Israel from the bondage of slavery and He commanded us to observe this holiday. We are not to celebrate in vain, but to give thanks to Him and to recognize an even greater Passover and deliverance. Through the death of the foretold Messiah-Yeshua, we too will be passed over from death and released from the bondage of sin.

I ask tonight that you consider each of the scriptures and prayers that we will be reading this evening and that you may truly observe and recognize our God, the God of Abraham, Isaac and Jacob. I also encourage you to seek God on your own. The truth is revealed in God's Word.

READER: Exodus 12:17 You are to observe the festival of matzah, for on this very day I brought your divisions out of the land of Egypt. Therefore, you are to observe this day from generation to generation by a perpetual regulation.

READER: Luke 22:19 Also, taking a piece of matzah, he made the b'rakhah, broke it, gave it to them and said, "This is my body, which is being given for you; do this in memory of me."

(Leader says a Prayer -- not scripted)

LEADER: Light is a symbol of God's presence.

Yeshua said - John 8:12 "I am the Light of the world"

He also said - Matthew 5:14 "You are light for the world.

Lighting 2 candles during holidays and on Shabbat remind us that God is our light, we are to be light, and we should stand as one of two witnesses to testify of the faithfulness of YHWH

It is also written in Genesis that the offspring of a woman would crush the serpent's head.

64

Genesis 3:15 I will put animosity between you and the woman, and between your descendant and her descendant; he will bruise your head, and you will bruise his heel."

It is through a woman that our salvation would come (Messiah would be born), our hope, our light. It is by the seed of a woman that Yeshua was born. Let us kindle the festival lights.

WOMAN: *Ba-rukh A-tah A-do-nai E-lo-hey-nu Me-lekh ha-'o-lam a-sher kid-sha-nu B'-mi-tzvo-tav v'-tzi-va-nu l'-had-lik ner shel (shabbat) yom tov.* Blessed are you, O Lord our God, King of the Universe, who has sanctified us by your commandments, and has commanded us to kindle the Festival lights. Amen.

Ba-rukh A-tah A-do-nai E-lo-hey-nu Me-lekh ha-'o-lam a-sher she-he-che-ya-nu v'-ki-yi-mo-nu v'-hi-gi-a-nu l'z-man ha-zey. Blessed are you, O Lord our God, King of the Universe, who has kept us in life and has preserved us, and has enabled us to reach this season. Amen.

LEADER: The Seder plate has many items that we will use to experience the Passover using our senses. We will now begin reading the Haggadah, which means "the telling". We are called to celebrate Passover -- Jew and Gentile. For Yeshua said:

Matthew 5:17-20 "Don't think that I have come to abolish the Torah or the Prophets. I have come not to abolish but to complete. (18) Yes indeed! I tell you that until heaven and earth pass away, not so much as a yud (י) or a stroke will pass from the Torah — not until everything that must happen has happened. (19) So whoever disobeys the least of these mitzvot and teaches others to do so will be called the least in the Kingdom of Heaven. But whoever obeys them and so teaches will be called great in the Kingdom of Heaven. (20) For I tell you that unless your righteousness is far greater than that of the Torah-teachers and P'rushim, you will certainly not enter the Kingdom of Heaven!

Paul told us --1 Corinthians 5:7-8 Get rid of the old hametz, so that you can be a new batch of dough, because in reality you are unleavened. For our Pesach lamb, the Messiah, has been sacrificed. (8) So let us celebrate the Seder not with leftover hametz, the hametz of wickedness and evil, but with the matzah of purity and truth.

READER: Exodus 6:1 Adonai said to Moshe, "Now you will see what I am going to do to Pharaoh. With a mighty hand he will send them off; with force he will drive them from the land!"

ALL: Exodus 6:6-7 "Therefore, say to the people of Isra'el: 'I am Adonai. I will free you from the forced labor of the Egyptians, rescue you from their oppression, and redeem you with an outstretched arm and with great judgments. (7) I will take you as my people, and I will be your God. Then you will know that I am Adonai your God, who freed you from the forced labor of the Egyptians.

LEADER: During the Seder we drink four glasses of wine:

The Cup of Sanctification, the Cup of Plagues, The Cup of Redemption and the Cup of Praise. We will say the traditional prayer before drinking each cup. I would also like to point out that there is traditional meaning with each cup as well as Yeshua's fulfillment.

SANCTIFICATION:

Traditional - We are to be clean of yeast.

Fulfillment - We are to be clean of sin -- Yeshua

is the only way to be cleansed of our sins.

PLAGUES:

Traditional - Remembrance of the Plagues in

Egypt

Fulfillment - Remembrance of our trials and

66

tribulations - develops perseverance, humility and maturity in our walk with the Lord

REDEMPTION:

Traditional - Symbolizes the blood of the Passover lamb who saved the Israelites from death

Fulfillment - Yeshua is our Passover Lamb who's blood saved us from death. This cup is the cup used in communion or The Lord's Supper.

PRAISE:

Traditional - Give thanks to God for guiding Israel out of Egypt

Fulfillment - We are to always have praise on our lips for our salvation that is given through Yeshua.

READER: Hebrews 10:22-29 Therefore, let us approach the Holiest Place with a sincere heart, in the full assurance that comes from trusting — with our hearts sprinkled clean from a bad conscience and our bodies washed with pure water. (23) Let us continue holding fast to the hope we acknowledge, without wavering; for the One who made the promise is trustworthy. (24) And let us keep paying attention to one another, in order to spur each other on to love and good deeds, (25) not neglecting our own congregational meetings, as some have made a practice of doing, but, rather, encouraging each other. And let us do this all the more as you see the Day approaching. (26) For if we deliberately continue to sin after receiving the knowledge of the truth, there no longer remains a sacrifice for sins, (27) but only the terrifying prospect of Judgment, of raging fire that will consume the enemies. (28) Someone who disregards the Torah of Moshe is put to death without mercy on the word of two or three witnesses. (29) Think how much worse will be the punishment deserved by someone who has trampled underfoot the Son of God; who has treated as something common the blood of the covenant which made him holy; and who has insulted the Spirit, giver of God's grace!

READER: Luke 22:14-18 When the time came, Yeshua and the emissaries reclined at the table, (15) and he said to them, "I have really wanted so much to celebrate this Seder with you before I die! (16) For I tell you, it is certain that I will not celebrate it again until it is given its full meaning in the Kingdom of God." (17) Then, taking a cup of wine, he made the b'rakhah and said, "Take this and share it among yourselves. (18) For I tell you that from now on, I will not drink the 'fruit of the vine' until the Kingdom of God comes."

LEADER: Sanctification is the first step to drawing close to the Father. God is holy and we can not enter His presence with sin. He established the sacrificial system to make atonement for us and to cover us in order to allow us to draw near to Him. Exodus 19:22 Even the cohanim, who are allowed to approach Adonai, must keep themselves holy; otherwise, Adonai may break out against them." Leviticus 10:3 Moshe said to Aharon, "This is what Adonai said: 'Through those who are near me I will be consecrated, and before all the people I will be glorified.' " Aharon kept silent.

Yeshua is the ultimate sacrifice, so we can be in the presence of the Father. May we all be sanctified through the blood of the Lamb, Yeshua.

Please fill your cup. 1 Corinthians 11:26-29 For as often as you eat this bread and drink the cup, you proclaim the death of the Lord, until he comes. (27) Therefore, whoever eats the Lord's bread or drinks the Lord's cup in an unworthy manner will be guilty of desecrating the body and blood of the Lord! (28) So let a person examine himself first, and then he may eat of the bread and drink from the cup; (29) for a person who eats and drinks without recognizing the body eats and drinks judgment upon himself.

Let us lift our cups, the Cup of Sanctification, and bless the Lord for His abundant giving.

ALL: *Ba-rukh a-tah A-do-nai E-lo-hey-nu Me-lekh ha-'o-lam bo-rey pri ha-ga-fen.* Blessed are you, O Lord our God, Ruler of the Universe, who creates the fruit of the vine.

(Drink the first cup of wine.)

URECHATZ – Ritual hand washing

READER: Psalms 24:1-10 *[By David. A psalm:]* The earth is Adonai's, with all that is in it, the world and those who live there; (2) for he set its foundations on the seas and established it on the rivers. (3) Who may go up to the mountain of Adonai? Who can stand in his holy place? (4) Those with clean hands and pure hearts, who don't make vanities the purpose of their lives or swear oaths just to deceive. (5) They will receive a blessing from Adonai and justice from God, who saves them. (6) Such is the character of those who seek him, of Ya`akov, who seeks your face. (Selah) (7) Lift up your heads, you gates! Lift them up, everlasting doors, so that the glorious king can enter! (8) Who is he, this glorious king? Adonai, strong and mighty, Adonai, mighty in battle. (9) Lift up your heads, you gates! Lift them up, everlasting doors, so that the glorious king can enter! (10) Who is he, this glorious king? Adonai-Tzva'ot - he is the glorious king. (Selah)

LEADER: Let us wash our hands. As we wash, let us renew our commitment to God to have "clean hands and a clean heart".

(wash hands and then dry.)

ALL: *Ba-rukh A-tah A-do-nai E-lo-hey-nu Me-lekh ha-'o-lam a-sher kid-sha-nu B'-mitz-vo-tav v'-tzi-va-nu ahl na-tie-lat ya-da-yim.* Blessed are you, O Lord our God, King of the Universe, who has sanctified us by your commandments, and has commanded us to wash our hands.

69

the last phrase and has commanded us to wash our hands has been added into the blessing it is not a direct commandment of the LORD. However, I do believe that it is good practice to wash our hands before we eat. The point here though is not dirt free hands. The idea is that we approach the Father with clean hands and a pure heart. In this aspect we are commanded to have clean hands before Him. Which means that the working of our hands are clean before a Holy God and that our deeds or doings are clean before Him as well.

Psalms 24:3-5 KJV

(3) Who shall ascend into the hill of the LORD? or who shall stand in his holy place?

(4) He that hath clean hands, and a pure heart; who hath not lifted up his soul unto vanity, nor sworn deceitfully.

(5) He shall receive the blessing from the LORD, and righteousness from the God of his salvation.

James 4:8 KJV

(8) Draw nigh to God, and he will draw nigh to you. Cleanse your hands, ye sinners; and purify your hearts, ye double minded.

KARPAS - Parsley

READER: Exodus 2:23-25 Sometime during those many years the king of Egypt died, but the people of Isra'el still groaned under the yoke of slavery, and they cried out, and their cry for rescue from slavery came up to God. (24) God heard their groaning, and God remembered his covenant with Avraham, Yitz'chak and Ya`akov. (25) God saw the people of Isra'el, and God acknowledged them.

70

LEADER: We will take the parsley, called *kar-pas* and we will dip it into the salt water. We do this to symbolize the tears and pain of the Israelites. After the following prayer, take the parsley and dip it twice into the salt water and remember that even though we have painful circumstances in our lives, we will always have the hope of God to free us from our tribulations.

ALL: *Ba-rukh a-tah A-do-nai E-lo-hey-nu Me-lekh ha-'o-lam b-orey pri ha-'a-da-mah.* Blesssed are you, O Lord our God, Ruler of the Universe, who creates the fruit of the earth.

(Dip the parsley in the salt water twice, then eat it.)

YACHATZ –Divide, breaking the matzah

READER: 1 Corinthians 5:6-8 Your boasting is not good. Don't you know the saying, "It takes only a little hametz to leaven a whole batch of dough?" (7) Get rid of the old hametz, so that you can be a new batch of dough, because in reality you are unleavened. For our Pesach lamb, the Messiah, has been sacrificed. (8) So let us celebrate the Seder not with leftover hametz, the hametz of wickedness and evil, but with the matzah of purity and truth.

READER: Exodus 12:34 The people took their dough before it had become leavened and wrapped their kneading bowls in their clothes on their shoulders.

LEADER: (Take three matzohs and put them in the matzoh pouch, one per section.)

Take your matzah pouch and three slices of matzah and put one matzah in each section. In a moment we will break the middle one.

Many different explanations are offered as to why we do this and what it represents. One is that the three matzahs represent the patriarchs: Abraham, Isaac, and Jacob. However, why would we break the matzah representing Isaac? Abraham offered his son Isaac at the *a-ke-dat Yitz-chak,* the binding of Isaac, but Isaac was not broken.

Another explanation offered is that the three matzahs represent God, Israel and the Jewish people. Again, why break the matzah representing Israel and that one only?

The broken piece is called "the bread of affliction." Yet another explanation offered is that slaves could not be sure where their next meal was coming from and so they might hide some away just in case.

The Hebrew scriptures say *Adonai e-chad u-sh-mo e-chad,* "The Lord is One and His Name is One" (Zechariah 14:9). However, the word *e-chad* carries with it the concept of some sort of plural *aspect.* For example, in Genesis 2:24 we read, "Therefore a man shall leave his father and mother and be joined to his wife, and they shall become *e-chad* flesh—*one* flesh." Also, the Hebrew scriptures refer to God as *Elohim,* a *plural* form.

Perhaps the three *ma-tzot* hint at the *triune* nature of God--a single indivisible spirit who manifests to us as our Father, and as Yeshua, the Mashiach, the *living* Torah, the Word of God and Son of God, and also as *Ruach HaKodesh,* the Holy Spirit of God. Perhaps the middle matzah is broken to remind us of what

Yeshua, the Bread of Life, endured to be our *ki-pur-ah,* the sacrifice that atoned for our sins.

(Remove and break the middle matzah in two relatively equal pieces.)

The matzah is bruised, striped and pierced

We now break the middle piece, the bread of affliction. We will eat one half and the other half is called the *a-fi-ko-men,* [ah-fee-KOH-men] the dessert.- **that which follows**

(Wrap the afikomen in a cloth or put it in the <u>afikomen pouch</u>.)

I will hide the *afikomen* and later the children can try to find it to return it for a reward.

(Hide the wrapped afikomen, but don't make it too difficult to find. If the children can't find it later, the Seder can't continue. Put the <u>other half</u> back in the middle section of the pouch.)

ALL: In haste we went out of Egypt.

MAGGID - Telling the Story of the Exodus

READER: Deuteronomy 6:4-9   "Sh'ma, Yisra'el! Adonai Eloheinu, Adonai echad *[Hear, Isra'el! Adonai our God, Adonai is one]*; (5) and you are to love Adonai your God with all your heart, all your being and all your resources. (6) These words, which I am ordering you today, are to be on your heart; (7) and you are to teach them carefully to your children. You are to talk about them when you sit at home, when you are traveling on the road, when you lie down and when you get up. (8) Tie them on your hand as a sign, put them at the front of a headband around your forehead, (9) and write them on the door-frames of your house and on your gates.

READER: Deuteronomy 6:20-25 "Some day your child will ask you, 'What is the meaning of the instructions, laws and rulings which Adonai our God has laid down for you?' (21) Then you will tell your child, 'We were slaves to Pharaoh in Egypt, and Adonai brought us out of Egypt with a strong hand. (22) Adonai worked great and terrible signs and wonders against Egypt, Pharaoh and all his household, before our very eyes. (23) He brought us out from there in order to bring us to the land he had sworn to our ancestors that he would give us. (24) Adonai ordered us to observe all these laws, to fear Adonai our God, always for our own good, so that he might keep us alive, as we are today. (25) It will be righteousness for us if we are careful to obey all these mitzvot before Adonai our God, just as he ordered us to do.' "

READER: Exodus 12:26-28 When your children ask you, 'What do you mean by this ceremony?' (27) say, 'It is the sacrifice of Adonai's Pesach [Passover], because [Adonai] passed over the houses of the people of Isra'el in Egypt, when he killed the Egyptians but spared our houses.' " The people of Isra'el bowed their heads and worshipped. (28) Then the people of Isra'el went and did as Adonai had ordered Moshe and Aharon — that is what they did.

YOUNG CHILD: (Rising to ask the four questions)

Ma nish-ta-nah ha-lai-lah ha-zeh mi-kol ha-ley-lot!

How different this night is from all other nights!

- *She-be-khol ha-ley-lot a-nu okh-lin cha-meytz u-ma-tzah. Ha-lai-lah ha-zeh ku-lo ma-tzah.*
- On all other nights we eat bread or matzah. On this night why do we eat *only* matzah?
- *She-be-khol ha-ley-lot a-nu okh-lin she'ar yerakot. Ha-lai-lah ha-zeh a-ror.*
- On all other nights we eat all kinds of vegetables. On this night why do we eat only bitter herbs?
- *She-be-khol ha-ley-lot eyn a-nu mat-bi-lin a-fi-lu pa-'am e-chet. Ha-lai-lah ha-zeh shtey f'a-min.*

- On all other nights we do not dip our vegetables even once. On this night why do we dip them twice? (This refers to dipping the parsely twice in salt water before eating it.)

- *She-be-khol ha-ley-lot a-nu okh-lin beyn yo-she-vin u-veyn me-su-bin. Ha-lai-lah ha-zeh ku-la-nu me-su-bin.*

- On all other nights we eat our meals sitting or reclining. On this night why do we eat only reclining?

LEADER: Tonight is different from all other nights because tonight we will remember what God has done for his people.

ALL: Blessed is the Almighty God who has given the Torah to His people.

LEADER: The Torah speaks concerning the four sons:

- a Wise one,
- a Wicked one,
- a Simple one, and
- one Who is unable to ask.

What does the Wise son say?

The Wise son seeks knowledge:

Deuteronomy 6:20 "Some day your child will ask you, 'What is the meaning of the instructions, laws and rulings which Adonai our God has laid down for you?'

What does the Wicked son say?

the Wicked son looks down on the beliefs of his

people and scoffs:

Exodus 12:26 When your children ask you, 'What do you mean by this ceremony?'

What does the Simple son say?

The Simple son asks a simple question,

Exodus 13:14 When, at some future time, your son asks you, 'What is this?' then say to him, 'With a strong hand Adonai brought us out of Egypt, out of the abode of slavery.

What does the son say Who is unable to ask?

And the son Who is unable to ask, the parent must teach:

Exodus 13:8 On that day you are to tell your son, 'It is because of what Adonai did for me when I left Egypt.'

We will now tell the story of Passover.

READER: The Israelites were already in the land of Egypt. They became fertile and multiplied and increased very greatly, so that the land was filled with them. A new king arose over Egypt, who did not know Joseph, and imposed great labor and hardship on Israel. But the more Israel was oppressed, the more they increased and spread out. The king then ordered that all newborn baby boys be killed. The Pharaoh charged all his people, saying "every boy that is born you shall throw into the Nile, but let every girl live."

READER: A Levite woman conceived and bore a son and hid him for three months. After that time, she prepared a wicker basket and laid the child in the basket and placed it among the reeds by the bank of the Nile. The daughter of Pharaoh came down to bathe in the Nile and saw the basket among the reeds and had her slave girl fetch the basket. The Pharaoh's daughter took pity on the child and made him her own son. She named him Moses, explaining, "I drew him out of water."

READER: Moses grew and had learned of his heritage. After witnessing an Egyptian beating an Israelite, he struck down the

Egyptian and hid him in the sand. When Pharaoh learned of the matter, he sought to kill Moses, but Moses fled from Pharaoh. He arrived in the land of Midian, where he married his wife, Zipporah.

READER: A long time had gone by and the king of Egypt died. The Israelites were groaning under bondage and cried out to God. God heard their cries. God appeared to Moses in a burning bush telling him that he would use Moses to lead His people out of Egypt into a land "flowing with milk and honey." So Moses returned to Egypt and Moses took the rod of God with him.

READER: Moses and his brother Aaron went to the Pharaoh to ask for the release of their people. But the Pharaoh's heart was hardened against Israel and would not release them from the bondage of slavery. Each time the Pharaoh refused to let Israel go, the land of Egypt came under a great plague. With the tenth and most awful plague, the heart of Pharaoh would be pierced.

ALL: Exodus 12:12 For that night, I will pass through the land of Egypt and kill all the firstborn in the land of Egypt, both men and animals; and I will execute judgment against all the gods of Egypt; I am Adonai.

READER: Exodus 12:13 The blood will serve you as a sign marking the houses where you are; when I see the blood, I will pass over *[Hebrew: פָסַח pasach]* you — when I strike the land of Egypt, the death blow will not strike you.

READER: Exodus 12:14-17 " 'This will be a day for you to remember and celebrate as a festival to Adonai; from generation to generation you are to celebrate it by a perpetual regulation. (15) " 'For seven days you are to eat matzah - on the first day remove the leaven from your houses. For whoever eats hametz *[leavened bread]* from the first to the seventh day is to be cut off from Isra'el. (16) On the first and seventh days, you are to have an assembly set aside for God. On these days no work is to be done, except what each must do to prepare his food; you may do only that. (17) You are to observe the festival of matzah, for on this very day I brought your divisions out of the land of Egypt. Therefore, you are to observe this day from generation to generation by a perpetual regulation.

LEADER: Let us fill our cups a second time.

A full cup is a sign of joy and on this night we are filled with joy in remembrance of God's mighty deliverance.

We must also remember the great sacrifice at which redemption was purchased. Many died in the process of delivering Israel from the bondage of Egypt.

As we recite each plague, let us dip our little finger into the cup, allowing a drop of wine to fall, on the plate reducing the fullness of our cup of joy this night.

ALL:
- **Blood!**
- **Frogs!**
- **Gnats!**
- **Wild Beasts!**
- **Disease to Livestock!**
- **Boils!**
- **Hail!**
- **Locusts!**
- **Darkness!**
- **Death of the Firstborn!**

LEADER: Rabbi Gamaliel, grandson of Rabbi Hillel and teacher of Rabbi Saul (Paul, the Apostle), taught that in recounting the Passover story one must explain three things: The Passover Lamb, Unleavened Bread, and the Bitter Herbs.

LEADER: (Lifting the shank bone of a lamb) **PASSOVER:** It is God that we honor in remembering that He passed over the houses of the children of Israel in Egypt when He struck the Egyptians. The shank bone reminds us of the lamb whose blood marked the doors of Israel.

- We read in Exodus that the lamb was to be without defect, brought into the household and cared for.
- It was not to have broken bones
- It was then at twilight, the fourteenth day of the month, that the Israelites were to slaughter the lamb and put the blood on the sides and tops of the doorframes.
- God gave His people instructions that only through obedience would they be spared from the angel of death.
- Isaiah told of the coming Messiah, that He would be led like a lamb to the slaughter. We know that Yeshua was our final blood atonement so that we would be freed from the bondage of sin and we would be passed over from death.
- Revelation 5:12 and they shouted out, "Worthy is the slaughtered Lamb to receive power, riches, wisdom, strength, honor, glory and praise!"
- John 19:32-34 The soldiers came and broke the legs of the first man who had been put on a stake beside Yeshua, then the legs of the other one; (33) but when they got to Yeshua and saw that he was already dead, they didn't break his legs. (34) However, one of the soldiers stabbed his side with a spear, and at once blood and water flowed out.

READER: Israel was saved by God and not an angel or seraph or any other messenger. For it is written: Exodus 12:12 For that night, I will pass through the land of Egypt and kill all the firstborn in the land of Egypt, both men and animals; and I will execute judgment against all the gods of Egypt; I am Adonai.

LEADER: I shall pass through the land of Egypt

ALL: "I" -- not "an angel"

LEADER: I shall strike down every first-born.

ALL: "I" -- not "a seraph"

LEADER: I shall destroy all the Egyptian gods.

ALL: "I" -- not "a messenger"

ALL: I am the Lord, I am the One God, and there is none besides Me.

LEADER: MATZAH (Lifting the other half of the Middle Matzah): Why do we eat this unleavened bread? The dough did not have time to rise before their redemption was complete. God revealed Himself to them and redeemed them and they had to move at the appointed time. As it is written:

Exodus 12:39 They baked matzah loaves from the dough they had brought out of Egypt, since it was unleavened; because they had been driven out of Egypt without time to prepare supplies for themselves.

LEADER: MAROR (Lifting the Bitter Herb): **Why do we eat bitter herb? We eat bitter herb because of the hardship that Israel had to bear. As it is written:**
Exodus 1:14 making their lives bitter with hard labor — digging clay, making bricks, all kinds of field work; and in all this toil they were shown no mercy.

LEADER: (Lifting the egg) The egg has also been added to the Seder. The egg was added during the Babylonian exile. The egg does not have a great significance in the Seder. The traditional teaching says it symbolizes the hardness of Pharaoh's heart. It is also said it symbolizes mourning the loss of the Temple. I see no *biblical* standpoint for the egg in the Exodus telling of Passover.

LEADER: And now we bless our second cup of wine, the cup of plagues. Even with plagues around us our Father (Adoneinu) takes care of His Children, so we serve Him with joy.

ALL: *Ba-rukh a-tah A-do-nai E-lo-hey-nu Me-lekh ha-'o-lam bo-rey pri ha-ga-fen.* Blesssed are you, O Lord our God, Ruler of the Universe, who created the fruit of the vine.

(Drink the second cup of wine.)

RACHTZAH –performing the hand washing

ALL: *Ba-rukh A-tah A-do-nai E-lo-hey-nu Me-lekh ha-'o-lam a-sher kid-sha-nu B'-mitz-vo-tav v'-tzi-va-nu ah-'na-tie-lat yah-da-yim.* Blessed are you, O Lord our God, King of the Universe, who has sanctified us with His commandments, and has commanded us to wash our hands.

MOTZI – blessing over food

LEADER: We will now bless the matzah as a food.

ALL: (Leader holding all the matzah on the seder plate) *Ba-rukh A-tah Adonai E-lo-hey-nu Me-lekh ha-'o-lam ha-mo-tzi le-khem min ha-'a-retz.* Blessed are You, O Lord our God, King of the Universe, who brings forth bread from the earth.

(*This is the bread blessing Yeshua pronounced at the Last Supper.*)

(Do not eat the Matzah at this time.)

ᴍᴀᴛᴢᴀʜ – **unleavened bread**

LEADER: (Leader holding the top and middle-half pieces of matzah) The matzah of Passover is not just food, but a fulfillment of a commandment -- let us bless the Matzah.

ALL: *Ba-rukh A-tah A-do-nai El-o-hey-nu Me-lekh ha-'o-lam a-sher kid-sha-nu B'-mitz-vo-tav v'-tzi-va-nu a-he-lot ma-tza.* Blessed are You, O Lord our God, King of the Universe, Who has sanctified us with His commandments, and has commanded us concerning the eating of the matzah.

(Do not eat the Matzah at this time.)

ᴍᴀʀᴏʀ – **bitter herb**

ALL: *Ba-rukh A-tah A-do-nai El-o-hey-nu Me-lekh ha-'o-lam a-sher kid-sha-nu B'-mitz-vo-tav v'-tzi-va-nu a-he-lot Ma-ror.* Blessed are you, O Lord our God, King of the Universe, Who has sanctified us with His commandments, and has commanded us concerning the eating of the Maror.

(Everone eat the **top** Matzah with Maror.)

ᴋᴏʀᴇᴄʜ - **"wrap" and "make a sandwich"**

READER: Exodus 12:11 " 'Here is how you are to eat it: with your belt fastened, your shoes on your feet and your staff in your hand; and you are to eat it hurriedly. It is Adonai's Pesach .

ALL: They are to celebrate it on the fourteenth day of the second month at twilight. They are to eat the lamb, together with unleavened bread and bitter herbs. (Numbers 9:11)

(Everyone eat the **bottom** Matzah with Maror.)

LEADER: Let us now eat and remember the grace, mercy and love that God has for each of us, for He sent Yeshua, our Messiah, to be our Passover Lamb. We too, like Israel, have been released from the bondage of slavery and have been saved from the bondage of sin.

(Eat the **broken** half-Matzah with Maror and Charoset.)

LEADER: How great is God's goodness to us! For each of His acts of mercy and kindness we declare *dayenu* [die-YAY-new] - it would have been sufficient.

LEADER: If the Lord had merely rescued us, but had not judged the Egyptians.

　ALL: *day-ye-nu*!

LEADER: If He had only destroyed their gods, but had not parted the Red Sea.

　ALL: *day-ye-nu*!

LEADER: If He had only drowned our enemies, but had not fed us with manna.

　ALL: *day-ye-nu*!

LEADER: If He had only led us through the desert, but had not given us the Sabbath.

　ALL: *day-ye-nu*!

LEADER: If He had only given us the Torah, but not the land of Israel.

　ALL: *day-ye-nu*!

The *Shulchan Orech* is not read -- these are directions

- Leader says a prayer.
- Psalms 113:1-114:8 Halleluyah! Servants of Adonai, give praise! Give praise to the name of Adonai! (2) Blessed be the name of Adonai from this moment on and forever! (3) From sunrise until sunset Adonai's name is to be praised. (4) Adonai is high above all nations, his glory above the heavens. (5) Who is like Adonai our God, seated in the heights, (6) humbling himself to look on heaven and on earth. (7) He raises the poor from the dust, lifts the needy from the rubbish heap, (8) in order to give him a place among princes, among the princes of his people. (9) He causes the childless woman to live at home happily as a mother of children. Halleluyah!
- (114:1) When Isra'el came out of Egypt, the house of Ya`akov from a people of foreign speech, (2) Y'hudah became *[God's]* sanctuary, Isra'el his domain. (3) The sea saw this and fled; the Yarden turned back; (4) the mountains skipped like rams, the hills like young sheep. (5) Why is it, sea, that you flee? Why, Yarden, do you turn back? (6) Why, mountains, do you skip like rams; and you hills like young sheep? (7) Tremble, earth, at the presence of the Lord, at the presence of the God of Ya`akov, (8) who turned the rock into a pool of water, flint into flowing spring.
- Break to eat the Passover Supper.
- Everyone returns to finish reading the Haggadah.

After the meal

- The *afikomen* must be found (by the children) and returned to the Leader for a reward. The reward is a symbol of the fact that Yeshua *purchased* our Redemption at the *price* of His own life.

(Even in a non-Messianic Seder, if the *afikomen* is not found, the Seder cannot continue! -- So when the Leader hides it, don't make it very hard to find!)

- Save room for the dessert -- the *afikomen*.

TZAFON - hidden

LEADER: (Lifting the afikomen) We will now eat the *afikomen*, the dessert. The taste of the *afikomen* should linger in our mouths. It is about the *afikomen* that Yeshua said "This is my body given for you; do this in remembrance of me." (Luke 22:19) The Passover can not be completed without the *afikomen*, nor can our redemption be complete without Yeshua, the Bread of Life, our Messiah!

ALL: *Ba-rukh A-tah A-do-nai El-o-hey-nu Me-lekh ha-'o-lam ha-mo-tzi le-khem min ha-'a-retz.* Blessed are You, O Lord our God, King of the Universe, who brings forth bread from the earth.

(All eat the Afikoman)

LEADER: Many ask, "How does the Messiah, Yeshua, fit into the Passover Story?" God gave us many signs and prophecies about our coming Messiah. Yeshua fulfilled all the prophecies foretold of the first coming of the Messiah, in the Torah, the prophets and the writings. Just as the lamb's blood protected Israel from death, Yeshua's blood will protect us from death.

READER:

Prophecy: Fulfilled Micah 5:2 But you, Beit-Lechem near Efrat, so small among the clans of Y'hudah, out of you will come forth to me the future ruler of Isra'el, whose origins are far in the past, back in ancient times.

85

Prophecy: Now Micah 5:3 Therefore he will give up *[Isra'el]* only until she who is in labor gives birth. Then the rest of his kinsmen will return to the people of Isra'el.

Prophecy: Future Micah 5:4-5 He will stand and feed his flock in the strength of Adonai, in the majesty of the name of Adonai his God; and they will stay put, as he grows great to the very ends of the earth; (5) and this will be peace.

READER: Isaiah 52:13-53:8 "See how my servant will succeed! He will be raised up, exalted, highly honored! (14) Just as many were appalled at him, because he was so disfigured that he didn't even seem human and simply no longer looked like a man, (15) so now he will startle many nations; because of him, kings will be speechless. For they will see what they had not been told, they will ponder things they had never heard." (53:1) Who believes our report? To whom is the arm of Adonai revealed? (2) For before him he grew up like a young plant, like a root out of dry ground. He was not well-formed or especially handsome; we saw him, but his appearance did not attract us. (3) People despised and avoided him, a man of pains, well acquainted with illness. Like someone from whom people turn their faces, he was despised; we did not value him. (4) In fact, it was our diseases he bore, our pains from which he suffered; yet we regarded him as punished, stricken and afflicted by God. (5) But he was wounded because of our crimes, crushed because of our sins; the disciplining that makes us whole fell on him, and by his bruises *[Or: and in fellowship with him]* we are healed. (6) We all, like sheep, went astray; we turned, each one, to his own way; yet Adonai laid on him the guilt of all of us. (7) Though mistreated, he was submissive — he did not open his mouth. Like a lamb led to be slaughtered, like a sheep silent before its shearers, he did not open his mouth. (8) After forcible arrest and sentencing, he was taken away; and none of his generation protested his being cut off from the land of the living for the crimes of my people, who deserved the punishment themselves.

BARECH - Blessing after the meal

ALL: Psalms 116:12-14 How can I repay Adonai for all his generous dealings with me? (13) I will raise the cup of salvation and call on the name of Adonai. (14) I will pay my vows to Adonai in the presence of all his people.

LEADER: Let us fill our cups for the third time this evening. (Lifting the cup) **This is the Cup of Redemption, symbolizing the blood of the Passover Lamb. It was the cup "after supper", which Yeshua identified himself --** Luke 22:20 He did the same with the cup after the meal, saying, "This cup is the New Covenant, ratified by my blood, which is being poured out for you.

ALL: *Ba-rukh A-tah A-do-nai E-lo-hey-nu Me-lekh ha-'o-lam bo-rey pri ha-ga-fen.*

Blesssed are you, O Lord our God, Ruler of the Universe, who created the fruit of the vine. (Drink the third cup of wine.)

HALLEL - Praise

Psalm 113-118
LEADER:

Matthew 26:30 After singing the Hallel, they went out to the Mount of Olives.

Psalms 118:1-29 Give thanks to Adonai; for he is good, for his grace continues forever. (2) Now let Isra'el say, "His grace continues forever." (3) Now let the house of Aharon say, "His grace continues forever." (4) Now let those who fear Adonai say, "His grace continues forever." (5) From my being hemmed in I called on Yah; he answered and gave me more room. (6) With Adonai on my side, I fear nothing - what can human beings do to me? (7) With Adonai on my side as my help, I will look with triumph at those who hate me. (8) It is better to take refuge in Adonai than to trust in human beings; (9) better to take refuge in Adonai than to put one's trust in princes. (10) The nations all surrounded me; in the name of Adonai I cut them down. (11) They surrounded me on every side in the name of Adonai I cut them down. (12) They surrounded me like bees but were extinguished [as quickly] as a fire in thorns; in the name of Adonai I cut them down. (13) You pushed me hard to make me fall, but Adonai helped me. (14) Yah is my strength and my song, and he has become my salvation. (15) The sound of rejoicing and victory is heard in the tents of the righteous: "Adonai's right hand struck powerfully! (16) Adonai's right hand is raised in triumph! Adonai's right hand struck powerfully!" (17) I will not die; no, I will live and proclaim the great deeds of Yah! (18) Yah disciplined me severely, but did not hand me over to death. (19) Open the gates of righteousness for me; I will enter them and thank Yah. (20) This is the gate of Adonai; the righteous can enter it. (21) I am thanking you because you answered me; you became my salvation. (22) The very rock that the builders rejected has become the cornerstone! (23) This has come from Adonai, and in our eyes it is amazing. (24) This is the day Adonai has made, a day for us to rejoice and be glad. (25) Please, Adonai! Save us! Please, Adonai! Rescue us! (26) Blessed is he who comes in the name of Adonai. We bless you from the house of Adonai. (27) Adonai is God, and he gives us light. Join in the pilgrim festival with branches all the way to the horns of the altar. (28) You are my God, and I thank you. You are my God; I exalt you. (29) Give thanks to Adonai; for he is good, for his grace continues forever.

LEADER: (Lifting the extra cup for Elijah) **The theme of this part of the Haggadah before the meal was the redemption of the Israelites from Egypt. In keeping with tradition, we now move to the Messianic redemption. We open the door, indicating our readiness to receive the Prophet Elijah, herald of the Messiah. We must also now open our hearts to the truth.**

(Have a child open the door.)

ALL: Malachi 4:5-6 Look, I will send to you Eliyahu the prophet before the coming of the great and terrible Day of Adonai. (6) He will turn the hearts of the fathers to the children and the hearts of the children to their fathers; otherwise I will come and strike the land with complete destruction." [Look, I will send to

88

you Eliyahu the prophet before the coming of the great and terrible Day of Adonai.]

LEADER: Elijah was taken up by a great whirlwind in a chariot of fire. We wait for him today to announce the second coming of our Messiah, Son of David.

READER: Before the birth of John the Baptizer, an angel of the Lord said,

Luke 1:16-17 He will turn many of the people of Isra'el to Adonai their God. (17) He will go out ahead of Adonai in the spirit and power of Eliyahu to turn the hearts of fathers to their children and the disobedient to the wisdom of the righteous, to make ready for Adonai a people prepared."

READER: Later, Yeshua spoke of John,

Matthew 11:14 Indeed, if you are willing to accept it, he is Eliyahu, whose coming was predicted.

READER: It was this same John who saw Yeshua and declared,

John 1:29 The next day, Yochanan saw Yeshua coming toward him and said, "Look! God's lamb! The one who is taking away the sin of the world!

LEADER: Let us fill our cups, the Cup of Praise and give thanks to God!

ALL: *Ba-rukh A-tah A-do-nai E-lo-he-ynu Me-lekh ha-'o-lam bo-rey pri ha-ga-fen.*

Blesssed are you, O Lord our God, Ruler of the Universe, who created the fruit of the vine.

(Drink the fourth cup of wine.)

NIRTZAH - acceptance

READER: Jeremiah 31:31-34 "Here, the days are coming," says Adonai, "when I will make a new covenant with the house of Isra'el and with the house of Y'hudah. (32) It will not be like the covenant I made with their fathers on the day I took them by their hand and brought them out of the land of Egypt; because

89

they, for their part, violated my covenant, even though I, for my part, was a husband to them," says Adonai. (33) "For this is the covenant I will make with the house of Isra'el after those days," says Adonai: "I will put my Torah within them and write it on their hearts; I will be their God, and they will be my people. (34) No longer will any of them teach his fellow community member or his brother, 'Know Adonai'; for all will know me, from the least of them to the greatest; because I will forgive their wickednesses and remember their sins no more."

READER: Revelation 4:8b "Holy, holy, holy is Adonai, God of heaven's armies the One who was, who is and who is coming!"

READER: Isaiah 6:3 They were crying out to each other, "More holy than the holiest holiness is Adonai-Tzva'ot! The whole earth is filled with his glory!"

READER: 2 Corinthians 3:12-18 Therefore, with a hope like this, we are very open — (13) unlike Moshe, who put a veil over his face, so that the people of Isra'el would not see the fading brightness come to an end. (14) What is more, their minds were made stonelike; for to this day the _same veil remains_ over them when they read the Old Covenant; it has not been unveiled, because only by the Messiah is the **_veil_** taken away. (15) Yes, till today, whenever Moshe is read, a veil lies over their heart. (16) "But," says the Torah, "whenever someone turns to Adonai, the **_veil_** is taken away." (17) Now, "Adonai" in this text means the Spirit. And where the Spirit of Adonai is, there is freedom. (18) So all of us, with faces unveiled, see as in a mirror the glory of the Lord; and we are being changed into his very image, from one degree of glory to the next, by Adonai the Spirit.

LEADER: With these prayers we will **finish our Seder.**

We are all called to live the Shema -- to love the Lord our God with all our heart, soul and might, and to treat others with kindness.

Seek a relationship with God, not a "religion".

There are many today that do not believe the Yeshua is the Son of God. To deny this, is to deny the Torah, the prophets and the writings. There is no mystery -- it's all there. All the prophecies pertaining to the first coming of the Messiah have already been fulfilled by Yeshua.

If you were to go back and read the prophecies, you would clearly see that it would be impossible for anyone else to fulfill these prophecies.

So we can look into and study the Torah and prophets and study Yeshua's ministry and see the true fulfillment of God's word.

SHEMA – Hear and Obey

Deuteronomy 6:4-9

"Sh'ma, Yisra'el! Adonai Eloheinu, Adonai echad
[Hear, Isra'el! Adonai our God, Adonai is one]; (5) and you are to love Adonai your God with all your heart, all your being and all your resources. (6) These words, which I am ordering you today, are to be on your heart; (7) and you are to teach them carefully to your children. You are to talk about them when you sit at home, when you are traveling on the road, when you lie down and when you get up. (8) Tie them on your hand as a sign, put them at the front of a headband around your forehead, (9) and write them on the door-frames of your house and on your gates.

Deuteronomy 11:13-21

"So if you listen carefully to my mitzvot which I am giving you today, to love Adonai your God and serve him with all your heart and all your being; (14) then, *[says Adonai,]* 'I will give your land its rain at the right seasons, including the early fall rains and the late spring rains; so that you can gather in your wheat, new wine and olive oil; (15) and I will give your fields grass for your livestock; with the result that you will eat and be satisfied.' (16) But be careful not to let yourselves be seduced, so that you turn aside, serving other gods and worshipping them. (17) If you do, the anger of Adonai will blaze up against you. He will shut up the sky, so that there will be no rain. The ground will not yield its produce, and you will quickly pass away from the good land Adonai is giving you. (18) Therefore, you are to store up these words of mine in your heart and in all your being; tie them on your hand as a sign; put them at the front of a headband around your forehead; (19) teach them carefully to your children, talking about them when you sit at home, when you are traveling on the road, when you lie down and when you get up; (20) and write them on the door-frames of your house and on your gates - (21) so that you and your children will live long on the land Adonai swore to your ancestors that he would give them for as long as there is sky above the earth.

93

Adonai said to Moshe, (38) "Speak to the people of Isra'el, instructing them to make, through all their generations, tzitziyot on the corners of their garments, and to put with the tzitzit on each corner a blue thread. (39) It is to be a tzitzit for you to look at and thereby remember all of Adonai's mitzvot and obey them, so that you won't go around wherever your own heart and eyes lead you to prostitute yourselves; (40) but it will help you remember and obey all my mitzvot and be holy for your God. (41) I am Adonai your God, who brought you out of the land of Egypt in order to be your God. I am Adonai your God."

Shemoneh Esrei--Amidah

The 18 – Prayer of Standing
My Lord, open my lips, that my mouth may declare your praise.

First Blessing- THE GOD OF HISTORY
Blessed are You, O Yahweh our Elohim and Elohim of our fathers, the Elohim of Abraham, the Elohim of Isaac and the Elohim of Jacob, the great, mighty and revered Elohim, the Most High Elohim who bestows loving kindnesses, the creator of all things, who remembers the good deeds of the patriarchs and in love will bring a redeemer to their children's children for his name's sake. O king, helper, savior and shield.Blessed are You, O Yahweh, the shield of Abraham

Second Blessing- THE GOD OF NATURE
*You, O Yahweh, are mighty forever, You revive the dead, You have the power to save. * You sustain the living with loving kindnesses, You revive the dead with great mercy, You support the falling, heal the sick, set free the bound and keep faith with those who sleep in the dust. Who is like You, O doer of mighty acts? Who resembles You, a king who puts to death and restores to life, and causes salvation to flourish? And You are certain to revive the dead.*
Blessed are You, O Yahweh, who revives the dead.

Third Blessing- SANCTIFICATION OF GOD
We will sanctify Your name in this world just as it is sanctified in the highest heavens, as it is written by Your prophet: "And they call out to one another and say:

- 'Holy, holy, holy is Yahweh of hosts; the whole earth is full of his glory.' [Isaiah 6:3]

Those facing them praise Elohim saying:

- "Blessed be the Presence of Yahweh in his place." [Ezekiel 3:12] And in Your Holy Words it is written, saying,
- "Yahweh reigns forever, Your Elohim, O Zion, throughout all generations. Hallelujah." [Ps. 146:10] Throughout all generations we will declare Your

greatness, and to all eternity we will proclaim your holiness. Your praise, O our Elohim, shall never depart from our mouth, for You are a great and holy Elohim and King. Blessed are You, O Yahweh, the holy Elohim. You are holy, and Your name is holy, and holy beings praise You daily. (Selah.) Blessed are You, O Yahweh, the holy Elohim.

Fourth Blessing- PRAYER FOR UNDERSTANDING

You favor men with knowledge, and teach mortals understanding. O favor us with the knowledge, the understanding and the insight that come from You. Blessed are You, O Yahweh, the gracious giver of knowledge.

Fifth Blessing- FOR REPENTANCE

Bring us back, O our father, to Your Instruction; draw us near, O our King, to Your service; and cause us to return to You in perfect repentance. Blessed are You, O Yahweh, who delights in repentance.

Sixth Blessing- FOR FORGIVENESS

Forgive us, O our Father, for we have sinned; pardon us, O our King, for we have transgressed; for You pardon and forgive. Blessed are You, O Yahweh, who is merciful and always ready to forgive.

Seventh Blessing- FOR DELIVERANCE FROM AFFLICTION

Look upon our affliction and plead our cause, and redeem us speedily for Your name's sake, for You are a mighty redeemer. Blessed are You, O Yahweh, the redeemer of Israel.

Eighth Blessing- FOR HEALING

Heal us, O Yahweh, and we will be healed; save us and we will be saved, for You are our praise. O grant a perfect healing to all our ailments, may it be Your will, Yahweh my Elohim, and the Elohim of my forefathers, that You quickly send a complete recovery from heaven, spiritual healing and physical healing to all our loved ones who are in need of healing from You today, for You, almighty King, are a faithful and merciful healer. Blessed are You, O Yahweh, the healer of the sick of his people Israel.

Ninth Blessing- FOR DELIVERANCE FROM WANT
Bless this year for us, O Yahweh our Elohim, together with all the varieties of its produce, for our welfare. Bestow a blessing upon the face of the earth. O satisfy us with Your goodness, and bless our year like the best of years. Blessed are You, O Yahweh, who blesses the years.

Tenth Blessing- FOR GATHERING OF EXILES
Sound the great shofar for our freedom, raise the ensign to gather our exiles, and gather us from the four corners of the earth. Blessed are You, O Yahweh, who gathers the dispersed of his people Israel.

Eleventh Blessing- FOR THE RIGHTEOUS REIGN OF GOD
Restore our judges as in former times, and our counselors as at the beginning; and remove from us sorrow and sighing. Reign over us, You alone, O Yahweh, with loving kindness and compassion, and clear us in judgment. Blessed are You, O Yahweh, the King who loves righteousness and justice.

Twelfth Blessing - FOR THE DESTRUCTION OF APOSTATES AND THE ENEMIES OF GOD
Let there be no hope for slanderers, and let all wickedness perish in an instant. May all Your enemies quickly be cut down, and may You soon in our day uproot, crush, cast down and humble the dominion of arrogance. Blessed are You, O Yahweh, who smashes enemies and humbles the arrogant.

Thirteenth Blessing- FOR THE RIGHTEOUS AND PROSELYTES
May Your compassion be stirred, O Yahweh our Elohim, towards the righteous, the pious, the elders of Your people the house of Israel, the remnant of their scholars, towards proselytes, and

towards us also. Grant a good reward to all who truly trust in Your name. Set our lot with them forever so that we may never be put to shame, for we have put our trust in You. Blessed are You, O Yahweh, the support and stay of the righteous.

Fourteenth Blessing- FOR THE REBUILDING OF JERUSALEM
Return in mercy to Jerusalem Your city (Your people), and dwell in it as You have promised. Rebuild it soon in our day as an eternal structure, and quickly set up in it the throne of David. Blessed are You, O Yahweh, who rebuilds Jerusalem.

Fifteenth Blessing - FOR THE MESSIANIC KING
Speedily cause the offspring of Your servant David to flourish, and let him be exalted by Your saving power, for we wait all day long for Your salvation. Blessed are You, O Yahweh, who causes salvation to flourish.

Sixteenth Blessing- FOR THE ANSWERING OF PRAYER
Hear our voice, O Yahweh our Elohim; spare us and have pity on us. Accept our prayer in mercy and with favor, for You are a Elohim who hears prayers and supplications. O our King, do not turn us away from Your presence empty-handed, for You hear the prayers of Your people Israel with compassion. Blessed are You, O Yahweh, who hears prayer.

Seventeenth Blessing- FOR RESTORATION OF TEMPLE SERVICE
Be pleased, O Yahweh our Elohim, with Your people Israel and with their prayers. Restore the service to the inner sanctuary of Your Temple, and receive in love and with favor both the fire-offerings of Israel and their prayers. May the worship of Your people Israel always be acceptable to You. And let our eyes behold Your return in mercy to Zion. Blessed are You, O Yahweh, who restores his divine presence to Zion.

Eighteenth Blessing- THANKSGIVING FOR GOD'S UNFAILING MERCIES

We give thanks to You that You are Yahweh our Elohim and the Elohim of our fathers forever and ever. Through every generation You have been the rock of our lives, the shield of our salvation. We will give You thanks and declare Your praise for our lives that are committed into Your hands, for our souls that are entrusted to You, for Your miracles that are daily with us, and for Your wonders and Your benefits that are with us at all times, evening, morning and noon. O beneficent one, Your mercies never fail; O merciful one, Your loving-kindnesses never cease. We have always put our hope in You. For all these acts may Your name be blessed and exalted continually, O our King, forever and ever. Let every living thing give thanks to You and praise Your name in truth, O Elohim, our salvation and our help. (Selah.) Blessed are You, O Yahweh, whose Name is the Beneficent One, and to whom it is fitting to give thanks.

Nineteenth Blessing -FOR PEACE

My Elohim, guard my tongue from evil and my lips from speaking deceitfully. To those who curse me, let my soul be silent; and let my soul be like dust to everyone. Open my heart to Your Torah, then my soul will pursue Your commandments. As for all those who design evil against me, speedily nullify their counsel and disrupt their design. Act for Your Name's sake; act for Your right hand's sake; act for Your sanctity's sake; act for Your Torah's sake. That Your beloved ones may be given rest; let Your right hand save, and respond to me. May they be acceptable the words of my mouth and the thoughts of my heart, before You Yeshua, my rock and my redeemer. He Who makes peace in His heights may He make peace among us and upon all Israel. Grant peace, welfare, blessing, grace, lovingkindness and mercy to us and to all Israel your people. Bless us, O our Father, one and all, with the light of your countenance; for by the light of your countenance you have given us, O Lord our God, a Torah of life, lovingkindness and salvation, blessing, mercy, life and peace. May it please you to bless your people Israel at all times and in every hour with your peace. Blessed are you, O Lord, who blesses his people Israel with peace.. Amein.

Num 6:24-26

יְבָרֶכְךָ יְהוָֹה וְיִשְׁמְרֶךָ:

יָאֵר יְהוָֹה פָּנָיו אֵלֶיךָ וִיחֻנֶּךָ:

יִשָּׂא יְהוָֹה פָּנָיו אֵלֶיךָ

וְיָשֵׂם לְךָ שָׁלוֹם:

(The Aaronic priestly blessing)

May the Lord bless you and protect you.

May the Lord deal kindly and graciously with you.

May the Lord bestow His favor upon you

and grant you peace.

(Numbers 6:24-26 NJPS)

La-sha-nah *ha-ba-'ah* *bi-ru-sha-la-yim!* Next year in Jerusalem!

Verse 1: I-lu ho-tzi ho-tzi-a-nu, ho-tzi-a-nu mi-mitz-ra-yim, ho-tzi-a-nu mi-mitz-ra-yim day-yey-nu

Verse 2: I-lu na-tan, na-tan la-nu, na-tan la-nu et ha-sha-bat, na-tan la-nu et ha-sha-bat, day-yey-nu

Verse 3: I-lu na-tan, na-tan la-nu, na-tan la-nu et ha-to-rah, na-tan la-nu et ha-to-rah, day-yey-nu

Chorus: Day day-yey-nu, Day day-yey-nu, Day day-yey-nu, Day-yey-nu, Day-yey-nu

Unleavened bread

חַג הַמַצּוֹת

Chag Hamatzot

What is the Feast of Unleavened Bread?
How is the Feast of Unleavened Bread observed?
Is this different than Passover?
How does Firstfruits tie in to this time?

Exodus 12:15
" 'For seven days you are to eat matzah - on the first day remove the leaven from your houses. For whoever eats hametz [leavened bread] from the first to the seventh day is to be cut off from Isra'el.

The Feast of Unleavened Bread was for a duration of seven days. It was during the time of Passover. According to Exodus chapter twelve, a lamb was selected on the tenth of the first month, called Aviv. This lamb was then brought into the home and was to be carefully inspected for four days. On the fourteenth day of the month, the lamb was slaughtered around three in the afternoon (many translations say between the evenings or at twilight).

The lamb would then be roasted and would be eaten as night set in, which in the Hebrew calendar would now be the fifteenth day of the month. This is because sundown to sundown is one day in the Hebrew calendar, not sunrise to sunrise or midnight to midnight as we typically think of the calendar.

As the lamb was being eaten the sun would set and it is now the next day. It is now the first day of the Feast of Unleavened Bread. As was stated, this is a festival for seven days. It would last from the fifteenth of the month to the twenty-first of the month. After sundown on the twenty-second (remember, evening comes first) this festival is over.

The observation of this festival, was to not eat anything with leaven in it for the duration of the festival. Further, it was to be extracted from your homes so it would not be found with you. You were to be "leaven free" for this whole period of time.

1 Corinthians 5:6-8 (CJB)
(6) Your boasting is not good. Don't you know the saying, "It takes only a little hametz to leaven a whole batch of dough?"
(7) Get rid of the old hametz, so that you can be a new batch of dough, because in reality you are unleavened. For our Pesach lamb, the Messiah, has been sacrificed.
(8) So let us celebrate the Seder not with leftover hametz, the hametz of wickedness and evil, but with the matzah of purity and truth.

The Apostle Paul makes the connection here that we can also see in the book of Matthew. Leaven, in this case, represents sin. This passage even shows how the effects of sin can operate in our lives. It only takes a little bit to cause defilement. Once it is there, it will grow and feed on the other things that are present in our lives until it takes us over. As James chapter 1 states, sin ultimately produces death.

This time of unleavened bread was not just the ideal time for all of the children of Israel to do a physical "yeast cleanse." It was also the time that the Father told His children to do a spiritual yeast cleanse. This time was given for us to inspect ourselves. This appointed time was set aside to teach us how to do that. The problem that we have though, is that we are still natural people trying to learn spiritual concepts. Even Paul makes the point that the natural man came first and then the spiritual.

1 Corinthians 15:46
Howbeit that was not first which is spiritual, but that which is natural; and afterward that which is spiritual.

1 Corinthians 2:14-16
(14) But the natural man receiveth not the things of the Spirit of God: for they are foolishness unto him: neither can he know them, because they are spiritually discerned.
(15) But he that is spiritual judgeth all things, yet he himself is judged of no man.

(16) For who hath known the mind of the Lord, that he may instruct him? But we have the mind of Christ.

There are times in our life when our discernment is not as sharp as it should be. The Father gives us His word to teach us how to discern. Another way to put this is, sometimes we just have to see it in order to comprehend it. The problem is, how do you see spirit with natural eyes? The word now comes in and teaches us how to deal with ourselves and to be able to discern things within ourselves that would count as "leaven".

1 Corinthians 11:31-32
(31) For if we would judge ourselves, we should not be judged.
(32) But when we are judged, we are chastened of the Lord, that we should not be condemned with the world.

If leaven represents sin, then what is leaven? How does it act or behave? What does it look like?

Exodus 12:15
" 'For seven days you are to eat matzah - on the first day remove the leaven from your houses. For whoever eats hametz [leavened bread] from the first to the seventh day is to be cut off from Isra'el.

In the prior verse, there are two words used for leaven. You see "leaven" and "hametz". We are told first that we should eat matzah. What does matzah represent? We will address this later. When leaven is mentioned in regard to this appointed time, we are told to remove it from our houses. The word used for leaven is the Hebrew word;
H7603
שְׂאֹר śe'ôr
From H7604; barm or yeast cake (as swelling by fermentation): - leaven.

It is from the word;
H7604

שָׁאַר shâ'ar - shaw-ar'
A primitive root; properly to swell up, that is, be (causatively make) redundant: - leave, (be) left, let, remain, remnant, reserve, the rest.

This is the process of swelling up, the fermenting process. Once something ferments, it will continue to do so unless an agent is added to stop the fermentation. If the fermentation process is stopped, can the process be undone? Can you take a loaf of dough that had fermented and extract the yeast from it? Or has the property of the dough changed?

The word "sha'ar" could be remnant in the idea of something left. If you make a sourdough bread, you are following this biblical principle. You take something called a starter and mix it with flour and water and wait for the process to take over. Before you bake the bread you reserve a portion of it and set it aside for the purpose of making more bread. In this process, you can have bread being made indefinitely from the same starter.

When we are told to remove the leaven from our houses, we are being told to inspect our dwellings and remove anything that will cause or start this process. This is done physically in order to teach us the spiritual principle. Have you ever read the label of everything you pick up at the grocery store in order to search for leaven or yeast? I am not saying some or most, I mean literally every single thing. If you do this for a seven day period (not counting the time of preparation looking through the cabinets) I guarantee you will learn a spiritual lesson if you do it with the idea that we are to inspect ourselves this same way. You will find out more than you realize.

The second word used here is the word "chametz". This is the Hebrew word H2557 in the Strongs concordance;
חָמֵץ - châmêts
From H2556; ferment, (figuratively) extortion: - leaven, leavened (bread).

It is from the word
H2556
חָמֵץ - châmêts

A primitive root; to be pungent; that is, in taste (sour, that is, literally fermented, or figuratively harsh), in color (dazzling): - cruel (man), dyed, be grieved, leavened.

This would be something that has been fermented. In leavened bread versus unleavened bread, what is the major difference? The major difference between the two is yeast. This is something that has gone through the process of fermentation and will be served out to others.

Yeshua our Messiah told His followers to keep away from leaven. What did He mean by Leaven? He called corrupt teaching leaven. Even if there was some good there originally, now there was some leaven there. Once something has been leavened (the teaching) can you "unleaven" it?

Matthew 16:6, 11&12 (CJB)
(6) So when Yeshua said to them, "Watch out! Guard yourselves against the hametz of the P'rushim (Pharisees) and Tz'dukim, (Sadducees)"
(11) How can you possibly think I was talking to you about bread? Guard yourselves from the hametz of the P'rushim and Tz'dukim!"
(12) Then they understood — they were to guard themselves not from yeast for bread but from the teaching of the P'rushim and Tz'dukim.

Improper teaching can corrupt. It doesn't take much to do so. All you need is enough to be a "starter" for you.

2 Peter 3:14
Wherefore, beloved, seeing that ye look for such things, be diligent that ye may be found of him in peace, without spot, and blameless.

Matthew 5:48
Be ye therefore perfect, even as your Father which is in heaven is perfect.

Exodus 12:16-20

(16) On the first and seventh days, you are to have an assembly set aside for God. On these days no work is to be done, except what each must do to prepare his food; you may do only that.

(17) You are to observe the festival of matzah, for on this very day I brought your divisions out of the land of Egypt. Therefore, you are to observe this day from generation to generation by a perpetual regulation.

(18) From the evening of the fourteenth day of the first month until the evening of the twenty-first day, you are to eat matzah.

(19) During those seven days, no leaven is to be found in your houses. Whoever eats food with hametz in it is to be cut off from the community of Isra'el — it doesn't matter whether he is a foreigner or a citizen of the land.

(20) Eat nothing with hametz in it. Wherever you live, eat matzah.' "

The Feast of Unleavened Bread is one of the Moedim (appointed times) of the LORD. If we go once again to Leviticus chapter 23 we will see more regarding this appointed time.

Leviticus 23:4-8

(4) " 'These are the designated times of Adonai, the holy convocations you are to proclaim at their designated times.

(5) " 'In the first month, on the fourteenth day of the month, between sundown and complete darkness, comes Pesach for Adonai.

(6) On the fifteenth day of the same month is the festival of matzah; for seven days you are to eat matzah.

(7) On the first day you are to have a holy convocation; don't do any kind of ordinary work.

(8) Bring an offering made by fire to Adonai for seven days. On the seventh day is a holy convocation; do not do any kind of ordinary work.' "

In this passage from Leviticus, we see Passover and unleavened bread mentioned separately.

How is the feast of Matzohs observed? Wee see the answer in Leviticus 23 and Exodus 12.

- FOR SEVEN DAYS YOU SHALL EAT MATZAH.
- YOU SHALL NOT EAT LEAVEN (YEAST).
- THE FIRST DAY AND THE SEVENTH DAY ARE HOLY CONVOCATIONS WHICH MEANS THAT WE GATHER.
- FOR SEVEN DAYS THERE SHALL BE NO LEAVEN IN YOUR HOUSES.

What do we learn from the Matzah (unleavened bread) itself? As you look at a piece of Matzah, you will notice a few things concerning it.

- Matzah has no leaven.
- Matzah is striped.
- Matzah is pierced.
- As matzah is partaken of, it is first broken

John 1:29 declares that Yeshua has no leaven,
The next day John seeth Jesus coming unto him, and saith, Behold the Lamb of God, which taketh away the sin of the world.

Isaiah 53:4-7 says that he was striped for us,
(4) In fact, it was our diseases he bore, our pains from which he suffered; yet we regarded him as punished, stricken and afflicted by God.
(5) But he was wounded because of our crimes, crushed because of our sins; the disciplining that makes us whole fell on him, and by his bruises (stripes) [Or: and in fellowship with him] we are healed.
(6) We all, like sheep, went astray; we turned, each one, to his own way; yet Adonai laid on him the guilt of all of us.
(7) Though mistreated, he was submissive — he did not open his mouth. Like a lamb led to be slaughtered, like a sheep silent before its shearers, he did not open his mouth.

Yeshua was pierced for us as well.

Psalms 22:16
For dogs have compassed me: the assembly of the wicked have inclosed me: they pierced my hands and my feet.

Zechariah 12:10
And I will pour upon the house of David, and upon the inhabitants of Jerusalem, the spirit of grace and of supplications: and they shall look upon me whom they have pierced, and they shall mourn for him, as one mourneth for his only son, and shall be in bitterness for him, as one that is in bitterness for his firstborn.

John 19:34
But one of the soldiers with a spear pierced his side, and forthwith came there out blood and water.

Revelation 1:7
Behold, he cometh with clouds; and every eye shall see him, and they also which pierced him: and all kindreds of the earth shall wail because of him. Even so, Amen.

He was without sin, we are called to be in Him. We should be like Him.

1 John 3:1-11
(1) Behold, what manner of love the Father hath bestowed upon us, that we should be called the sons of God: therefore the world knoweth us not, because it knew him not.
(2) Beloved, now are we the sons of God, and it doth not yet appear what we shall be: but we know that, when he shall appear, we shall be like him; for we shall see him as he is.
(3) And every man that hath this hope in him purifieth himself, even as he is pure.
(4) Whosoever committeth sin transgresseth also the law: for sin is the transgression of the law.
(5) And ye know that he was manifested to take away our sins; and in him is no sin.

(6) Whosoever abideth in him sinneth not: whosoever sinneth hath not seen him, neither known him.

(7) Little children, let no man deceive you: he that doeth righteousness is righteous, even as he is righteous.

(8) He that committeth sin is of the devil; for the devil sinneth from the beginning. For this purpose the Son of God was manifested, that he might destroy the works of the devil.

(9) Whosoever is born of God doth not commit sin; for his seed remaineth in him: and he cannot sin, because he is born of God.

(10) In this the children of God are manifest, and the children of the devil: whosoever doeth not righteousness is not of God, neither he that loveth not his brother.

(11) For this is the message that ye heard from the beginning, that we should love one another.

The Apostle Paul tells us to get rid of the leaven in our lives. If we decide to keep only a little leaven, it will grow. We ourselves are to be unleavened bread before the Father. We are told that Messiah is our Passover offering and that we should partake of that offering. Given these things, we see that this time is relevant to our lives because we can see how it was and is relevant to Yeshua's life.

1 Corinthians 5:6-8 (CJB)

(6) Your boasting is not good. Don't you know the saying, "It takes only a little hametz to leaven a whole batch of dough?"

(7) Get rid of the old hametz, so that you can be a new batch of dough, because in reality you are unleavened. For our Pesach lamb, the Messiah, has been sacrificed.

(8) So let us celebrate the Seder not with leftover hametz, the hametz of wickedness and evil, but with the matzah of purity and truth.

All Scripture is to reveal the Messiah and impart His character and life to His people. Let us do as Paul says and keep the Passover and celebrate it as a memorial of the provision of the Messiah in our lives.

Colossians 2:16-17

(16) So don't let anyone pass judgment on you in connection with eating and drinking, or in regard to a festival or Rosh-Hodesh or Shabbat.

(17) These are a shadow of things that are coming, but the body is of the Messiah.

Firstfruits

בִּכּוּרִים

Bikkurim

What is the significance of Firstfruits?
What does Firstfruits mean?
What is the history of it?
How was this feast observed?
How was this feast fulfilled in the Messiah?

The quick answer regarding Firstfruits is implied in the name itself. Firstfruits would be the first portion of the fruit of your crop, the fruit of your labors. The first of every portion was to be presented to the LORD by the priests and be accepted by the LORD. If the first portion was accepted, it was considered holy. If the first portion was considered a representative of the whole harvest, and it was considered holy, the whole harvest was considered dedicated to God and was now holy.

We as believers in the Messiah can understand the idea of first portion to God, or first fruit. However, we don't understand why this is called a feast day. There is a specific time that was called Firstfruits. It was set aside at this time in order to reveal the Messiah. To see and understand more regarding this feast, we will start in the chapter of festivals, Leviticus 23.

Leviticus 23:9-10
(9) And the LORD spake unto Moses, saying,
(10) Speak unto the children of Israel, and say unto them, When ye be come into the land which I give unto you, and shall reap the harvest thereof, then ye shall bring a sheaf of the firstfruits of your harvest unto the priest:

The first thing to note here in these verses is that Firsfruits was to be observed once the people came into the land. This time could not be observed while they were in the wilderness. They had no crop and without a crop, there could be no harvest. The only gathering the children of Israel did in the wilderness was to collect manna.

Why did they have to wait? Other than the obvious, it was commanded that they had to first go into the land. In Hebraic thought the land is synonymous with the promise. Look at what has happened so far. The children of Israel were

116

redeemed and brought out of bondage and slavery. They were now testified of to be the children of God, a people called by His name. They were now told to walk out their redemption (a process we would call sanctification) by eating manna and avoiding leaven. Now, they were waiting for the promise to be fulfilled in order to acknowledge the Firstfruit.

The Hebrew word for Firstfruit is the word,
H1061
בִּכּוּר – bikkûr - bik-koor'
From H1069; the first fruits of the crop: - first fruit (-ripe [figuratively), hasty fruit.

This was ripe fruit and was the first of the crops. It is from the Hebrew word,

H1069
בָּכַר
bâkar
baw-kar'
A primitive root; properly to burst the womb, that is, (causatively) bear or make early fruit (of woman or tree); also (as denominatively from H1061) to give the birthright: - make firstborn, be firstling, bring forth first child (new fruit).

Now we can see a little more in-depth what is being said here. According to the Hebrew, a firstfruit can be a first born, one with birthright. We can see a little more of the shadows that point to the Messiah here.

What was our part in the Feast of Firstfruit? Where Firstfruits are mentioned in scripture...
- Your responsibility was to set it aside and bring it as an offering.
- The rest was performed by the Cohen (Priest).

Let's look at some Scriptures mentioning firstfruits;

Exodus 23:16 - And the feast of harvest, the firstfruits of thy labours, which thou hast sown in the field: and the feast of ingathering, which is in the end of the year, when thou hast gathered in thy labours out of the field.

Exodus 23:19 - The first of the firstfruits of thy land thou shalt bring into the house of the LORD thy God. Thou shalt not seethe a kid in his mother's milk.

Exodus 34:22 - And thou shalt observe the feast of weeks, of the firstfruits of wheat harvest, and the feast of ingathering at the year's end.

Exodus 34:26 - The first of the firstfruits of thy land thou shalt bring unto the house of the LORD thy God. Thou shalt not seethe a kid in his mother's milk.

Leviticus 2:12 - As for the oblation of the firstfruits, ye shall offer them unto the LORD: but they shall not be burnt on the altar for a sweet savour.

Leviticus 2:14 - And if thou offer a meat offering of thy firstfruits unto the LORD, thou shalt offer for the meat offering of thy firstfruits green ears of corn dried by the fire, even corn beaten out of full ears.

Leviticus 23:10 - Speak unto the children of Israel, and say unto them, When ye be come into the land which I give unto you, and shall reap the harvest thereof, then ye shall bring a sheaf of the firstfruits of your harvest unto the priest:

Leviticus 23:17 - Ye shall bring out of your habitations two wave loaves of two tenth deals: they shall be of fine flour; they shall be baken with leaven; they are the firstfruits unto the LORD.

Leviticus 23:20 - And the priest shall wave them with the bread of the firstfruits for a wave offering before the LORD, with the two lambs: they shall be holy to the LORD for the priest.

Numbers 18:12 - All the best of the oil, and all the best of the wine, and of the wheat, the firstfruits of them which they shall offer unto the LORD, them have I given thee.

Numbers 28:26 - Also in the day of the firstfruits, when ye bring a new meat offering unto the LORD, after your weeks be out, ye shall have an holy convocation; ye shall do no servile work:

Deuteronomy 26:10 - And now, behold, I have brought the firstfruits of the land, which thou, O LORD, hast given me. And thou shalt set it before the LORD thy God, and worship before the LORD thy God:

2 Kings 4:42 - And there came a man from Baalshalisha, and brought the man of God bread of the firstfruits, twenty loaves of barley, and full ears of corn in the husk thereof. And he said, Give unto the people, that they may eat.

2 Chronicles 31:5 - And as soon as the commandment came abroad, the children of Israel brought in abundance the firstfruits of corn, wine, and oil, and honey, and of all the increase of the field; and the tithe of all things brought they in abundantly.

Nehemiah 10:35 - And to bring the firstfruits of our ground, and the firstfruits of all fruit of all trees, year by year, unto the house of the LORD:

Nehemiah 10:37 - And that we should bring the firstfruits of our dough, and our offerings, and the fruit of all manner of trees, of wine and of oil, unto the priests, to the chambers of the house of our God; and the tithes of our ground unto the Levites, that the same Levites might have the tithes in all the cities of our tillage.

Nehemiah 12:44 - And at that time were some appointed over the chambers for the treasures, for the offerings, for the firstfruits, and for the tithes, to gather into them out of the fields of the cities the portions of the law for the priests and Levites: for Judah rejoiced for the priests and for the Levites that waited.

Nehemiah 13:31 - And for the wood offering, at times appointed, and for the firstfruits. Remember me, O my God, for good.

Proverbs 3:9 - Honour the LORD with thy substance, and with the firstfruits of all thine increase:

Jeremiah 2:3 - Israel was holiness unto the LORD, and the firstfruits of his increase: all that devour him shall offend; evil shall come upon them, saith the LORD.

Ezekiel 20:40 - For in mine holy mountain, in the mountain of the height of Israel, saith the Lord GOD, there shall all the house of Israel, all of them in the land, serve me: there will I accept them, and there will I require your offerings, and the firstfruits of your oblations, with all your holy things.

Ezekiel 44:30 - And the first of all the firstfruits of all things, and every oblation of all, of every sort of your oblations, shall be the priest's: ye shall also give unto the priest the first of your dough, that he may cause the blessing to rest in thine house.

Let us go back to Leviticus 23 to look a little further at this appointed time.
Leviticus 23:9-16
(9) Adonai said to Moshe,
(10) "Tell the people of Isra'el, 'After you enter the land I am giving you and harvest its ripe crops, you are to bring a sheaf of the firstfruits of your harvest to the cohen.
(11) He is to wave the sheaf before Adonai, so that you will be accepted; the cohen is to wave it on the day after the Shabbat.
(12) On the day that you wave the sheaf, you are to offer a male lamb without defect, in its first year, as a burnt offering for Adonai.

120

(13) Its grain offering is to be one gallon of fine flour mixed with olive oil, an offering made by fire to Adonai as a fragrant aroma; its drink offering is to be of wine, one quart.

(14) You are not to eat bread, dried grain or fresh grain until the day you bring the offering for your God; this is a permanent regulation through all your generations, no matter where you live."

(15) " 'From the day after the day of rest — that is, from the day you bring the sheaf for waving — you are to count seven full weeks,

(16) until the day after the seventh week; you are to count fifty days; and then you are to present a new grain offering to Adonai.

How was a person to observe this Feast of Firstfruit? You brought the first fruit of your crop to the priest. That's it! You gave it to the Cohen, He took it and waved it as an offering to Yahweh. You brought it. He drew it near to the Father to be accepted. Because of this service, the whole harvest was considered holy and acceptable for use.

Firstfruits are given at different times but they all are according to the harvest of the seasons. For the Festival (Moed) of Firstfruits , the sheaf was brought and presented to be offered on the day after the Sabbath.

Leviticus 23:11
And he shall wave the sheaf before the LORD, to be accepted for you: on the morrow after the sabbath the priest shall wave it.

Leviticus 23:15 (looking forward to Shavuot)
And ye shall count unto you from the morrow after the sabbath, from the day that ye brought the sheaf of the wave offering; seven sabbaths shall be complete:

As we look a little further, we will see the significance of this in relation to the Messiah. There is a blessing involved for us any time we offer ourselves to the Father. This time was set aside for a specific purpose though.

121

Yeshua, our Messiah, rose from the grave on Firstfruits and presented Himself as the firstfruit offering to the Father on behalf of the rest of the harvest which is us! The harvest is the gathering of all of the people of YHWH. A people called out of the world and called by the name above every name.

On the preparation day, (which is the 14th of Aviv) about 3pm is when the lambs were slaughtered for Pesach. It was at this time that our Messiah was on the cross. We will look at this in Matthew 27.

Matthew 27:45-46
(45) Now from the sixth hour there was darkness over all the land unto the ninth hour.
(46) And about the ninth hour (3 pm) Jesus cried with a loud voice, saying, Eli, Eli, lama sabachthani? that is to say, My God, my God, why hast thou forsaken me?

Matthew 27:50
Jesus, when he had cried again with a loud voice, yielded up the ghost.

Leviticus 23:5-8
(5) In the fourteenth day of the first month at even is the LORD'S passover.
(6) And on the fifteenth day of the same month is the feast of unleavened bread unto the LORD: seven days ye must eat unleavened bread.
(7) In the first day ye shall have an holy convocation: ye shall do no servile work therein.
(8) But ye shall offer an offering made by fire unto the LORD seven days: in the seventh day is an holy convocation: ye shall do no servile work therein.

Exodus 12:6

And ye shall keep it up until the fourteenth day of the same month: and the whole assembly of the congregation of Israel shall kill it in the evening.

Taken literally from the Hebrew this would be between the evenings, this would be in the afternoon, before sundown.

Matthew 27:57-60 – 14th of Aviv

(57) When the even was come (before night), there came a rich man of Arimathaea, named Joseph, who also himself was Jesus' disciple:

(58) He went to Pilate, and begged the body of Jesus. Then Pilate commanded the body to be delivered.

(59) And when Joseph had taken the body, he wrapped it in a clean linen cloth,

(60) And laid it in his own new tomb, which he had hewn out in the rock: and he rolled a great stone to the door of the sepulchre, and departed.

Mark 15:42-43

(42) And it, becoming evening already, since it was the Preparation, that is, the day before sabbath,

(43) Joseph of Arimathea, an honorable counsellor, who also waited for the kingdom of God, came and went in boldly to Pilate and asked for the body of Jesus.

A lot of problems have come in because of the phrases, "preparation day" and "day before the Sabbath". One thing we need to remember is that Passover leads into the first day of unleavened bread, which is a Sabbath. The fourteenth of Aviv is a time of preparation because they had to have all of the leaven out and preparations had to be made for Passover.

In other words, because of the High Holy days, there can be more than one Sabbath in a single week. There would also be another day of preparation. One would have to prepare for the coming Sabbath so Friday afternoon would also be considered a time or day of preparation.

Yeshua died on the fourteenth of Aviv going into the fifteenth, which is the first day of unleavened bread, a Sabbath and a high holy day (a high holy day does not have to fall on a Saturday.) This would be day one of Him being in the grave.

The body of Yeshua had to be taken down before sundown, before the fifteenth of Aviv set in. This was for two reasons, first, it was in the scriptures that if the body of one who was put to death was left overnight it would defile the land.

Deuteronomy 21:22-23
(22) And if a man have committed a sin worthy of death, and he be to be put to death, and thou hang him on a tree:
(23) His body shall not remain all night upon the tree, but thou shalt in any wise bury him that day; (for he that is hanged is accursed of God;) that thy land be not defiled, which the LORD thy God giveth thee for an inheritance.

The second reason being, Yeshua was to be in the tomb for three nights and days.

Matthew 12:40
(40) For as Jonah was three days and three nights in the belly of the huge fish, so the Son of Man shall be three days and three nights in the heart of the earth.

We see in other Scriptures that Messiah had said that He would rise in three days. Here in Matthew twelve, He gives more detail. He said that He would be three days and three nights. Remember, in the Hebraic reckoning of time, evening comes first.

Back to the Matthew telling, Matthew 27:61-62
(61) And there was Mary Magdalene, and the other Mary, sitting over against the sepulchre.

(62) Now the next day, that followed the day of the preparation, the chief priests and Pharisees came together unto Pilate,

This would be the 15th of Aviv which is the first day of unleavened bread.

Matthew 27:61-66
(61) And there was Mary Magdalene, and the other Mary, sitting over against the sepulchre.
(62) Now the next day, that followed the day of the preparation, the chief priests and Pharisees came together unto Pilate,
(63) Saying, Sir, we remember that that deceiver said, while he was yet alive, After three days I will rise again.
(64) Command therefore that the sepulchre be made sure until the third day, lest his disciples come by night, and steal him away, and say unto the people, He is risen from the dead: so the last error shall be worse than the first.
(65) Pilate said unto them, Ye have a watch: go your way, make it as sure as ye can.
(66) So they went, and made the sepulchre sure, sealing the stone, and setting a watch.

After three nights and three days, the first day of the week would be approaching. This first day of the week, during the feast of unleavened bread, would be Firstfruits. So, the time in scripture when Mary went to the tomb, would be on Firsfruits. Ironically, it is not declared a Sabbath, but Scripture makes a point to say it is the day after the Sabbath.

Matthew 28:1-7
(1) In the end of the sabbath, as it began to dawn toward the first day of the week, came Mary Magdalene and the other Mary to see the sepulchre.
(2) And, behold, there was a great earthquake: for the angel of the Lord descended from heaven, and came and rolled back the stone from the door, and sat upon it.
(3) His countenance was like lightning, and his raiment white as snow:

(4) And for fear of him the keepers did shake, and became as dead men.

(5) And the angel answered and said unto the women, Fear not ye: for I know that ye seek Jesus, which was crucified.

(6) He is not here: for he is risen, as he said. Come, see the place where the Lord lay.

(7) And go quickly, and tell his disciples that he is risen from the dead; and, behold, he goeth before you into Galilee; there shall ye see him: lo, I have told you.

The angel rolled the stone away to show that Yeshua had already been raised. Sometime between the close of the Sabbath (evening of Saturday) and the dawn of the first day (sunrise on Sunday), Yeshua had risen! If you look at the biblical reckoning of time and realize that due to the High Holy day there could be more than one Sabbath in a single week. If you look closely to the time you will see that He was in the ground three days and three nights as was predicted in Matthew 12:40.

Yeshua rose and presented Himself as a firsfruit offering as well as He Himself being our High Priest. Remember, the priest is the one who presented your firstfruit offering to the Father. When was the firstfruit offering presented to the Father?

Leviticus 23:11
And he shall wave the sheaf before the LORD, to be accepted for you: on the morrow after the sabbath the priest shall wave it.

Leviticus 23:15
And ye shall count unto you from the morrow after the sabbath, from the day that ye brought the sheaf of the wave offering; seven sabbaths shall be complete:

YESHUA ROSE FROM THE GRAVE ON FIRSTFRUITS AND PRESENTED HIMSELF AS THE FESTIVAL OF FIRSTFRUIT OFFERING TO THE FATHER!

Romans 11:16 - For if the firstfruit be holy, the lump is also holy: and if the root be holy, so are the branches.

1 Corinthians 15:20 & 23
(20) But now is Christ risen from the dead, and become the firstfruits of them that slept.
(23) But every man in his own order: Christ the firstfruits; afterward they that are Christ's at his coming.

Messiah is a firstfruit offering. If He is the offering that is received as Holy and acceptable to God then the whole harvest is received as Holy and acceptable to God! The harvest of Messiah is all those that He gathers into the Kingdom.

Revelation 14:4-5
(4) These are the ones who have not defiled themselves with women, for they are virgins; they follow the Lamb wherever he goes; they have been ransomed from among humanity as firstfruits for God and the Lamb;
(5) on their lips no lie was found — they are without defect.

The Spring feasts in order are listed below.
- Passover
- Unleavened bread
- Firstfruits
- And now comes time to prepare for SHAVUOT. THIS TIME OF PREPARING FOR SHAVUOT IS CALLED "COUNTING THE OMER."

We will cover the counting of the omer in our next portion covering Shavuot, the Feast of Weeks.

Shavuot
שבעת
The Feast of Weeks
(Pentecost)

Pentecost, most of what we have been taught concerning Pentecost is found in the book of Acts in chapter two. It's only recent that it is becoming common knowledge in Christian circles that the day of Pentecost was not just a onetime event. Pentecost is named so, because it means fiftieth, from the Greek word pentekoste.

Why would this day be called fiftieth? This day was counted off from the time of Passover. The number of that count was fifty days. What we are coming to understand is that the day we have called Pentecost had a prior name. The original name for the day of Pentecost was "Shavuot" and it is found in the Torah and Tanakh (Old Testament). I believe that in order to get a better understanding of what happened in Acts chapter two, we should look a little deeper into the foundations and history of this feast.

There were three feasts of the LORD that were called "foot feasts." This meant that three times a year, for these three feasts, you were to travel to Jerusalem in honor of these feasts in order to serve the LORD in them. The three feasts, in order, are; Pesach (Passover), Shavuot (Pentecost) and Sukkot (Tabernacles).

Exodus 34:21-24 KJV
(21) Six days thou shalt work, but on the seventh day thou shalt rest: in earing time and in harvest thou shalt rest.
(22) And thou shalt observe the feast of weeks, of the firstfruits of wheat harvest, and the feast of ingathering at the year's end.
(23) Thrice in the year shall all your men children appear before the Lord GOD, the God of Israel.
(24) For I will cast out the nations before thee, and enlarge thy borders: neither shall any man desire thy land, when thou shalt go up to appear before the LORD thy God thrice in the year.

Pentecost is how we have known this day in the New Testament (Brit Hadashah in Hebrew). Pentecost means fiftieth. Shavuot is how this day was referred to in the Old Testament. So, we can assume Shavuot means fifty right? Wrong. The Hebrew word for fifty would be the word "Chamesheem." Shavuot actually means weeks. It is the plural of the word Shavua, or week. If you looked it up in the Strongs concordance it would be the word H7620 Shavua.

130

Strong's concordance H7620
שָׁבֻעַ שָׁבֻעַ שְׁבֻעָה
shâbûa' shâbûa' shebû'âh
literally sevened, that is, a week (specifically of years): - seven, week.

In the Old Testament, you will see this called the feast of weeks. Why is it called the feast of weeks? It is called the feast of weeks because we have to count the weeks in order to figure out when to celebrate it. The only thing that we have been told about the date, is to count the weeks to determine the date. Unlike most other feasts, there was no set day of the month to coincide with this day. We eagerly count off the days and weeks in anticipation of the completion of the counting.

We know that at the completion of the counting and the completion of the harvesting there will be a feast. We are told to start counting on the day after the Sabbath. The day after the Sabbath during the feast of Unleavened Bread would be Firstfruits. We are to count seven weeks, which is forty nine days. During this counting of seven weeks, we pass seven Sabbath's and then the next day, being the fiftieth day, is Shavuot.

Is counting the only thing we do during this time? No, it is also a time of harvest. We then set aside the harvest for Him and at the ingathering of the festival, we present a portion of the harvest to the LORD.

The Counting of the weeks is referred to as counting the omer.
An omer is a Hebrew word for a unit of measure that is often translated as a sheaf.

Strong's concordance H6016 '- עֹמֶר omer -o'-mer
From H6014; properly a heap, that is, a sheaf; also an omer, as a dry measure: - omer, sheaf.

We see this appointed time in what I like to call "the feast chapter," which is Leviticus 23. This chapter of Leviticus is rich in understanding the appointed times of the LORD. Let's look at Shavuot starting with verse fifteen.

Leviticus 23:15-16

(15) " 'From the day after the day of rest — that is, from the day you bring the sheaf for waving — you are to count seven full weeks,

(16) until the day after the seventh week; you are to count fifty days; and then you are to present a new grain offering to Adonai.

We read in verse fifteen to bring the sheaf. We just saw that a sheaf was called an omer in Hebrew. The countdown to Shavuot was to start with the waving of the omer. An omer is a unit of measure that alludes to the perfect provision of every man. In other words, it's "our daily bread." We see in the book of Exodus that every person was to receive a daily portion of manna by the hand of the Father. The measurement of this daily portion was an omer.

Exodus 16:15-19

(15) And when the children of Israel saw it, they said one to another, It is manna: for they wist not what it was. And Moses said unto them, This is the bread which the LORD hath given you to eat.

We call the food that they received manna because that was what the children of Israel said when they saw it. In our minds we picture the people rejoicing as they came out of their tents because they saw bread falling from the sky. Some of us may even picture a side of honey or date spread to go with it. This, however, was not quite the scene.

What was literally said by Israel when they saw what the Father had given to them , in the Hebrew, is מָן הוּא "Man Hu." "Man" is the word "mah" which means What. "Hu" is the Hebrew word for "he" it also can mean "it" in the masculine form. What was said when they saw the provision of God is literally... "what is it?"

The children of Israel were told by Moses that they would have the provision of food, or the daily bread, that they needed. When it came, they didn't recognize it. They didn't know what it was or what to do with it, because they had not seen it before. The Father gave them physical provision of spirit. He sent bread (food) that they would have to go out and collect and prepare in order to eat. The portion that they were to gather was measured out as an omer for each person. Every man, woman and child each received an omer.

Exodus 16:15-19

(16) This is the thing which the LORD hath commanded, Gather of it every man according to his eating, an omer for every man, according to the number of your persons; take ye every man for them which are in his tents.

(17) And the children of Israel did so, and gathered, some more, some less.

(18) And when they did mete it with an omer, he that gathered much had nothing over, and he that gathered little had no lack; they gathered every man according to his eating.

(19) And Moses said, Let no man leave of it till the morning.

This time of gathering an omer was to be remembered forever among all of Israel.

Exodus 16:32-34

(32) And Moses said, This is the thing which the LORD commandeth, Fill an omer of it to be kept for your generations; that they may see the bread wherewith I have fed you in the wilderness, when I brought you forth from the land of Egypt.

(33) And Moses said unto Aaron, Take a pot, and put an omer full of manna therein, and lay it up before the LORD, to be kept for your generations.

(34) As the LORD commanded Moses, so Aaron laid it up before the Testimony, to be kept.

This whole scenario echoes into the New Testament when Yeshua says, Give us this day our daily bread in Matthew chapter 6 verse 11 and in the book of Luke chapter 11 and verse 3.

This time of Shavuot alludes to us giving thanks to God for the provision of the daily bread that we receive from the Father. We thank Him daily for the omer that we have received from Him and we count off the fifty days until the festival. We also know that there is more, the bread that the Father gives is the bread of life, HIS WORD.

Deuteronomy 8:1-3

(1) All the commandments which I command thee this day shall ye observe to do, that ye may live, and multiply, and go in and possess the land which the LORD sware unto your fathers.

(2) And thou shalt remember all the way which the LORD thy God led thee these forty years in the wilderness, to humble thee,

and to prove thee, to know what was in thine heart, whether thou wouldest keep his commandments, or no.

(3) And he humbled thee, and suffered thee to hunger, and fed thee with manna, which thou knewest not, neither did thy fathers know; that he might make thee know that man doth not live by bread only, but by every word that proceedeth out of the mouth of the LORD doth man live.

These are the words that were quoted by our Messiah Yeshua when Hasatan came to Him. We read in Matthew chapter 4 verses 3-4:

(3) And when the tempter came to him, he said, If thou be the Son of God, command that these stones be made bread.

(4) But he answered and said, It is written, Man shall not live by bread alone, but by every word that proceedeth out of the mouth of God.

We see again in Luke chapter 4 verses 3-4:

(3) And the devil said unto him, If thou be the Son of God, command this stone that it be made bread.

(4) And Jesus answered him, saying, It is written, That man shall not live by bread alone, but by every word of God.

It is well established that the bread is the Word. Something that we also see is that Yeshua is the living bread. It makes perfect sense that He would be called the Living Bread because He is the Living Word that was in the beginning according to John chapter 1. We see the bread of life in John chapter 6.

John 6:47-51

(47) Verily, verily, I say unto you, He that believeth on me hath everlasting life.

(48) I am that bread of life.

(49) Your fathers did eat manna in the wilderness, and are dead.

(50) This is the bread which cometh down from heaven, that a man may eat thereof, and not die.

(51) I am the living bread which came down from heaven: if any man eat of this bread, he shall live for ever: and the bread that I will give is my flesh, which I will give for the life of the world.

As is done with any other adherence to the Word, there is a traditional blessing that is said every day of these fifty days of counting and bringing the omer.

THE TRADITIONAL BLESSING FOR COUNTING THE OMER

BLESSED ARE YOU LORD OUR GOD KING OF THE UNIVERSE, WHO HAS SANCTIFIED US BY THY COMMANDMENTS, AND HAS COMMANDED US CONCERNING THE COUNTING OF THE OMER.

You would then insert the day, then the count of weeks, then how many days into the week. For instance,
THIS IS THE 7th DAY BEING -1- WEEK AND NO DAYS OF THE OMER
THIS IS THE 10th DAY BEING -1- WEEKS AND THREE DAYS OF THE OMER
THIS IS THE 40th DAY BEING -6- WEEKS AND FOUR DAYS OF THE OMER
THIS IS THE 50th DAY BEING -7- WEEKS AND ONE DAY OF THE OMER

The offerings brought for the feast of weeks are called, first fruit offerings. We can see this in Numbers chapter twenty eight.

Numbers 28:26 (HNV) - Also in the day of the first fruits, when you offer a new meal offering to the LORD in your [feast of] weeks, you shall have a holy convocation; you shall do no servile work;

The time of this passage is Shavuot. We also see this in a few other Scriptures.

Deuteronomy 16:10 (HNV)
You shall keep the feast of weeks to the LORD your God with a tribute of a freewill offering of your hand, which you shall give, according as the LORD your God blesses you:

Leviticus 23:15-22 (HNV)
"'You shall count from the next day after the Shabbat, from the day that you brought the sheaf of the wave offering; seven Shabbatot shall be completed:
(16) even to the next day after the seventh Shabbat you shall number fifty days; and you shall offer a new meal offering to the LORD.

(17) You must bring bread from your homes for waving — two loaves made with one gallon of fine flour, baked with leaven — as firstfruits for Adonai.

(18) Along with the bread, present seven lambs without defect one year old, one young bull and two rams; these will be a burnt offering for Adonai, with their grain and drink offerings, an offering made by fire as a fragrant aroma for Adonai.

(19) Offer one male goat as a sin offering and two male lambs one year old as a sacrifice of peace offerings.

(20) The cohen will wave them with the bread of the firstfruits as a wave offering before Adonai, with the two lambs; these will be holy for Adonai for the cohen.

(21) On the same day, you are to call a holy convocation; do not do any kind of ordinary work; this is a permanent regulation through all your generations, no matter where you live.

(22) " 'When you harvest the ripe crops produced in your land, don't harvest all the way to the corners of your field, and don't gather the ears of grain left by the harvesters; leave them for the poor and the foreigner; I am Adonai your God.' "

During Shavuot there was an increase in burnt (olah) offerings. This symbolizes an increased dedication to YHWH during this season. During this time we are to prepare ourselves and dedicate ourselves to YHWH. The idea is, now that you have been redeemed, what do you do? It is this time of counting the omer, the counting of the fifty days and all of the waiting and preparing that is done that make the connection to Shavuot. Shavuot is not a "stand alone" festival. It is connected to what came before, which is Passover.

Essentially, you would not be ready or prepared for Shavuot, if you had not observed Passover. Passover is so essential to Shavuot that the people who were unable to observe Passover at its appropriate time, due to uncleanness or adverse conditions, were given another chance to do so. They were to keep it on the same day in the second month. This would be during the time of counting.

Numbers 9:1-14

(1) And the LORD spake unto Moses in the wilderness of Sinai, in the first month of the second year after they were come out of the land of Egypt, saying,

(2) Let the children of Israel also keep the passover at his appointed season.

136

(3) In the fourteenth day of this month, at even, ye shall keep it in his appointed season: according to all the rites of it, and according to all the ceremonies thereof, shall ye keep it.

(4) And Moses spake unto the children of Israel, that they should keep the passover.

(5) And they kept the passover on the fourteenth day of the first month at even in the wilderness of Sinai: according to all that the LORD commanded Moses, so did the children of Israel.

(6) And there were certain men, who were defiled by the dead body of a man, that they could not keep the passover on that day: and they came before Moses and before Aaron on that day:

(7) And those men said unto him, We are defiled by the dead body of a man: wherefore are we kept back, that we may not offer an offering of the LORD in his appointed season among the children of Israel?

(8) And Moses said unto them, Stand still, and I will hear what the LORD will command concerning you.

(9) And the LORD spake unto Moses, saying,

(10) Speak unto the children of Israel, saying, If any man of you or of your posterity shall be unclean by reason of a dead body, or be in a journey afar off, yet he shall keep the passover unto the LORD.

(11) The fourteenth day of the second month at even they shall keep it, and eat it with unleavened bread and bitter herbs.

(12) They shall leave none of it unto the morning, nor break any bone of it: according to all the ordinances of the passover they shall keep it.

(13) But the man that is clean, and is not in a journey, and forbeareth to keep the passover, even the same soul shall be cut off from among his people: because he brought not the offering of the LORD in his appointed season, that man shall bear his sin.

(14) And if a stranger shall sojourn among you, and will keep the passover unto the LORD; according to the ordinance of the passover, and according to the manner thereof, so shall he do: ye shall have one ordinance, both for the stranger, and for him that was born in the land.

The Passover Shavuot connection

Pesach symbolizes the physical redemption of God's people. They had to literally and physically accept the word and apply the blood to the doorpost. It was a literal physical walk out of the bondage and slavery of Egypt. This was a physical redemption. They physically were slaves, and Yahweh physically crushed their oppressors. Pesach emphasizes the blood because without the blood there was no Pesach (redemption).

Then for the Feast of Firstfruits, you (through the priest) had to wave a barley sheaf before the LORD. Barley was the first crop of the year because it was the first month. This was literally the firstfruits of what God has given and symbolizes the first coming of Messiah. When Yeshua came, He was that Passover, and He did physically set you free.

Shavuot was also the giving of the word and the Spirit. It was a spiritual redemption. You could even call it an empowerment. On this day the LORD revealed to His people how He was going to equip them to walk in His blessings, provisions and covenant. He delivered them in the natural. Then He took them to the place where He delivered them in the spirit. We are to receive the covenant and walk in spirit and in truth.

We see in the Scriptures again that you were to bring a firstfruit offering for Shavuot. Wasn't this done at Passover? Yes. Can there be more than one firstfruit? Yes. In both of these you will see pictures of the Messiah, as well as, pictures of yourself.

What was the difference between the firstfruit offering of Pesach and that of Shavuot? The offering for Passover was a barley sheaf and the offering for Shavuot was bread made from wheat. The barley for Pesach was a sheaf, or unprocessed, it was not refined. It was just harvested and gathered, during this time, you had to eat unleavened bread for seven days. The offering for Shavuot was two loaves of processed and baked wheat bread that was presented to the Father. This represents the work that is finished and now is presented to the Father as a finished, refined product.

The time of Shavuot is when the word was proclaimed from Mt. Sinai and the Ruach HaKodesh (HOLY SPIRIT) was poured out. In order to get a good look at this we will start with the promise of the Master. After the resurrection, the disciples were gathered together and they watched Yeshua as He ascended to the Father. Let us take note that this was during the time of the counting of the omer and was also the fortieth day of it. There were only ten days left until Shavuot.

Acts 1:1-9

(1) The former treatise have I made, O Theophilus, of all that Jesus began both to do and teach,

(2) Until the day in which he was taken up, after that he through the Holy Ghost had given commandments unto the apostles whom he had chosen:

(3) To whom also he shewed himself alive after his passion by many infallible proofs, being seen of them forty days, and speaking of the things pertaining to the kingdom of God:

(4) And, being assembled together with them, commanded them that they should not depart from Jerusalem, but wait for the promise of the Father, which, saith he, ye have heard of me.

(5) For John truly baptized with water; but ye shall be baptized with the Holy Ghost not many days hence.

(6) When they therefore were come together, they asked of him, saying, Lord, wilt thou at this time restore again the kingdom to Israel?

(7) And he said unto them, It is not for you to know the times or the seasons, which the Father hath put in his own power.

(8) But ye shall receive power, after that the Holy Ghost is come upon you: and ye shall be witnesses unto me both in Jerusalem, and in all Judaea, and in Samaria, and unto the uttermost part of the earth.

(9) And when he had spoken these things, while they beheld, he was taken up; and a cloud received him out of their sight.

What Luke is writing of is found in the Gospel of Luke chapter twenty four.

Luke 24:44-49

(44) Then he said to them, "These are my words that I spoke to you while I was still with you, that everything written about me in the Law of Moses and the Prophets and the Psalms must be fulfilled."

(45) Then he opened their minds to understand the Scriptures,

(46) and said to them, "Thus it is written, that the Christ should suffer and on the third day rise from the dead,

(47) and that repentance and forgiveness of sins should be proclaimed in his name to all nations, beginning from Jerusalem.

(48) You are witnesses of these things.

(49) And behold, I am sending the promise of my Father upon you. But stay in the city until you are clothed with power from on high."

The disciples were told to wait in Jerusalem for the promise of power that they would be baptized in. What were they waiting for? The promise! The power of the Ruach HaKodesh (Holy Spirit)! They were also waiting for a certain time, Shavuot. It was during this time that the word was given. It only made sense to these men that this day would be chosen to reveal more of the Father to His children. They had been through Passover, were faithfully waiting, and now were expecting to see the promise.

Matthew 3:10-12
(10) Even now the axe is laid to the root of the trees. Every tree therefore that does not bear good fruit is cut down and thrown into the fire.
(11) "I baptize you with water for repentance, but he who is coming after me is mightier than I, whose sandals I am not worthy to carry. He will baptize you with the Holy Spirit and fire.
(12) His winnowing fork is in his hand, and he will clear his threshing floor and gather his wheat into the barn, but the chaff he will burn with unquenchable fire."

Isaiah 44:1-3
(1) "But now hear, O Jacob my servant, Israel whom I have chosen!
(2) Thus says the LORD who made you, who formed you from the womb and will help you: Fear not, O Jacob my servant, Jeshurun whom I have chosen.
(3) For I will pour water on the thirsty land, and streams on the dry ground; I will pour my Spirit upon your offspring, and my blessing on your descendants.

Zechariah 12:10
and I will pour out on the house of David and on those living in Yerushalayim a spirit of grace and prayer; and they will look to me, whom they pierced." They will mourn for him as one mourns for an only son; they will be in bitterness on his behalf like the bitterness for a firstborn son.

Joel 2:28-30
(28) "After this, I will pour out my Spirit on all humanity. Your sons and daughters will prophesy, your old men will dream dreams, your young men will see visions;

(29) and also on male and female slaves in those days I will pour out my Spirit.
(30) I will show wonders in the sky and on earth — blood, fire and columns of smoke.

Spirit, Wind and Fire
• Spirit and wind is the Hebrew word Ruach- רוח
• These two are connected
• Fire is often used speaking of the presence of YHWH
• Fire was used for purification
• The Spirit, Wind and Fire together testify of the presence of the Father

1 Kings 19:11-13
(11) And he said, Go forth, and stand upon the mount before the LORD. And, behold, the LORD passed by, and a great and strong wind rent the mountains, and brake in pieces the rocks before the LORD; but the LORD was not in the wind: and after the wind an earthquake; but the LORD was not in the earthquake:
(12) And after the earthquake a fire; but the LORD was not in the fire: and after the fire a still small voice.
(13) And it was so, when Elijah heard it, that he wrapped his face in his mantle, and went out, and stood in the entering in of the cave. And, behold, there came a voice unto him, and said, What doest thou here, Elijah?

On Shavuot the Spirit was poured out, as had been promised. The Scriptures testify that this is what was happening and this was what the prophets were making reference to. We see this in Acts 2:1-5, Joel 2:27-32, Acts 2:16-21 and Acts 2:44-47.

Acts 2:1-5
(1) And when the day of Pentecost was fully come, they were all with one accord in one place.
(2) And suddenly there came a sound from heaven as of a rushing mighty wind, and it filled all the house where they were sitting.
(3) And there appeared unto them cloven tongues like as of fire, and it sat upon each of them.
(4) And they were all filled with the Holy Ghost, and began to speak with other tongues, as the Spirit gave them utterance.
(5) And there were dwelling at Jerusalem Jews, devout men, out of every nation under heaven.

Joel 2:27-32
(27) And ye shall know that I *am* in the midst of Israel, and *that* I *am* the LORD your God, and none else: and my people shall never be ashamed.
(28) And it shall come to pass afterward, *that* I will pour out my spirit upon all flesh; and your sons and your daughters shall prophesy, your old men shall dream dreams, your young men shall see visions:
(29) And also upon the servants and upon the handmaids in those days will I pour out my spirit.
(30) And I will shew wonders in the heavens and in the earth, blood, and fire, and pillars of smoke.
(31) The sun shall be turned into darkness, and the moon into blood, before the great and the terrible day of the LORD come.
(32) And it shall come to pass, *that* whosoever shall call on the name of the LORD shall be delivered: for in mount Zion and in Jerusalem shall be deliverance, as the LORD hath said, and in the remnant whom the LORD shall call.

Acts 2:16-21
(16) But this is that which was spoken by the prophet Joel;
(17) And it shall come to pass in the last days, saith God, I will pour out of my Spirit upon all flesh: and your sons and your daughters shall prophesy, and your young men shall see visions, and your old men shall dream dreams:
(18) And on my servants and on my handmaidens I will pour out in those days of my Spirit; and they shall prophesy:
(19) And I will shew wonders in heaven above, and signs in the earth beneath; blood, and fire, and vapour of smoke:
(20) The sun shall be turned into darkness, and the moon into blood, before that great and notable day of the Lord come:
(21) And it shall come to pass, that whosoever shall call on the name of the Lord shall be saved.

What was the result of these events?

Acts 2:44-47
(44) And all that believed were together, and had all things common;
(45) And sold their possessions and goods, and parted them to all *men,* as every man had need.
(46) And they, continuing daily with one accord in the temple, and breaking bread from house to house, did eat their meat with gladness and singleness of heart,

(47) Praising God, and having favour with all the people. And the Lord added to the church daily such as should be saved.

Keep in mind the experience of Acts chapter two. What did they see? What did they hear? What did they experience? What was the testimony of the people? There was no doubt that they had quite an encounter with God Himself. As we keep this account fresh in our mind, let us now go back and look in Exodus 19 to see what exactly happened at Mt. Sinai.

Exodus 19:1-8
(1) In the third month, when the children of Israel were gone forth out of the land of Egypt, the same day came they into the wilderness of Sinai.
(2) For they were departed from Rephidim, and were come to the desert of Sinai, and had pitched in the wilderness; and there Israel camped before the mount.
(3) And Moses went up unto God, and the LORD called unto him out of the mountain, saying, Thus shalt thou say to the house of Jacob, and tell the children of Israel;
(4) Ye have seen what I did unto the Egyptians, and how I bare you on eagles' wings, and brought you unto myself.
(5) Now therefore, if ye will obey my voice indeed, and keep my covenant, then ye shall be a peculiar treasure unto me above all people: for all the earth is mine:
(6) And ye shall be unto me a kingdom of priests, and an holy nation. These are the words which thou shalt speak unto the children of Israel.
(7) And Moses came and called for the elders of the people, and laid before their faces all these words which the LORD commanded him.
(8) And all the people answered together, and said, All that the LORD hath spoken we will do. And Moses returned the words of the people unto the LORD.

The time frame of Exodus nineteen is the third Biblical month. Israel Left Egypt on the fourteenth day of the first month. This would have been during the time of the counting of the omer. Even though they were not counting yet, the precedent for it is given and the Father was laying the foundation for what He was going to do.

Before we look at Exodus nineteen, we should look forward to chapter twenty four to see what the result was of the word of God being given to the people.

Exodus 24:3-8
(3) And Moses came and told the people all the words of the LORD, and all the judgments: and all the people answered with one voice, and said, All the words which the LORD hath said will we do.
(4) And Moses wrote all the words of the LORD, and rose up early in the morning, and builded an altar under the hill, and twelve pillars, according to the twelve tribes of Israel.
(5) And he sent young men of the children of Israel, which offered burnt offerings, and sacrificed peace offerings of oxen unto the LORD.
(6) And Moses took half of the blood, and put it in basons; and half of the blood he sprinkled on the altar.
(7) And he took the book of the covenant, and read in the audience of the people: and they said, All that the LORD hath said will we do, and be obedient. (kol asher devar YHWH na'aseh v'neeshma)

כֹּל אֲשֶׁר־דִּבֶּר יְהוָה נַעֲשֶׂה וְנִשְׁמָע

(8) And Moses took the blood, and sprinkled it on the people, and said, Behold the blood of the covenant, which the LORD hath made with you concerning all these words.

Moses wrote a book with the covenant contained within it. They then sacrificed burnt offerings and peace offerings. The blood was applied to the altar and the covenant was read to the people. The people accepted the covenant and literally said, we will do and we will hear.
It is interesting that the phrase "we will do" came out of their mouths first. God's ways are much higher than ours. When He says that He wants something for us, it is in our best interest to do it, even if we do not fully understand why it is to be done this way. After the declaration of obedience to the word, the people were sprinkled with what Moses calls "the blood of the covenant!" What an amazing picture!

On to Exodus nineteen, the Father makes a declaration to His people.

Exodus 19:5 Now if you will obey Me and keep My covenant,

144

The Hebrew for "Now if you will obey Me" literally reads – "now if you will hear my voice." To hear ones voice means obedience. How many of us use this same terminology today. We might say "Are you hearing me?" What are we saying? It's not just hearing that we desire, it is to hear, comprehend and follow through with what was said.

John 10:26-28
(26) But ye believe not, because ye are not of my sheep, as I said unto you.
(27) My sheep hear my voice, [obey His word] and I know them, and they follow me:
(28) And I give unto them eternal life; and they shall never perish, neither shall any [man] pluck them out of my hand.

The event that we see happening at the foot of the mountain in the book of Exodus is called a betrothal. Yahweh now betroths his bride. At a betrothal, a covenant is written and vows are exchanged. Allow me to paraphrase what is being said here at the mountain. "I want to reveal myself to you in a very literal and intimate way. I want to keep you, hold you and protect you. This place of relationship is only reserved for a covenant that is given to my bride."

Exodus 19:4-6
(4) 'You have seen what I did to the Egyptians, and how I carried you on eagles' wings and brought you to myself.
(5) Now if you will pay careful attention to what I say and keep my covenant, then you will be my own treasure from among all the peoples, for all the earth is mine;
(6) and you will be a kingdom of cohanim for me, a nation set apart.' These are the words you are to speak to the people of Isra'el."

I love the phrase "my own treasure" from the above passage. If you look at this closely, it is the Hebrew word Segulah.

Strong's concordance H5459 סגלה
segûllâh an unused root meaning to shut up; wealth (as closely shut up): (as in a safe) - jewel, peculiar (treasure), proper good, special.

145

This word is what we would use to say that we have locked something up in a safe in order to safeguard it and protect it. Peter testifies of this same event later in first Peter. He calls us God's own possession.

1 Peter 2:9 for you are a chosen people. You are royal priests, a holy nation, God's very own possession. As a result, you can show others the goodness of God, for He called you out of the darkness into His wonderful light.

Titus 2:14 He gave His life to free us from every kind of sin, to cleanse us, and to make us His very own people, totally committed to doing good deeds.

Deuteronomy 7:6 For you are a holy people, who belong to the LORD your God. Of all the people on earth, the LORD your God has chosen you to be His own special treasure.

What we see in Exodus nineteen is a betrothal. We could say it is a proposal to the bride. All the people in agreement say "I do." The bridegroom says to prepare for His coming. The people of Israel were to wash their clothing and perform a mikveh (which is a baptism, or ritual immersion.) Israel was to be clean and have clean garments as they stood before their bridegroom.

He also says do not come near a woman. This is an issue of ritual cleanness. According to the Torah, if you were intimate with a woman, you were ritually unclean until you immersed and the sun went down which would be a new day. The people of YHWH are to keep themselves pure for Him, their Bridegroom.

Then we are told to prepare for the third day. It is in the third day that He will be revealed to His people. Despite all the things the people had seen, they had yet to see how the Bridegroom would reveal Himself to His beloved.

Revelation 3:5 He that overcometh, the same shall be clothed in white raiment; and I will not blot out his name out of the book of life, but I will confess his name before my Father, and before his angels.

1 Timothy 5:22 Lay hands hastily on no one, neither be a participant in other men's sins. Keep yourself pure.

146

Luke 3:4 As it is written in the book of the words of Esaias the prophet, saying, The voice of one crying in the wilderness, Prepare ye the way of the Lord, make his paths straight.

In the Exodus nineteen story, we are given further preparation as to what to expect during the time we await our bridegroom. Boundaries were placed for our protection. God is Holy. He desires to be with us but that doesn't change His holiness. If we are to approach Him, it must be the way He declares.

Exodus 19:12 says
You are to set limits (boundaries) for the people all around; and say, 'Be careful not to go up on the mountain or even touch its base; whoever touches the mountain will surely be put to death.

Deuteronomy 19:14 "You shall not move your neighbor's landmark, which the men of old have set, in the inheritance that you will hold in the land that the LORD your God is giving you to possess.

The boundaries are for our own protection and for our inheritance. At the mountain, protection was established and we were given boundaries of time and space. The boundaries were to let us know when we could approach Him. There was a set time established by the Father for His revealing and for our entering of covenant.

Back to the question, What did they see on this day? It is quite an awesome account by reading it. In the Hebrew we see even more depth to it.

Exodus 19:16
And it came to pass on the third day in the morning, that there were thunders and [קלת – Kolot- voices] lightnings [וּבְרָקִים – oovrakeem – and lightning, flashing, gleaming sword]
and a thick cloud[thunder cloud] upon the mount, and the voice of the trumpet [shofar] exceeding loud;[strong] so that all the people that [was] in the camp trembled.

On the mountain, they saw flashes of light, flame, fire and heard voices. They didn't just hear a voice, they heard voices, plural. Look at the following verses to see what happened next.

Exodus 19:16-19
(16) On the morning of the third day, there was thunder, lightning and a thick cloud on the mountain. Then a shofar blast sounded so loudly that all the people in the camp trembled.
(17) Moshe brought the people out of the camp to meet God; they stood near the base of the mountain.
(18) Mount Sinai was enveloped in smoke, because Adonai descended onto it in fire — its smoke went up like the smoke from a furnace, and the whole mountain shook violently.
(19) As the sound of the shofar grew louder and louder, Moshe spoke; and God answered him with a voice.

In the midst of all that went on, a shofar sounded one long great blast. The call was to tell the people to come up and approach the mountain. Moses spoke to the Father, and a single voice rose out over the rest. In the end, only one man answered the call to come up. Would the people come later?

Exodus 19:20
And the LORD came down upon mount Sinai, on the top of the mount: and the LORD called Moses [up] to the top of the mount; and Moses went up.

Yahweh stepped down and spoke directly to all of Israel from the mountain. Most major religions can trace their faith back to a spiritual revelation of one individual. When the Torah was given, YHWH spoke to the ENTIRE NATION! What other people can say as an entire nation, "We all heard the voice of God!"

When Yahweh revealed Himself to His people, He did NOT give; theology, creeds, recipes, diagrams, equations, formulas or doctrine. He did give His Torah, which properly translated from the Hebrew means teachings, Commandments, Customs and Decrees. In the Hebrew all of these are listed separately and are taught differently. Today, we have only known them as a whole group together that we call from the Greek "nomos" which means law. What the Father gave us goes far beyond what we would call "laws." He gave us His covenant and taught us how to walk in His blessing.

Yeshua, our Messiah said in the gospel of Luke,
Luke 6:45 The good person produces good things from the store of good in his heart, while the evil person produces evil things

from the store of evil in his heart. For his mouth speaks what overflows from his heart.

When you speak, it is from the overflow of your heart. When Yahweh spoke to His people, it was out of the overflow of His heart. When He spoke, it was to give His Torah, His teaching to His people. We were not given rules and regulations. The "laws" or teaching and instruction of the Torah is a reflection of the "Lawgiver" or teacher. Each mitzvah (command) He gave no matter how small or irrelevant we see it as being, is a reflection of the heart of the Father. Therefore, each mitzvah is another revelation of Yahweh and His character.

Yeshua said of having life in our relationships,
Matthew 22:35-40
(35) Then one of them, which was a lawyer, asked him a question, tempting him, and saying,
(36) Master, which is the great commandment in the law?
(37) Jesus said unto him, Thou shalt love the Lord thy God with all thy heart, and with all thy soul, and with all thy mind.
(38) This is the first and great commandment.
(39) And the second is like unto it, Thou shalt love thy neighbour as thyself.
(40) On these two commandments hang all the law and the prophets.

Yeshua said that on these two things hang all of the things that were given prior. If we would approach these two things wholeheartedly and unselfishly, we would be transformed.

The first thing proclaimed from the mountain was...
Exodus 20:2 (CJB) "I am Adonai your God, who brought you out of the land of Egypt, out of the abode of slavery.

The first commandment is to believe in YHWH who delivered us, redeemed us, and receive His claim of ownership over us. Redemption always precedes the commandment. Salvation and relationship precedes the Torah. Did you notice that while in Egypt, the Father did not tell Moses to tell Israel if they behaved and were good enough they would be redeemed? They were redeemed first!

Now that they are redeemed, they have no idea what a relationship with God and their brothers is to look like. They

149

knew how to be slaves. They knew how to be oppressed. They knew how to serve Pharaoh, the god of this world. Now that they are redeemed, they need to understand how to walk with Yahweh.

Exodus 20:3-7 (CJB)
(3) "You are to have no other gods before me.
(4) You are not to make for yourselves a carved image or any kind of representation of anything in heaven above, on the earth beneath or in the water below the shoreline.
(5) You are not to bow down to them or serve them; for I, Adonai your God, am a jealous God, punishing the children for the sins of the parents to the third and fourth generation of those who hate me,
(6) but displaying grace to the thousandth generation of those who love me and obey my mitzvot.
(7) "You are not to use lightly the name of Adonai your God, because Adonai will not leave unpunished someone who uses his name lightly.

Matthew 5:33&37 "Again, you have heard that our fathers were told, 'Do not break your oath,' and 'Keep your vows to Adonai.'
(37) Just let your 'Yes' be a simple 'Yes,' and your 'No' a simple 'No'; anything more than this has its origin in evil.

Exodus 20:8-17
(8) "Remember the day, Shabbat, to set it apart for God.
(9) You have six days to labor and do all your work,
(10) but the seventh day is a Shabbat for Adonai your God. On it, you are not to do any kind of work — not you, your son or your daughter, not your male or female slave, not your livestock, and not the foreigner staying with you inside the gates to your property.
(11) For in six days, Adonai made heaven and earth, the sea and everything in them; but on the seventh day he rested. This is why Adonai blessed the day, Shabbat, and separated it for himself.
(12) "Honor your father and mother, so that you may live long in the land which Adonai your God is giving you.
(13) "Do not murder.
(14) "Do not commit adultery.
(15) "Do not steal.
(16) "Do not give false evidence against your neighbor.

(17) "Do not covet your neighbor's house; do not covet your neighbor's wife, his male or female slave, his ox, his donkey or anything that belongs to your neighbor."

After all of these we see something very interesting in Exodus 20 verse 18. We read that all the people experienced the thunder, the lightning, the sound of the shofar, and the mountain smoking. When the people saw it, they trembled.

Take a second look at Exodus 20:18. Before it says all the people heard the thunder. Here it says that all the people experienced it. The voice of the LORD is not to hear only, but to experience! If we would genuinely hear Him, we would experience Him!

Psalms 29:1-11
(1) A Psalm of David. Give unto the LORD, O ye mighty, give unto the LORD glory and strength.
(2) Give unto the LORD the glory due unto his name; worship the LORD in the beauty of holiness.
(3) The voice of the LORD is upon the waters: the God of glory thundereth: the LORD is upon many waters.
(4) The voice of the LORD is powerful; the voice of the LORD is full of majesty.
(5) The voice of the LORD breaketh the cedars; yea, the LORD breaketh the cedars of Lebanon.
(6) He maketh them also to skip like a calf; Lebanon and Sirion like a young unicorn.
(7) The voice of the LORD divideth the flames of fire.
(8) The voice of the LORD shaketh the wilderness; the LORD shaketh the wilderness of Kadesh.
(9) The voice of the LORD maketh the hinds to calve, and discovereth the forests: and in his temple doth every one speak of his glory.
(10) The LORD sitteth upon the flood; yea, the LORD sitteth King for ever.
(11) The LORD will give strength unto his people; the LORD will bless his people with peace.

Ezekiel 39:27-29
(27) When I have brought them again from the people, and gathered them out of their enemies' lands, and am sanctified in them in the sight of many nations;

151

(28) Then shall they know that I am the LORD their God, which caused them to be led into captivity among the heathen: but I have gathered them unto their own land, and have left none of them any more there.

(29) Neither will I hide my face any more from them:
- for I have poured out my Spirit (רוח) upon the house of Israel, saith the Lord GOD.

Exodus 20:18
• All the people experienced (saw ראים - r'eem)
• the thunder, (voices –אֶת הַקֹולֹת – Et haKolot)
• the lightning, (torches –וְאֵת הַלַּפִּידִם- v'et halpedam)
• the sound (voice) of the shofar, and the mountain smoking. When the people saw it, they trembled.

The whole nation heard the voice of Yahweh in the midst of the fire on the mountain.

Deuteronomy 4:12 And the LORD spake unto you out of the midst of the fire: ye heard the voice of the words, but saw no similitude; only ye heard a voice.

Deuteronomy 4:36 Out of heaven he made thee to hear his voice, that he might instruct thee: and upon earth he shewed thee his great fire; and thou heardest his words out of the midst of the fire.

Deuteronomy 5:4 The LORD talked with you face to face in the mount out of the midst of the fire,

Deuteronomy 5:23-25
(23) And it came to pass, when ye heard the voice out of the midst of the darkness, (for the mountain did burn with fire,) that ye came near unto me, even all the heads of your tribes, and your elders;
(24) And ye said, Behold, the LORD our God hath shewed us his glory and his greatness, and we have heard his voice out of the midst of the fire: we have seen this day that God doth talk with man, and he liveth.
(25) Now therefore why should we die? for this great fire will consume us: if we hear the voice of the LORD our God any more, then we shall die.

Again, take note that the people heard the voice of Yahweh in the fire. Paul says, of his conversion experience, that he saw a great and blinding light. Did Paul possibly see the fire and glory of God?

Acts 9:3-4
(3) And as he journeyed, he came near Damascus: and suddenly there shined round about him a light from heaven:
(4) And he fell to the earth, and heard a voice saying unto him, Saul, Saul, why persecutest thou me?

The word use here for light is the Strong's concordance word, G5457
φῶς
phōs
to shine or make manifest, luminousness, fire, light

Acts 26:13-14
(13) At midday, O king, I saw in the way a light from heaven, above the brightness of the sun, shining round about me and them which journeyed with me.
(14) And when we were all fallen to the earth, I heard a voice speaking unto me, and saying in the Hebrew tongue, Saul, Saul, why persecutest thou me? it is hard for thee to kick against the pricks.

From Mt. Sinai and Mt. Horev, Yahweh called out to the whole nation. They SAW, and experienced, the voices. They SAW the fire. The people were called out in a similar way that Paul was called out. We could say that Paul had his own Sinai experience. How do you think He will manifest to His people again? Let us look again at the mountain experience.

Exodus 20:18-19
(18) And all the people saw the thunderings, and the lightnings, and the noise of the trumpet, and the mountain smoking: and when the people saw it, they removed, and stood afar off.
(19) And they said unto Moses, Speak thou with us, and we will hear: but let not God speak with us, lest we die.

This is why Yeshua said...

John 5:44-47
(44) How can ye believe, which receive honour one of another, and seek not the honour that cometh from God only?
(45) Do not think that I will accuse you to the Father: there is one that accuseth you, even Moses, in whom ye trust.
(46) For had ye believed Moses, ye would have believed me: for he wrote of me.
(47) But if ye believe not his writings, how shall ye believe my words?

Yeshua said that if we really believed what Moses wrote, we would believe Him! He further states that it was Yeshua Himself that Moses was writing about. Our Messiah is revealed in the pages of the Torah and the writings of the prophets. After all, isn't He the Word that was from the beginning mentioned in John chapter 1?

Exodus 20:20-21
(20) And Moses said unto the people, Fear not: for God is come to prove you, and that his fear may be before your faces, that ye sin not.
(21) And the people stood afar off, and Moses drew near unto the thick darkness where God was.

If we are faithful to approach Him, He will be revealed to us. Once He is revealed, we will never walk the same way again. We are given hope and a witness, a counselor, a comforter.

John 14:12-17
(12) Yes, indeed! I tell you that whoever trusts in me will also do the works I do! Indeed, he will do greater ones, because I am going to the Father.
(13) In fact, whatever you ask for in my name, I will do; so that the Father may be glorified in the Son.
(14) If you ask me for something in my name, I will do it.
(15) "If you love me, you will keep my commands;
(16) and I will ask the Father, and he will give you another comforting Counselor like me, the Spirit of Truth, to be with you forever.
(17) The world cannot receive him, because it neither sees nor knows him. You know him, because he is staying with you and will be united with you.

We will be equipped through the Spirit of Truth.

John 15:26-27
(26) "When the Counselor comes, whom I will send you from the Father — the Spirit of Truth, who keeps going out from the Father — he will testify on my behalf.
(27) And you testify too, because you have been with me from the outset.

The Spirit of truth will direct us in truth. What is truth? What do the psalms say is truth? What did Yeshua say is truth?

Psalms 119:142   Thy righteousness is an everlasting righteousness, and thy law is the truth.

John 17:14-17
(14) I have given them thy word; and the world hath hated them, because they are not of the world, even as I am not of the world.
(15) I pray not that thou shouldest take them out of the world, but that thou shouldest keep them from the evil.
(16) They are not of the world, even as I am not of the world.
(17) Sanctify them through thy truth: thy word is truth.

John 16:7-15 speaks of the instruction of truth.
(7) Nevertheless I tell you the truth; It is expedient for you that I go away: for if I go not away, the Comforter will not come unto you; but if I depart, I will send him unto you.
(8) And when he is come, he will reprove the world of sin, and of righteousness, and of judgment:
(9) Of sin, because they believe not on me;
(10) Of righteousness, because I go to my Father, and ye see me no more;
(11) Of judgment, because the prince of this world is judged.
(12) I have yet many things to say unto you, but ye cannot bear them now.
(13) Howbeit when he, the Spirit of truth, is come, he will guide you into all truth: for he shall not speak of himself; but whatsoever he shall hear, that shall he speak: and he will shew you things to come.
(14) He shall glorify me: for he shall receive of mine, and shall shew it unto you.
(15) All things that the Father hath are mine: therefore said I, that he shall take of mine, and shall shew it unto you.

The truth will open blind eyes.

Romans 11:25-27

(25) For I would not, brethren, that ye should be ignorant of this mystery, lest ye should be wise in your own conceits; that blindness in part is happened to Israel, until the fulness of the Gentiles be come in.

(26) And so all Israel shall be saved: as it is written, There shall come out of Sion the Deliverer, and shall turn away ungodliness from Jacob:

(27) For this is my covenant unto them, when I shall take away their sins.

The truth shall establish itself in our lives.

Isaiah 2:2-3

(2) And it shall come to pass in the last days, that the mountain of the LORD'S house shall be established in the top of the mountains, and shall be exalted above the hills; and all nations shall flow unto it.

(3) And many people shall go and say, Come ye, and let us go up to the mountain of the LORD, to the house of the God of Jacob;

- and he will teach us of his ways,
- and we will walk in his paths:
- for out of Zion shall go forth the law (תורה),
- and the word of the LORD from Jerusalem.

The Spirit will help in the harvest. It will help in bringing the nations to Yahweh. This is often called "the fullness" of the gentiles. It shall be that all nations will be given opportunity to come into the covenant that was established with Abraham.

Genesis 12:2-3

(2) I will make of you a great nation, I will bless you, and I will make your name great; and you are to be a blessing.

(3) I will bless those who bless you, but I will curse anyone who curses you; and by you
all the families of the earth will be blessed."

Genesis 22:18 and by your descendants all the nations of the earth will be blessed —
because you obeyed my order."

156

Paul says that this declaration to Abraham was the gospel being sent beforehand. The Gospel would be sent through the covenant and descendants of Abraham.

Galatians 3:8-9
(8) And the scripture, foreseeing that God would justify the heathen through faith, preached before the gospel unto Abraham, saying, In thee shall all nations be blessed.
(9) So then they which be of faith are blessed with faithful Abraham.

Being in covenant with the Father, we are to show our dedication to Him by allowing ourselves to be given over as a living sacrifice. We should lay our lives down and follow the examples of Abraham, Isaac and yes, Yeshua Himself. God desires an altar of earth to be given to worship Him.

Exodus 20:24
For me you need make only an altar of earth (אֲדָמָה adamah); on it you will sacrifice your burnt offerings, peace offerings, sheep, goats and cattle. In every place where I cause my name to be mentioned, I will come to you and bless you.

The word for earth is "adamah" from the word "adam." What was man (Adam) created from? The earth (adamah.)

Romans 12:1-3
(1) I beseech you therefore, brethren, by the mercies of God, that ye present your bodies a living sacrifice, holy, acceptable unto God, *which is* your reasonable service.
(2) And be not conformed to this world: but be ye transformed by the renewing of your mind, that ye may prove what *is* that good, and acceptable, and perfect, will of God.
(3) For I say, through the grace given unto me, to every man that is among you, not to think *of himself* more highly than he ought to think; but to think soberly, according as God hath dealt to every man the measure of faith.

Even the stone altar was a representation of man.

Exodus 20:25
If you do make me an altar of stone, you are not to build it of cut stones; for if you use a tool on it, you profane it.

If you fashioned the stone into your own idea of what it should look like, it would be profane before God. If you take the stones as He gave them and use them for His purposes, it would be acceptable.

1 Peter 2:5
Ye also, as lively stones, are built up a spiritual house, an holy priesthood, to offer up spiritual sacrifices, acceptable to God by Jesus Christ.

Revelation 21:14 The wall of the city (new Yerushalayim) had twelve foundation stones,
and on them were written the names of the twelve apostles of the Lamb.

Ultimately, what we see is the Father gathering His people. When they are gathered in His time, He will reveal Himself to them. He gathers, and is gathering, His people. He redeems whom He gathers. He blesses and equips them by His Spirit. The purpose is so that they can walk the word as a testimony to the nations.

What have we seen regarding this time called Shavuot? The Torah was given on Mt. Sinai. The Ruach HaKodesh (Holy Spirit) was poured out. Those who were prepared for it received it and fulfilled it's purpose. Those who were prepared for the Word, understood the Word. Those who do so today will walk in it and be the ones to proclaim repentance and advance the kingdom for the preparation of the returning King.

It is important that we understand that this time would be a time called Spirit and truth. On this day both were given. The truth is the word of Yahweh and the Spirit equips you for life in His Word. The Word of God is truth.

John 17:14-17
(14) I have given them thy word; and the world hath hated them, because they are not of the world, even as I am not of the world.
(15) I pray not that thou shouldest take them out of the world, but that thou shouldest keep them from the evil.
(16) They are not of the world, even as I am not of the world.
(17) Sanctify them through thy truth: thy word is truth.

Torah, as the Father gave it, is truth.
Psalms 119:142 Thy righteousness is an everlasting righteousness, and thy law (Torah) is the truth.

Daniel 9:13 As it is written in the law (Torah) of Moses, all this evil is come upon us: yet made we not our prayer before the LORD our God, that we might turn from our iniquities, and understand thy truth.

Romans 2:20 An instructor of the foolish, a teacher of babes, which hast the form of knowledge and of the truth in the law (Torah).

Torah, as the Father gave it, is good.
Romans 7:12 Wherefore the law (Torah) is holy, and the commandment holy, and just, and good.

Romans 7:16 If then I do that which I would not, I consent unto the law (Torah) that it is good.

1 Timothy 1:8 (CJB) We know that the Torah is good, provided one uses it in the way the Torah itself intends.

Torah, as the Father gave it, is spirit.
Romans 7:14 For we know that the law is spiritual: but I am carnal, sold under sin.

Romans 8:2(CJB) Why? Because the Torah of the Spirit, which produces this life in union with Messiah Yeshua, has set me free from the "Torah" of sin and death.

Romans 8:4(CJB) so that the just requirement of the Torah might be fulfilled in us who do not run our lives according to what our old nature wants but according to what the Spirit wants.

Galatians 5:18(CJB) But if you are led by the Spirit, then you are not in subjection to the system that results from perverting the Torah into legalism.

1 Corinthians 2:14
Now the natural (soulish) man does not receive the things from the Spirit of God to him they are nonsense! Moreover, he is

unable to grasp them, because they are evaluated through the Spirit.

To understand the Word of YHWH, we must approach it in the way that it was given. The Word was given by a loving God who wants nothing more than to bless His children. We however, as little children do so often do not understand what is for their (our) betterment. We tell a child not to run and play in the street because there are lawless ones out on the road who pay no attention to the laws that were given to protect us. If a child runs out in the road, there is potential that a car will soon come down that road.

We tell our children not to run with knives or scissors. Is it because we don't trust them that we say this? Or is the reason that we know their ability to walk or run is often impeded by their own excitement and they cease to pay attention to their feet and where they are going? We could even be saying this because we know there are bumps in the road ahead. Like a family pet who doesn't desire any harm but can't see sometimes past their own desires and wants, and at that moment decides to play with the child and causes them to fall.

Sometimes we can't see the forest for the trees. We should remove the hindrances to the Word and those things that keep it from being alive in our life, so that we can truly see the revelation that is waiting for us.

2 Corinthians 3:15-18
(15) But even unto this day, when Moses is read, the vail is upon their heart.
(16) Nevertheless when it shall turn to the Lord, the vail shall be taken away.
(17) Now the Lord is that Spirit: and where the Spirit of the Lord is, there is liberty.
(18) But we all, with open face beholding as in a glass the glory of the Lord, are changed into the same image from glory to glory, even as by the Spirit of the Lord.

We often have had a hard time seeing the revealing of the Messiah in the Torah (Old Testament). This is because we have been taught how to approach it with a veil. Don't forget that the Word was in the beginning. When we come to the LORD and ask Him to circumcise our hearts and take away anything that

160

doesn't belong to Him, we will change in how we see the word. Yeshua tells His disciples after he had risen that this is what he was talking about all along.

Luke 24:44-49
(44) And he said unto them, These are the words which I spake unto you, while I was yet with you, that all things must be fulfilled, which were written in the law of Moses, and in the prophets, and in the psalms, concerning me.
(45) Then opened he their understanding, that they might understand the scriptures,
(46) And said unto them, Thus it is written, and thus it behoved Christ to suffer, and to rise from the dead the third day:
(47) And that repentance and remission of sins should be preached in his name among all nations, beginning at Jerusalem.
(48) And ye are witnesses of these things.
(49) And, behold, I send the promise of my Father upon you: but tarry ye in the city of Jerusalem, until ye be endued with power from on high.

Jeremiah testifies of the covenant that was to be made with the children of God.

Jeremiah 31:31-34
(31) Behold, the days come, saith the LORD, that I will make a new covenant with the house of Israel, and with the house of Judah:
(32) Not according to the covenant that I made with their fathers in the day that I took them by the hand to bring them out of the land of Egypt; which my covenant they brake, although I was an husband unto them, saith the LORD:
(33) But this shall be the covenant that I will make with the house of Israel; After those days, saith the LORD, I will put my law in their inward parts, and write it in their hearts; and will be their God, and they shall be my people.
(34) And they shall teach no more every man his neighbour, and every man his brother, saying, Know the LORD: for they shall all know me, from the least of them unto the greatest of them, saith the LORD: for I will forgive their iniquity, and I will remember their sin no more.

Ezekiel touches on the concept of coming to the Father in repentance. He will clean you up, give you His heart and His desires. He will also give you His Spirit to equip you to walk in the Word and all of the promises that were given to His people.

Ezekiel 36:24-27
(24) For I will take you from among the nations, gather you from all the countries, and return you to your own soil.
(25) Then I will sprinkle clean water on you, and you will be clean; I will cleanse you from all your uncleanness and from all your idols.
(26) I will give you a new heart and put a new spirit inside you; I will take the stony heart out of your flesh and give you a heart of flesh.
(27) I will put my Spirit inside you and cause you to live by my laws, respect my rulings and obey them.

Remember, the equipping of the Spirit was to strengthen you to walk in the word and be about the Father's business.

Matthew 9:37-38
(37) Then saith he unto his disciples, The harvest truly is plenteous, but the labourers are few;
(38) Pray ye therefore the Lord of the harvest, that he will send forth labourers into his harvest.

The harvest is, a people who have prepared their hearts and are ready to come into the house. Let us go out and work the field to bring them in, equipped with the very presence of God.

John 4:35-38
(35) Don't you have a saying, 'Four more months and then the harvest'? Well, what I say to you is: open your eyes and look at the fields! They're already ripe for harvest!
(36) The one who reaps receives his wages and gathers fruit for eternal life, so that the reaper and the sower may be glad together
(37) for in this matter, the proverb, 'One sows and another reaps,' holds true.
(38) I sent you to reap what you haven't worked for. Others have done the hard labor, and you have benefited from their work."

Now, when we read Acts chapter two, we should see a little more to the picture.

162

Acts 2:1-4

(1) And when the day of Pentecost was fully come, they were all with one accord in one place.

(2) And suddenly there came a sound from heaven as of a rushing mighty wind, and it filled all the house where they were sitting.

(3) And there appeared unto them cloven tongues like as of fire, and it sat upon each of them.

(4) And they were all filled with the Holy Ghost, and began to speak with other tongues, as the Spirit gave them utterance.

The Ruach HaKodesh (Holy Spirit) was manifested to them with the promise that they would be immersed in fire.

Matthew 3:11 It's true that I am immersing you in water so that you might turn from sin to God; but the one coming after me is more powerful than I — I'm not worthy even to carry his sandals — and he will immerse you in the Ruach HaKodesh and in fire.

The fire (Spirit) was given in order to start the harvesting that was needed to gather in people for the kingdom.

Acts 2:14-21

(14) But Peter, standing up with the eleven, lifted up his voice, and said unto them, Ye men of Judaea, and all ye that dwell at Jerusalem, be this known unto you, and hearken to my words:

(15) For these are not drunken, as ye suppose, seeing it is but the third hour of the day.

(16) But this is that which was spoken by the prophet Joel;

(17) And it shall come to pass in the last days, saith God, I will pour out of my Spirit upon all flesh: and your sons and your daughters shall prophesy, and your young men shall see visions, and your old men shall dream dreams:

(18) And on my servants and on my handmaidens I will pour out in those days of my Spirit; and they shall prophesy:

(19) And I will shew wonders in heaven above, and signs in the earth beneath; blood, and fire, and vapour of smoke:

(20) The sun shall be turned into darkness, and the moon into blood, before that great and notable day of the Lord come:

(21) And it shall come to pass, that whosoever shall call on the name of the Lord shall be saved.

The Ruach HaKodesh was revealed in Jerusalem and it was poured out on a people who were seeking the way, the truth and the life.

Acts 2:38-42
(38) Then Peter said unto them, Repent, and be baptized every one of you in the name of Jesus Christ for the remission of sins, and ye shall receive the gift of the Holy Ghost.
(39) For the promise is unto you, and to your children, and to all that are afar off, even as many as the Lord our God shall call.
(40) And with many other words did he testify and exhort, saying, Save yourselves from this untoward generation.
(41) Then they that gladly received his word were baptized: and the same day there were added unto them about three thousand souls.
(42) And they continued stedfastly in the apostles' doctrine and fellowship, and in breaking of bread, and in prayers.

It is further testified of that after the Spirit fell, much unity was spread across the body. This is not saying that everyone agreed with everything that was said by everyone else all of the time. This means that people now cared more for their brothers than themselves.

Acts 2:46-47
(46) Continuing faithfully
• and with singleness of purpose
• to meet in the Temple courts daily,
• and breaking bread in their several homes, they shared their food in joy and simplicity of heart,
• (47) praising God and having the respect of all the people. And day after day the Lord
kept adding to them those who were being saved.

We should be the same. After all, aren't we to have the light of the world living in us?

Matthew 5:15-17
(15) Likewise, when people light a lamp, they don't cover it with a bowl but put it on a lampstand, so that it shines for everyone in the house.
(16) In the same way, let your light shine before people, so that they may see the good things you do and praise your Father in heaven.

(17) "Don't think that I have come to abolish the Torah or the Prophets. I have come not to abolish but to complete.

You have been given a holy fire, what are you doing with it?

Mark 4:21 He said to them, "A lamp isn't brought in to be put under a bowl or under the bed, is it? Wouldn't you put it on a lampstand?

Luke 11:33 "No one who has kindled a lamp hides it or places it under a bowl; rather, he puts it on a stand, so that those coming in may see its light.

Isaiah 2:3-5
(3) Many peoples will go and say, "Come, let's go up to the mountain of Adonai, to the house of the God of Ya`akov! He will teach us about his ways, and we will walk in his paths." For out of Tziyon will go forth Torah, the word of Adonai from Yerushalayim.
(4) He will judge between the nations and arbitrate for many peoples. Then they will hammer their swords into plow-blades and their spears into pruning-knives; nations will not raise swords at each other, and they will no longer learn war.
(5) Descendants of Ya`akov, come! Let's live in the light of Adonai!

We see in Scripture the light and fire of Yeshua our Messiah and the response that happens when we see it.

Isaiah 60:1-3
(1) "Arise, shine [Yerushalayim], for your light has come, the glory of Adonai has risen over you.
(2) For although darkness covers the earth and thick darkness the peoples; on you Adonai will rise; over you will be seen his glory.
(3) Nations will go toward your light and kings toward your shining splendor.

We see that Shavuot is about being in communion with Yahweh, and your brother. When we walk in the unity of the Messiah, we stand together for one common purpose, to hear from the LORD and to walk in His ways. Once that happens, Then we will see the promises in Acts 2 and Psalm 133 fulfilled.

Acts 2:1
And when the day of Pentecost was fully come, they were all with one accord in one place.

Psalms 133:1-3
(1) [A song of ascents. By David:] Oh, how good, how pleasant it is for brothers to live together in harmony.
(2) It is like fragrant oil on the head that runs down over the beard, over the beard of Aharon, and flows down on the collar of his robes.
(3) It is like the dew of Hermon that settles on the mountains of Tziyon. For it was there that Adonai ordained the blessing of everlasting life.

This time of Shavuot and counting the omer is traditionally used to examine ourselves. This is a time to look at our relationship with Yahweh, and our relationship with each other. The Scriptures often state that our unity comes when we are walking in obedience to the Father.

Psalms 139:23-24
(23) Examine me, God, and know my heart; test me, and know my thoughts.
(24) See if there is in me any hurtful way, and lead me along the eternal way.

Matthew 5:21-24
(21) "You have heard that our fathers were told, 'Do not murder,' and that anyone who commits murder will be subject to judgment.
(22) But I tell you that anyone who nurses anger against his brother will be subject to judgment; that whoever calls his brother, 'You good-for-nothing!' will be brought before the Sanhedrin; that whoever says, 'Fool!' incurs the penalty of burning in the fire of Gei-Hinnom!
(23) So if you are offering your gift at the Temple altar and you remember there that your brother has something against you,
(24) leave your gift where it is by the altar, and go, make peace with your brother. Then come back and offer your gift.

Ezekiel 11:18-20
(18) Then they will go there and remove all its loathsome things and disgusting practices,

166

(19) and I will give them <u>unity of heart</u>. "I will put a new spirit among you." I will remove from their bodies the hearts of stone and give them hearts of flesh;
(20) so that they will live by my regulations, obey my rulings and act by them. Then they will be my people, and I will be their God.

Ephesians 4:2-3
(2) Always be humble, gentle and patient, bearing with one another in love,
(3) and making every effort to preserve the unity the Spirit gives through the binding power of shalom.

One purpose of leaders in the body of Messiah is to train up and equip His people. Another is to teach His people how to live at peace with each other.

Ephesians 4:11-16 (CJB)
(11) Furthermore, he gave some people as emissaries, some as prophets, some as proclaimers of the Good News, and some as shepherds and teachers.
(12) Their task is to equip God's people for the work of service that builds the body of the Messiah,
(13) until we all arrive at the unity implied by trusting and knowing the Son of God, at full manhood, at the standard of maturity set by the Messiah's perfection.
(14) We will then no longer be infants tossed about by the waves and blown along by every wind of teaching, at the mercy of people clever in devising ways to deceive.
(15) Instead, speaking the truth in love, we will in every respect grow up into him who is the head, the Messiah.
(16) Under his control, the whole body is being fitted and held together by the support of every joint, with each part working to fulfill its function; this is how the body grows and builds itself up in love.

When we have a solid relationship with the Father, it becomes easier to have good and solid relationships with each other.

Galatians 5:13-26
(13) For, brothers, you were called to be free. Only do not let that freedom become an excuse for allowing your old nature to have its way. Instead, serve one another in love.
(14) For the whole of the Torah is summed up in this one sentence: "Love your neighbor as yourself";

(15) but if you go on snapping at each other and tearing each other to pieces, watch out, or you will be destroyed by each other! (16) What I am saying is this: run your lives by the Spirit. Then you will not do what your old nature wants.
(17) For the old nature wants what is contrary to the Spirit, and the Spirit wants what is contrary to the old nature. These oppose each other, so that you find yourselves unable to carry out your good intentions.
(18) But if you are led by the Spirit, then you are not in subjection to the system that results from perverting the Torah into legalism.
(19) And it is perfectly evident what the old nature does. It expresses itself in sexual immorality, impurity and indecency;
(20) involvement with the occult and with drugs; in feuding, fighting, becoming jealous and getting angry; in selfish ambition, factionalism, intrigue
(21) and envy; in drunkenness, orgies and things like these. I warn you now as I have warned you before: those who do such things will have no share in the Kingdom of God!
(22) But the fruit of the Spirit is love, joy, peace, patience, kindness, goodness, faithfulness,
(23) humility, self control. Nothing in the Torah stands against such things.
(24) Moreover, those who belong to the Messiah Yeshua have put their old nature to death on the stake, along with its passions and desires.
(25) Since it is through the Spirit that we have Life, let it also be through the Spirit that we order our lives day by day.
(26) Let us not become conceited, provoking and envying each other.

Our unity is testified of by being in relationship with Yeshua, our Messiah.

John 15:4-12
(4) Stay united with me, as I will with you — for just as the branch can't put forth fruit by itself apart from the vine, so you can't bear fruit apart from me.
(5) "I am the vine and you are the branches. Those who stay united with me, and I with them, are the ones who bear much fruit; because apart from me you can't do a thing.
(6) Unless a person remains united with me, he is thrown away like a branch and dries up. Such branches are gathered and thrown into the fire, where they are burned up.

(7) "If you remain united with me, and my words with you, then ask whatever you want, and it will happen for you.
(8) This is how my Father is glorified — in your bearing much fruit; this is how you will prove to be my talmidim.
(9) "Just as my Father has loved me, I too have loved you; so stay in my love.
(10) If you keep my commands, you will stay in my love — just as I have kept my Father's commands and stay in his love.
(11) I have said this to you so that my joy may be in you, and your joy be complete.
(12) "This is my command: that you keep on loving each other just as I have loved you.

All of these things in the spring feasts that we have discussed so far tell us of the work and relationship that was being established at Yeshua's first coming. Follow the progression of time and the feasts so far.

Man was created, he fell and was exiled. The promise was given. The people were redeemed and brought out of the bondage, slavery and exile of Egypt. Then they were given the word to show how to maintain their freedom along with the Spirit to equip them to walk in it. The festivals were given to prophesy of the coming Messiah and the work that He would do for His people.

- Shabbat – To enter His rest
- Pesach – Being redeemed by the blood of the Lamb.
- Matzah – Search yourselves for leaven, be like the One who was without leaven.
- Firstfruits – Give yourself to the Messiah who presented Himself as firstfruits to the Father in order to make the way for you (coming from the harvest) to be Holy and acceptable to Him.
- Shavuot – Walk in the Spirit, equipped to spread the gospel and overcome the world.

Shavuot/ The betrothal of the bride

Throughout this section, we have mentioned that this time was a betrothal or an engagement of the bride. This is reconciliation of a promised relationship with the Father. Many books have been written regarding this subject. We will not go into an exhaustive study here, But I do feel there are some things that should be shared. I believe that with the completion of the

169

prior section there would be a better understanding relating to this subject.

In Exodus nineteen, the feast on the mountain was a celebration of the giving of the word of Yahweh. Yahweh made a vow on the mountain. He was betrothing His people, and the people said, "I do." They entered into a covenant and Yahweh gave them a ketuba (a written legal marriage certificate) or wedding vows.

We see pictures of our betrothal in the Scriptures. It is not just in Exodus nineteen, but a few other places as well. Here are a few examples of our betrothal.

Hosea 2:19-20
(19) I will betroth you to me forever; yes, I will betroth you to me in righteousness, in justice, in grace and in compassion;
(20) I will betroth you to me in faithfulness, and you will know Adonai .

Isaiah 54:5
For thy Maker is thine husband; the LORD of hosts is his name; and thy Redeemer the Holy One of Israel; The God of the whole earth shall he be called.

Deuteronomy 29:10-15
(10) Ye stand this day all of you before the LORD your God; your captains of your tribes, your elders, and your officers, with all the men of Israel,
(11) Your little ones, your wives, and thy stranger that is in thy camp, from the hewer of thy wood unto the drawer of thy water:
(12) That thou shouldest enter into covenant with the LORD thy God, and into his oath, which the LORD thy God maketh with thee this day:
(13) That he may establish thee to day for a people unto himself, and that he may be unto thee a God, as he hath said unto thee, and as he hath sworn unto thy fathers, to Abraham, to Isaac, and to Jacob.
(14) Neither with you only do I make this covenant and this oath;
(15) But with him that standeth here with us this day before the LORD our God, and also with him that is not here with us this day:

We can now see that Shavuot was a betrothal ceremony. All of the elements were there. A drawing together of people as witnesses. A huppa, which is a wedding canopy, was provided by the cloud cover. A Ketubah, which is the written legal wedding vows, provided by the two tablets. An exchange of vows before the witnesses. Finally, there was a covenant meal.

Do you remember the declarations that were given while the bride was still in Egypt?
Exodus 6:6-7
(6) "Therefore, say to the people of Isra'el: 'I am Adonai.
- I will free you from the forced labor of the Egyptians,
- rescue you from their oppression,
- and redeem you with an outstretched arm and with great judgments.
- (7) I will take you as my people, and I will be your God. Then you will know that I am Adonai your God, who freed you from the forced labor of the Egyptians.

We see a beautiful promise of the bridegroom and redeemer. We have at times not been faithful but yet it was declared that we could come into the covenant.

Romans 9:25
As indeed he says in Hoshea, "Those who were not my people I will call my people; her who was not loved I will call loved;

Now that the betrothal has been done, we must put aside all other petitioners of courtship and keep our eyes focused on the one we have been given to. In other words, do not go back to the ways of the world but keep your eyes on your true love.

2 Corinthians 6:16-17
(16) What agreement can there be between the temple of God and idols? For we are the temple of the living God — as God said, "I will house myself in them, . . . and I will walk among you. I will be their God, and they will be my people."
(17) Therefore Adonai says, " 'Go out from their midst; separate yourselves; don't even touch what is unclean. Then I myself will receive you.

One thing that helps in remembering the word, is to keep it in a safe place where it will be protected but yet in view daily. The Ketubah is to be displayed in the dwelling place so all will be able to see that you belong to someone else and are not available to any other lover. This will help you in preparing to meet your bridegroom. You first give your heart to Him. Then as you prepare for the wedding day, you keep your wedding garment clean spotless and ready for the ceremony because you do not know the exact day that your bridegroom will come to get you and carry you away to the wedding feast.

Hebrews 8:10 says;
" 'For this is the covenant which I will make with the house of Isra'el after those days,' says Adonai: 'I will put my Torah in their minds and write it on their hearts; I will be their God, and they will be my people.

This Scripture is quoting Jeremiah 31:31-34

Jeremiah 31:31-34
(31) Behold, the days come, saith the LORD, that I will make a new covenant with the house of Israel, and with the house of Judah:
(32) Not according to the covenant that I made with their fathers in the day *that* I took them by the hand to bring them out of the land of Egypt; which my covenant they brake, although I was an husband unto them, saith the LORD:
(33) But this *shall be* the covenant that I will make with the house of Israel; After those days, saith the LORD, I will put my law in their inward parts, and write it in their hearts; and will be their God, and they shall be my people.
(34) And they shall teach no more every man his neighbour, and every man his brother, saying, Know the LORD: for they shall all know me, from the least of them unto the greatest of them, saith the LORD: for I will forgive their iniquity, and I will remember their sin no more.

Isaiah 54:5-6 reminds us that the LORD is our husband.
(5) For your husband is your Maker, Adonai-Tzva'ot is his name. The Holy One of Isra'el is your Redeemer. He will be called the God of all the earth.
(6) For Adonai has called you back like a wife abandoned and grief-stricken; "A wife married in her youth cannot be rejected," says your God.

172

Isaiah 61:10
I am so joyful in Adonai! My soul rejoices in my God, for he has clothed me in salvation, dressed me with a robe of triumph, like a bridegroom wearing a festive turban, like a bride adorned with her jewels.

Isaiah 62:5
as a young man marries a young woman, your sons will marry you; as a bridegroom rejoices over the bride, your God will rejoice over you.

The word Bridegroom is mentioned 11 times in the Brit Hadashah (New Testament).
- Matthew 9:15
- Matthew 25:5
- Matthew 25:6
- Matthew 25:10
- Mark 2:19
- Mark 2:20
- Luke 5:34
- Luke 5:35
- John 2:9
- John 3:29
- Revelation 18:23

Vows are exchanged when you come to Yahweh. You give your heart to Him and then declare faithful obedience to the one you love. You are the Bride of Messiah! We see that we are to treat our earthly brides as an example of the way that Yeshua treats His bride.

Ephesians 5:25-27
(25) Husbands, love your wives, even as Christ also loved the church, and gave himself for it;
(26) That he might sanctify and cleanse it with the washing of water by the word,
(27) That he might present it to himself a glorious church, not having spot, or wrinkle, or any such thing; but that it should be holy and without blemish.

Revelation 19:7-9
(7) "Let us rejoice and be glad! Let us give him the glory! For the time has come for the wedding of the Lamb, and his Bride has prepared herself —
(8) fine linen, bright and clean has been given her to wear." ("Fine linen" means the righteous deeds of God's people.)
(9) The angel said to me, "Write: 'How blessed are those who have been invited to the wedding feast of the Lamb!' " Then he added, "These are God's very words."

We must remember the words and promises of our bridegroom. A bride should always remember her vows. Deuteronomy 31:24-26 declares that the word of the LORD is to serve much like a Ketubah would. It would stand as a witness of the declarations made. The word was to remain as a witness for you. Remember, a witness can testify firsthand either for you, or against you.

Deuteronomy 31:24-26
(24) And it came to pass, when Moses had made an end of writing the words of this law in a book, until they were finished,
(25) That Moses commanded the Levites, which bare the ark of the covenant of the LORD, saying,
(26) Take this book of the law, and put it in the side of the ark of the covenant of the LORD your God, that it may be there for a witness against thee.

The word was meant to be within you. We see this as we look in Ezekiel.

Ezekiel 11:17-20
(17) Therefore say, Thus saith the Lord GOD; I will even gather you from the people, and assemble you out of the countries where ye have been scattered, and I will give you the land of Israel.
(18) And they shall come thither, and they shall take away all the detestable things thereof and all the abominations thereof from thence.
(19) And I will give them one heart, and I will put a new spirit within you; and I will take the stony heart out of their flesh, and will give them an heart of flesh:
(20) That they may walk in my statutes, and keep mine ordinances, and do them: and they shall be my people, and I will be their God.

Ezekiel 36:24-27
(24) For I will take you from among the heathen, and gather you out of all countries, and will bring you into your own land.
(25) Then will I sprinkle clean water upon you, and ye shall be clean: from all your filthiness, and from all your idols, will I cleanse you.
(26) A new heart also will I give you, and a new spirit will I put within you: and I will take away the stony heart out of your flesh, and I will give you an heart of flesh.
(27) And I will put my spirit within you, and cause you to walk in my statutes, and ye shall keep my judgments, and do *them*.

Yeshua said that He kept His Fathers word. So will His disciples.

John 14:15-27
(15) If ye love me, keep my commandments.
(16) And I will pray the Father, and he shall give you another Comforter, that he may abide with you for ever;
(17) *Even* the Spirit of truth; whom the world cannot receive, because it seeth him not, neither knoweth him: but ye know him; for he dwelleth with you, and shall be in you.
(18) I will not leave you comfortless: I will come to you.
(19) Yet a little while, and the world seeth me no more; but ye see me: because I live, ye shall live also.
(20) At that day ye shall know that I *am* in my Father, and ye in me, and I in you.
(21) He that hath my commandments, and keepeth them, he it is that loveth me: and he that loveth me shall be loved of my Father, and I will love him, and will manifest myself to him.
(22) Judas saith unto him, not Iscariot, Lord, how is it that thou wilt manifest thyself unto us, and not unto the world?
(23) Jesus answered and said unto him, If a man love me, he will keep my words: and my Father will love him, and we will come unto him, and make our abode with him.
(24) He that loveth me not keepeth not my sayings: and the word which ye hear is not mine, but the Father's which sent me.
(25) These things have I spoken unto you, being *yet* present with you.
(26) But the Comforter, *which is* the Holy Ghost, whom the Father will send in my name, he shall teach you all things, and bring all things to your remembrance, whatsoever I have said unto you.

(27) Peace I leave with you, my peace I give unto you: not as the world giveth, give I unto you. Let not your heart be troubled, neither let it be afraid.

We see here that Yeshua said He was going to reveal Himself and that the Holy Spirit is going to come to those who keep His word, to those who keep His commandments.

On this day of Shavuot, you were to make a proclamation. We see this in Leviticus 23.

Leviticus 23:20-21
(20) And the priest shall wave them with the bread of the first-fruits for a wave-offering before the LORD, with the two lambs; they shall be holy to the LORD for the priest.
(21) And ye shall make proclamation on the selfsame day; there shall be a holy convocation unto you; ye shall do no manner of servile work; it is a statute for ever in all your dwellings throughout your generations.

What proclamation were you supposed to make? What proclamation did Yahweh make on this day? We see the answer in Exodus nineteen.

Exodus 19:3-6
(3) Moshe went up to God, and Adonai <u>called</u> (קרא–KARA-PROCLAIMED) to him from the mountain: "Here is what you are to say to the household of Ya`akov, to tell the people of Isra'el:
(4) 'You have seen what I did to the Egyptians, and how I carried you on eagles' wings and brought you to myself.
(5) Now if you will pay careful attention to what I say and keep my covenant, then you will be my own treasure from among all the peoples, for all the earth is mine;
(6) and you will be a kingdom of cohanim for me, a nation set apart.' These are the words you are to speak to the people of Isra'el."

176

What words were proclaimed to the bride?

I HAVE DELIVERED YOU

I BROUGHT YOU TO MYSELF

IF YOU OBEY

AND KEEP MY COVENANT

YOU WILL BE A SPECIAL TREASURE

A KINGDOM OF PRIESTS

A HOLY NATION

- THIS WAS A KETUBA (A MARRIAGE CONTRACT)
- AN ENTERING OF A COVENANT
- AND HERE YHWH BETROTHED HIS BRIDE

OUR PROCLAMATION... "I DO!"

Let us recognize what the Father has done for us. Sometimes we just need to say something, a declaration if you will. Following are a few good declarations to keep and remember.

YOU HAVE DELIVERED ME

(YOU ARE MY LORD & SAVIOR)

YOU HAVE DRAWN ME TO YOU

I WILL KEEP YOUR WORD

I WILL BE A SPECIAL TREASURE

THAT SHINES FORTH THE GLORY OF YOU

I WILL WALK UPRIGHT AND HOLY

IN YOUR PRESENCE

Amen!

Yom Teruah

יום תרועה

Day of Alarm/
feast of trumpets

Yom Teruah, there really isn't much in scripture that specifically addresses this day. There are only two passages that address it directly. However, there is a lot of scripture that relates to this day, which we will see as we look further. As we take a look at it though, we will see how this day ties in with the work of the Messiah Yeshua (Jesus).

Before we go forward, let's take a real quick review. We will once again go to Leviticus twenty three to lay the foundation of our understanding for these times we are taking a closer look at.

Leviticus 23:1-2
(1) And the LORD spake unto Moses, saying,
(2) Speak unto the children of Israel, and say unto them, Concerning the feasts of the LORD, which ye shall proclaim to be holy convocations, even these are my feasts.

As we have addressed before, the word for "feasts" is often called designated times. It is the word from the Strong's concordance;
H4150 מועד מעד מועדה
   mô'âdâh   mô'êd
   • an appointment, a fixed time or season; a festival;
   • an assembly (as convened for a definite purpose);
   • appointed (sign, time),
   • (set, solemn) feast,
   • (appointed, due) season,
   • set time appointed

These set appointed times are to be holy convocations. We have learned that means a public gathering or a rehearsal. This would be from the Strong's concordance;
H4744 מקרא miqra' - From H7121; something called out, a public meeting; also a rehearsal: - assembly, calling, convocation, reading.

So far we have emphasized that a holy convocation is a public gathering. I do not want to lose that. However, I want to additionally stress the fact that they are rehearsals. When we observe the feasts of the LORD we are rehearsing for something.

This will be important to keep in mind as we start to open the understanding of the Fall feasts of YHWH.

Scripture does not specifically separate the feasts into two categories, Spring and Fall. We have done so in this study for the sole purpose of separation for clarification. It is no coincidence that these times fall into two separate seasons though. As we have seen, the feasts that are in the time of Spring reveal the Messiah and the work He would do at His coming. What we will see in these last studies is that the feasts in the Fall reveal the work of the Messiah in His coming AGAIN.

Remember, all of these set appointed times were given to...

Impart revelation from YHWH

Reveal the work of the Messiah

Show us how to draw close to the Father

Teach us how to gather in unity

Teach us how to come and worship with each other

So, as we take a closer look at what the Moedim are, we will better understand what they mean to us. If we take a look at Leviticus twenty three, we see a list of the Moedim of the LORD. The list starts with the foundation first and then lists the following times based on the foundation. The list below starts with the Spring and ends with the Fall. The Moedim in order are;

SHABBAT- the Sabbath

PESACH – Passover

MATZAH – Unleavened Bread

BIKKURIM –Firstfruits

SHAVUOT – Feast of Weeks

YOM TERUAH – Day of Trumpets (Day of Alarm)

YOM KIPPUR – Day of Atonement

SUKKOT – Feast of Tabernacles

While we continue on our journey through the Moedim, we will see a continuity of the work of the Messiah and the covenants that were made with the people of YHWH. Let me show you what I mean. If we take the festivals that we have looked at so far it will tell you a story based on the meanings of each festival. Let's start with the Sabbath.

-SHABBAT
- Stop all your pursuits and rest in your God. Enter His rest, a position of covenant.

-PESACH
- Redemption-the Blood has been applied and the plague of death has passed over you.

- MATZAH
- Go and sin no more. From this point on eat only a sinless life.

-BIKKURIM (FIRSTFRUIT)
- Yeshua HaMashiach is Risen as the Firstfruit of the Harvest.

-SHAVUOT
- We can now walk as people of YHWH, empowered by the Spirit and the Word.

It's quite a beautiful picture if we are willing to stop and look at it. The festivals begin their cycle in the spring. In the spring, everything all around us is bursting forth with life. It is a joyous time that shows us in the natural what the Father has done, and is doing, for us in the Spiritual realms of our lives. The Apostle Paul (Rabbi Shaul) helps us by explaining that sometimes we need to understand that the Father gave us things here with us in the Natural to teach us spiritual concepts.

1 Corinthians 15:46
Howbeit that was not first which is spiritual, but that which is natural; and afterward that which is spiritual.

We have already stated that the Moedim are not listed as two groupings. However, there is even a lesson to learn in how they are divided. In between spring and fall is summer. In the spring we have life bursting forth all around us and the coldness starts to go away. We are gently warmed with the presence of spring and the glow of the season around us.

Then comes the Summer! It's HOT! The heat at times can dry us out and make us lethargic and prone to wildfires. We start to look around and tell ourselves that we need time for some R&R (rest and relaxation). It's at these times that we take our minds off of our work and we lose focus. We tell ourselves that we need vacations or sabbaticals. What is disturbing though is the idea that when we do take a vacation, we tend to take a vacation from God as well. When we go on vacations do we look for a place to worship? Should we take a vacation from God?

We tell ourselves that we need to rest a little, relax some more. We take summer naps and seek to just exist and nothing else. Summer makes us lethargic, slow and lazy. It's now time to WAKE UP! What we see in this analogy are the tests of Summer. The test is, will we have faith when all around us it's just hot and dry? Even in our own souls?

Scripture speaks of the testing of faith during the summer. We must have faith and be faithful. We cannot grow weary in the summer. We must continue to work toward the reward.

Proverbs 10:5
He that gathereth in summer is a wise son: but he that sleepeth in harvest is a son that causeth shame.

We see a good example of faithfulness in the summer in the telling of the twelve spies in the book of Numbers chapter thirteen. Moses sent twelve men from the tribes of Israel to go and tour the land that they were to inhabit. A very interesting point here is that they were never asked their opinion about whether or not they thought that it was feasible to conquer the land.

The twelve were sent on a fact finding mission, not a feasibility study. They were told to do nothing else but to go and gather facts concerning the land and bring back some fruit. If these men had approached their task at hand in faith, they would have seen the promises of the Father wherever they went. Instead, they had an issue with a lack of faith. They rested their eyes on what they saw in front of them, but they were focused on the wrong things. Instead of saying we were like grasshoppers in their sight, they should have said "our God has given us this land and He goes before us into the battle! He declared it, so He will do it!"

There were twelve men who went into the land. What did they eat while they were in the land? Did they eat manna? Manna fell in the camp of Israel. When they went into the land, the manna stopped. These men walked into the promise of the Father, tasted of the promise that was told to them, and walked away from it saying it's too hard. The writer of the book of Hebrews puts it this way in Hebrews 6:4-6

(6:4) For it is impossible for those who were once enlightened, and have tasted of the heavenly gift, and were made partakers of the Holy Ghost,
(5) And have tasted the good word of God, and the powers of the world to come,
(6) If they shall fall away, to renew them again unto repentance; seeing they crucify to themselves the Son of God afresh, and put him to an open shame.

What happened when the men came back? Only two had held fast to the promise, Caleb and Joshua. There were two witnesses to stand and declare that the word of the LORD was true! It is also interesting to see the prophetic implications here. Caleb was from the tribe of Judah and Joshua was an Ephraimite (descended from Joseph). When you see all the people being regathered back into the land in Ezekiel 37 the tribes mentioned are Judah and Ephraim.

How does this story fit into the telling of the feasts? Numbers 13:20 gives the answer, it says that now was the time of the first ripe grapes. This was June/ July, the summer season.

After a long dreary summer, how quick are we to get back to the harvest? We must have faith.

In Leviticus 23, you have the Spring Feasts, then the Summer comes. After the long, hot & trying Summer we have the fall feasts. They are:
-YOM TERUAH
-YOM KIPPUR
-SUKKOT

We will start with Yom Teruah, a day for shouting and trumpet blasts. It testifies to the fact that YHWH is calling His people to WAKE UP and hear the sound of the shofar TODAY!

1 Corinthians 15:34 Awake to righteousness, and sin not; for some have not the knowledge of God: I speak this to your shame.

Ephesians 5:14 Wherefore he saith, Awake thou that sleepest, and arise from the dead, and Christ shall give thee light.

The telling of Yom Teruah starts in Leviticus chapter twenty three in verse twenty three.

Leviticus 23:23-25
(23) And the LORD spake unto Moses, saying,
(24) Speak unto the children of Israel, saying, In the seventh month, in the first day of the month, shall ye have a sabbath, a memorial of blowing of trumpets, an holy convocation.
(25) Ye shall do no servile work therein: but ye shall offer an offering made by fire unto the LORD.

Notice how much we are told about this day in the scripture we just read. The first day of the seventh month, that would be a Rosh Chodesh, a new moon, a new month. No man can predict with 100% accuracy when you will be able to see the new moon every month for years to come. We can come pretty close in our predictions, but can we really predict the sighting of it to make sure it is the right day? After all, we do see in Scripture where the sun and moon held it's place for a full day in the book of Joshua. Are we to predict if the Father sees fit to do another similar miracle?

We are then told that it is a Sabbath and we are to have a memorial. For the memorial, we are to blow the trumpets and have a holy convocation. We are not to work and we are to bring an offering to the LORD. We see more scripture concerning this day in the book of Numbers in chapter twenty-nine.

Numbers 29:1-6
(1) In the seventh month, on the first day of the month, you shall have a holy convocation; you shall do no servile work: it is a day of blowing of trumpets to you.
(2) You shall offer a burnt offering for a sweet savor to the LORD: one young bull, one ram, seven male lambs a year old without blemish;
(3) and their meal offering, fine flour mixed with oil, three tenth parts for the bull, two tenth parts for the ram,
(4) and one tenth part for every lamb of the seven lambs;
(5) and one male goat for a sin offering, to make atonement for you;
(6) besides the burnt offering of the new moon, and the meal offering of it, and the continual burnt offering and the meal offering of it, and their drink offerings, according to their ordinance, for a sweet savor, an offering made by fire to the LORD.

We see pretty much the same thing here that we saw in Leviticus. The only major difference is that here the offerings are defined a little more clearly. In both scriptures, we see that the fall festivals start with the first day of the seventh month. This could be referred to as the feast in which no one knows the day because we have to watch and wait for the appointed time to be at hand in order to properly observe it.

If we are to observe this time in the seventh month, it only makes sense to ask "When is the seventh month?" In order to answer the question, we should first ask "When is the first month?" We see the definition for the first, or the head of, the months in the book of Exodus chapter twelve.

Exodus 12:1-2
(1) And the LORD spake unto Moses and Aaron in the land of Egypt, saying,
(2) This month shall be unto you the beginning of months: it shall be the first month of the year to you.

The month of Aviv, also called Nisan, is the first month of the year. There will be six more revolutions or cycles of the moon in order to determine the first day of the seventh month. Remember why the lights in the firmament were put in order in the sky? Genesis 1:14 says; And God said: 'Let there be lights in the firmament of the heaven to divide the day from the night; and let them be for signs, and for seasons, and for days and years. Psalms 104:19 also says; He appointed the moon for seasons (moedim): the sun knoweth his going down.

Once the month is established, we are told to blow trumpets as a memorial. We see more regarding these trumpets in the book of Numbers chapter ten.

Numbers 10:1-10
(1) And the LORD spake unto Moses, saying,
(2) Make thee two trumpets of silver; of a whole piece shalt thou make them: that thou mayest use them for the calling of the assembly, and for the journeying of the camps.
(3) And when they shall blow with them, all the assembly shall assemble themselves to thee at the door of the tabernacle of the congregation.
(4) And if they blow but with one trumpet, then the princes, which are heads of the thousands of Israel, shall gather themselves unto thee.
(5) When ye blow an alarm, then the camps that lie on the east parts shall go forward.

(6) When ye blow an alarm the second time, then the camps that lie on the south side shall take their journey: they shall blow an alarm for their journeys.

(7) But when the congregation is to be gathered together, ye shall blow, but ye shall not sound an alarm.

(8) And the sons of Aaron, the priests, shall blow with the trumpets; and they shall be to you for an ordinance for ever throughout your generations.

(9) And if ye go to war in your land against the enemy that oppresseth you, then ye shall blow an alarm with the trumpets; and ye shall be remembered before the LORD your God, and ye shall be saved from your enemies.

(10) Also in the day of your gladness, and in your solemn days, and in the beginnings of your months, ye shall blow with the trumpets over your burnt offerings, and over the sacrifices of your peace offerings; that they may be to you for a memorial before your God: I am the LORD your God.

Israel was told to make two trumpets of silver. Silver in scripture was a representation of redemption. We see a good example of this when the half shekel ransom (redemption) price was to be given after the people were numbered for service in Exodus chapter thirty.

Exodus 30:11-16
(11) And the LORD spake unto Moses, saying,

(12) When thou takest the sum of the children of Israel after their number, then shall they give every man a ransom for his soul unto the LORD, when thou numberest them; that there be no plague among them, when thou numberest them.

(13) This they shall give, every one that passeth among them that are numbered, half a shekel after the shekel of the sanctuary: (a shekel is twenty gerahs:) an half shekel shall be the offering of the LORD.

(14) Every one that passeth among them that are numbered, from twenty years old and above, shall give an offering unto the LORD.

(15) The rich shall not give more, and the poor shall not give less than half a shekel, when they give an offering unto the LORD, to make an atonement for your souls.

(16) And thou shalt take the atonement money of the children of Israel, and shalt appoint it for the service of the tabernacle of the congregation; that it may be a memorial unto the children of Israel before the LORD, to make an atonement for your souls.

The redemption price for atonement was the same for every man who was numbered for military service. Every man had to pay the redemption price. The silver was then used in the service of the tabernacle.

The trumpets were to be used for different reasons. If one blew, it was only to assemble the leaders. If two blew, it meant something else. If they blew in succession it meant one thing but if they blew an alarm it meant something else. If you don't know what the trumpet calls are, you will not know what to do when you hear them.

There are four main traditional shofar sounds. They are:
- Tekiah: The "blast". One long blast with a clear tone. Signifies Rejoicing and Hope
- Shevarim: A "broken" sound of 3 short calls. Like the sighing. It is a reminder that we need to be broken before a coming King who will judge the earth.
- Teruah: An "alarm". A rapid series of 9 or more staccatoo notes. Like crying. It is a reminder to plead for mercy before the King who has come to judge the living and the dead
- Tekiah Gedolah: A single, unbroken blast held as long as possible. This call is a reminder that at the sound of the last great trumpet, the King will be back with power and glory to rule forever.

When we talked about Shavuot, we said that the sound the trumpets and shofars make is called a voice. You have been given a voice. Which of these four calls are you sounding? Let our voices raise up like a shofar to declare the word of the LORD.

Isaiah 58:1
Cry aloud, spare not, lift up thy voice like a trumpet, and shew my people their transgression, and the house of Jacob their sins.

Luke 3:4-6
(4) As it is written in the book of the words of Esaias the prophet, saying, The voice of one crying in the wilderness, Prepare ye the way of the Lord, make his paths straight.
(5) Every valley shall be filled, and every mountain and hill shall be brought low; and the crooked shall be made straight, and the rough ways shall be made smooth;
(6) And all flesh shall see the salvation of God.

1 Thessalonians 4:16
For the Lord himself shall descend from heaven <u>with a shout</u>, with the voice of the archangel, <u>and with the trump of God</u>(God's shofar): and the dead in Christ shall rise first:

We now return to the feast of trumpets in numbers chapter ten. We see that these trumpets that were made of pure silver were to be sounded over offerings, days of gladness, SET FEASTS, beginning of months and it that they will be a memorial.

Numbers 10:10
Also in the day of your gladness, and in your set feasts, and in the beginnings of your months, you shall blow the trumpets over your burnt offerings, and over the sacrifices of your shalom offerings; and they shall be to you for a memorial before your God: I am the LORD your God.

The word used in numbers ten for memorial is the Hebrew word זכר Zakar. It means to mark (so as to be recognized), to remember; to mention; be mindful, recount, record, remember, make to be remembered, bring (call, come, keep, put) to (in) remembrance, and to still think on.

Scripture says that when the trumpets blast you will be marked, recognized and be remembered before the LORD your God. The name of the call that is given in scripture in regards to this day is the call "Teruah." This is why the day is called Yom Teruah. The Hebrew word Teruah is the word;

H8643 תְּרוּעָה teru'ʿâh
From H7321; acclamation of joy or a battle cry; an alarm, blowing of the trumpets, joy, jubile, loud noise, rejoicing, shouting, (high, joyful) sound

This day called Yom Teruah in scripture literally translates as a day for shouting and rejoicing with a high and joyful sound. It is a day for jubilee. It is a reminder that we need to be waiting, watching and listening for this day because the King is coming and the Kingdom is at hand.

One problem is, there are many voices out there. We must be sure that we are listening to the right voice. We must discern the voices we hear to see which voices are for us, which are for others, and what is our appropriate action with the call going forth. Paul addresses this by relating people and the words given by them to the trumpets that were made to call forth the people of God.

1 Corinthians 14:8 - For if the trumpet give an uncertain sound, who shall prepare himself to the battle?

The word Teruah is from another word, the word Rua. It is the Strong's concordance #H7321 רוּעַ rûaʿ to mar (especially by breaking to split the ears with sound, shout (for alarm or joy: blow an alarm, cry aloud, make a joyful noise, shout for joy, sound an alarm, triumph.

This literally means a very loud cry. A sound so loud that it splits the ears. Do you remember what the sound on Mt. Sinai was that called the people forth? It was a shofar so loud that it shook the earth. We should also lift up our voices.

Isaiah 40:3-5
(3) The voice of him that crieth in the wilderness, Prepare ye the way of the LORD, make straight in the desert a highway for our God.
(4) Every valley shall be exalted, and every mountain and hill shall be made low: and the crooked shall be made straight, and the rough places plain:
(5) And the glory of the LORD shall be revealed, and all flesh shall see it together: for the mouth of the LORD hath spoken it.

Matthew 3:3 For this is he that was spoken of by the prophet Esaias, saying, The voice of one crying in the wilderness, Prepare ye the way of the Lord, make his paths straight.

Mark 1:3 The voice of one crying in the wilderness, Prepare ye the way of the Lord, make his paths straight.

Luke 3:4 As it is written in the book of the words of Esaias the prophet, saying, The voice of one crying in the wilderness, Prepare ye the way of the Lord, make his paths straight.

John 1:23 He said, I am the voice of one crying in the wilderness, Make straight the way of the Lord, as said the prophet Esaias.

We see that this day of Yom Teruah is to be a day in which the people of God were to give themselves over to making a joyful shout to the LORD as they prepare to meet with Him.

This is a time to rejoice!
This is a time to hear!
This is a time to proclaim!
This is a time to remember and act on behalf of the Kingdom of YHWH!

We saw in Exodus 19:13 that when the shofar sounds long,they shall come up to the mountain. When the people of the

LORD heard the voice of the shofar, they were to come up to the mount of the Lord AND MEET WITH HIM.

The people were told to prepare themselves to hear the voice of the shofar from Heaven. Part of the preparation, was to keep themselves clean and pure for the duration of the waiting process. When they heard the voice of the shofar, God Himself would come down to meet with them and the people were to go up to Him.

Exodus 19:13-20
(13) There shall not an hand touch it, but he shall surely be stoned, or shot through; whether it be beast or man, it shall not live: when the trumpet soundeth long, they shall come up to the mount.
(14) And Moses went down from the mount unto the people, and sanctified the people; and they washed their clothes.
(15) And he said unto the people, Be ready against the third day: come not at your wives.
(16) And it came to pass on the third day in the morning, that there were thunders and lightnings, and a thick cloud upon the mount, and the voice of the trumpet exceeding loud; so that all the people that was in the camp trembled.
(17) And Moses brought forth the people out of the camp to meet with God; and they stood at the nether part of the mount.
(18) And mount Sinai was altogether on a smoke, because the LORD descended upon it in fire: and the smoke thereof ascended as the smoke of a furnace, and the whole mount quaked greatly.
(19) And when the voice of the trumpet sounded long, and waxed louder and louder, Moses spake, and God answered him by a voice.
(20) And the LORD came down upon mount Sinai, on the top of the mount: and the LORD called Moses up to the top of the mount; and Moses went up.

When God came down on the mountain, only Moses went up. The people missed what the Father wanted for them. Were they really prepared for what they were to see and experience? Even if they were prepared for the shofar call, were they ready for the meeting that was to be experienced? The people were to prepare themselves, physically and spiritually for their meeting on the mountain. This scenario reminds me of another scripture from the book of Matthew.

Matthew 25:1-13
(1) Then shall the kingdom of heaven be likened unto ten virgins, which took their lamps, and went forth to meet the bridegroom.
(2) And five of them were wise, and five [were] foolish.
(3) They that [were] foolish took their lamps, and took no oil with them:
(4) But the wise took oil in their vessels with their lamps.
(5) While the bridegroom tarried, they _all_ slumbered and slept.

- Much like the sleepy summer months, this is the time between the feasts where we are told to watch for the first day of the seventh month. We know around the right time it will be there, but we are told to watch for it.

(6) And at midnight there was a cry made, Behold, the bridegroom cometh; go ye out to meet him.

- The cry, the sound of the shofar, was heard and a voice was lifted up as a shout. The shofar was blown before the bridegroom was announced. The sound of the shofar was given for all to hear. It was for all to come, gather and worship the King at the wedding feast of the Lamb.

(7) Then all those virgins arose, and trimmed their lamps.
(8) And the foolish said unto the wise, Give us of your oil; for our lamps are gone out.
(9) But the wise answered, saying, [Not so]; lest there be not enough for us and you: but go ye rather to them that sell, and buy for yourselves.
(10) And while they went to buy, the bridegroom came; and they that were ready went in with him to the marriage: and the door was shut.
(11) Afterward came also the other virgins, saying, Lord, Lord, open to us.
(12) But he answered and said, Verily I say unto you, I know you not....
(13) Watch therefore, for ye know neither the day nor the hour wherein the Son of man cometh.

We should watch and listen for the sound of the triumphant entrance of the Bridegroom and King. The King is coming for His Bride and the world will be judged. When the King returns and claims His bride, He will also separate all who are to be the bride and all who are invited to the wedding feast. When He returns, He will take His bride to the place that He has made ready for her.

Isaiah 66:22-23
(22) For as the new heavens and the new earth, which I will make, shall remain before me, says the LORD, so shall your seed and your name remain.
(23) It shall happen, that from one new moon to another, and from one Shabbat to another, shall all flesh come to worship before me, says the LORD.

We will all come and worship the King in the new Heaven and Earth. It is said that the LORD Himself will teach us and our children. We will all be taught by our Heavenly Father. We will be gathered together into His family forever.

Isaiah 54:13-14
(13) All your children shall be taught of the LORD; and great shall be the shalom of your children.
(14) In righteousness shall you be established: you shall be far from oppression, for you shall not be afraid; and from terror, for it shall not come near you.

Through Scripture we see that when the shofar is blown, great things happened.

Joshua had a great experience with the Shofar. The book of Joshua chapter 6 tells the story of Jericho. Verse 20 tells of the actual shofar call

- (6:20) So the people shouted, with the shofars blowing. When the people heard the sound of the shofars, the people let out a great shout; and the wall fell down flat; so that the people went up into the city, each one straight ahead of him; and they captured the city.

195

Joshua had a great experience with the shofar. Scripture says that the people let out a great shout when they heard the sound of the shofars. What's interesting is that the word used for "shofars" in the Hebrew, is singular. (Joshua 6:20) So the people shouted, with the shofars blowing. When the people heard the <u>sound of the shofars</u>, in the Hebrew this reads as "ET Kol HaShofar" (אֶת – קוֹל הַשׁוֹפָר) the Alef tav is used and it says they heard the voice (singular) of the shofar (singular). The verse continues to say that "the people let out a great shout"; this is the word Teruah – תְרוּעָה and the wall fell down flat; so that the people went up into the city, each one straight ahead of him; and they captured the city.

The thought is that the people sounded the shofars in unison so that they all heard one voice, one shofar, God's. When we all come together and put aside our own agendas on how we think something should be done in exchange for following the word of God, we will see great and mighty things and just like Jericho, the walls of division will come down.

There is a time coming when YHWH Himself will sound the shofar over His people.

Zechariah 9:11-16
(11) As for thee also, by the blood of thy covenant I have sent forth thy prisoners out of the pit wherein is no water.
(12) Turn you to the strong hold, ye prisoners of hope: even to day do I declare that I will render double unto thee;
(13) When I have bent Judah for me, filled the bow with Ephraim, and raised up thy sons, O Zion, against thy sons, O Greece, and made thee as the sword of a mighty man.
(14) And the LORD shall be seen over them, and his arrow shall go forth as the lightning: **and the Lord GOD shall blow the trumpet**, and shall go with whirlwinds of the south.
(15) The LORD of hosts shall defend them; and they shall devour, and subdue with sling stones; and they shall drink, and make a

noise as through wine; and they shall be filled like bowls, and as the corners of the altar.

(16) And the LORD their God shall save them in that day as the flock of his people: for they shall be as the stones of a crown, lifted up as an ensign upon his land.

Throughout Scripture, the shofar is used to sound an alarm calling the people to gather. There were other sounds that called the people to go out to war.

Nehemiah 4:19-20
(19) And I said unto the nobles, and to the rulers, and to the rest of the people, The work is great and large, and we are separated upon the wall, one far from another.
(20) In what place therefore ye hear the sound of the trumpet, resort ye thither unto us: our God shall fight for us.

When the shofar sounds, the people were to respond, either with worship or warfare. Both cases called for the people to have faith and answer the call. When the shofar sounds, we should hear the call and let out a sound of praise. When we worship, we come and bow down and declare His goodness. When we are called to war, we rejoice, knowing that our God said that He would go before us to fight for us and to deliver us from the adversary.

With the understanding of what we have learned so far, let us read the few verses that follow.

Psalms 98:6
With trumpets and sound of the ram's horn, make a joyful noise before the King, the LORD.

Joel 2:1
Blow the shofar in Tziyon, and sound an alarm in my holy mountain! Let all the inhabitants of the land tremble, for the day of the LORD comes, for it is close at hand:

Psalms 89:15
Blessed is the people that know the joyful sound (TERUAH): they shall walk, O LORD, in the light of thy countenance.

Psalms 98:1-9 A Psalm.
(1) O sing unto the LORD a new song; for He hath done marvellous things; His right hand, and His holy arm, hath wrought salvation for Him.
(2) The LORD hath made known His salvation; His righteousness hath He revealed in the sight of the nations.
(3) He hath remembered His mercy and His faithfulness toward the house of Israel; all the ends of the earth have seen the salvation of our God.
(4) Shout unto the LORD, all the earth; break forth and sing for joy, yea, sing praises.
(5) Sing praises unto the LORD with the harp; with the harp and the voice of melody.
(6) With (THE SILVER) trumpets and sound of the horn (SHOFAR) shout (RUAH) ye before the King, the LORD.
(7) Let the sea roar, and the fulness thereof; the world, and they that dwell therein;
(8) Let the floods clap their hands; let the mountains sing for joy together;
(9) Before the LORD, for He is come to judge the earth; He will judge the world with righteousness, and the peoples with equity.
(this could be a reference pointing forward to Yom Kippur after Yom Teruah)

Remember, the trumpets were a call to prepare yourself because the King is coming. Are you ready and prepared to hear His voice? Read Psalm twenty-nine and what it has to say concerning the voice of the LORD.

Psalms 29:1-11
(1) A Psalm of David. Give unto the LORD, O ye mighty, give unto the LORD glory and strength.
(2) Give unto the LORD the glory due unto his name; worship the LORD in the beauty of holiness.

(3) The voice of the LORD is upon the waters: the God of glory thundereth: the LORD is upon many waters.

(4) The voice of the LORD is powerful; the voice of the LORD is full of majesty.

(5) The voice of the LORD breaketh the cedars; yea, the LORD breaketh the cedars of Lebanon.

(6) He maketh them also to skip like a calf; Lebanon and Sirion like a young unicorn.

(7) The voice of the LORD divideth the flames of fire.

(8) The voice of the LORD shaketh the wilderness; the LORD shaketh the wilderness of Kadesh.

(9) The voice of the LORD maketh the hinds to calve, and discovereth the forests: and in his temple doth every one speak of his glory.

(10) The LORD sitteth upon the flood; yea, the LORD sitteth King for ever.

(11) The LORD will give strength unto his people; the LORD will bless his people with peace.

Yom Teruah is a time to rejoice, a time to sound the alarm of YHWH. We will list some scriptures and prayers that are appropriate for this day of Yom Teruah. There will not be much commentary on the following Scriptures. These are listed for you to read, speak out and meditate on as you prayerfully approach this day.

Isaiah fifty-eight is a good place to start and focus on what we should be listening for on the day of Yom Teruah.

Isaiah 58:1-2
(1) Cry aloud, spare not, lift up thy voice like a trumpet, and shew my people their transgression, and the house of Jacob their sins.
(2) Yet they seek me daily, and delight to know my ways, as a nation that did righteousness, and forsook not the ordinance of their God: they ask of me the ordinances of justice; they take delight in approaching to God.

Isaiah 40:3-5
(3) The voice of him that crieth in the wilderness, Prepare ye the way of the LORD, make straight in the desert a highway for our God.
(4) Every valley shall be exalted, and every mountain and hill shall be made low: and the crooked shall be made straight, and the rough places plain:
(5) And the glory of the LORD shall be revealed, and all flesh shall see it together: for the mouth of the LORD hath spoken it.

John 1:23
(23) He said, I am the voice of one crying in the wilderness, Make straight the way of the Lord, as said the prophet Esaias.

Ephesians 2:8-22 KJV
(8) For by grace are ye saved through faith; and that not of yourselves: it is the gift of God:

(9) Not of works, lest any man should boast.

(10) For we are his workmanship, created in Christ Jesus unto good works, which God hath before ordained that we should walk in them.

(11) Wherefore remember, that ye being in time past Gentiles in the flesh, who are called Uncircumcision by that which is called the Circumcision in the flesh made by hands;

(12) That at that time ye were without Christ, being aliens from the commonwealth of Israel, and strangers from the covenants of promise, having no hope, and without God in the world:

(13) But now in Christ Jesus ye who sometimes were far off are made nigh by the blood of Christ.

(14) For he is our peace, who hath made both one, and hath broken down the middle wall of partition between us;

(15) Having abolished in his flesh the enmity, even the law of commandments contained in ordinances; for to make in himself of twain one new man, so making peace;

(16) And that he might reconcile both unto God in one body by the cross, having slain the enmity thereby:

(17) And came and preached peace to you which were afar off, and to them that were nigh.

(18) For through him we both have access by one Spirit unto the Father.

(19) Now therefore ye are no more strangers and foreigners, but fellowcitizens with the saints, and of the household of God;

(20) And are built upon the foundation of the apostles and prophets, Jesus Christ himself being the chief corner stone;

(21) In whom all the building fitly framed together groweth unto an holy temple in the Lord:

(22) In whom ye also are builded together for an habitation of God through the Spirit.

Leviticus 23:23-25

(23) And the LORD spake unto Moses, saying,

(24) Speak unto the children of Israel, saying, In the seventh month, in the first day of the month, shall ye have a sabbath, a memorial of blowing of trumpets, an holy convocation.

(25) Ye shall do no servile work therein: but ye shall offer an offering made by fire unto the LORD.

Psalms 104:19
He appointed the moon for seasons (to Moedim לְמוֹעֲדִים): the sun knoweth his going down.

1 Thessalonians 4:16-17
(16) For the Lord himself shall descend from heaven with a shout, with the voice of the archangel, and with the trump of God: and the dead in Christ shall rise first:
(17) Then we which are alive and remain shall be caught up together with them in the clouds, to meet the Lord in the air: and so shall we ever be with the Lord.

Numbers 10:1-10
(1) And the LORD spake unto Moses, saying,
(2) Make thee two trumpets of silver; of a whole piece shalt thou make them: that thou mayest use them for the calling of the assembly, and for the journeying of the camps.
(3) And when they shall blow with them, all the assembly shall assemble themselves to thee at the door of the tabernacle of the congregation.
(4) And if they blow but with one trumpet, then the princes, which are heads of the thousands of Israel, shall gather themselves unto thee.
(5) When ye blow an alarm, then the camps that lie on the east parts shall go forward.
(6) When ye blow an alarm the second time, then the camps that lie on the south side shall take their journey: they shall blow an alarm for their journeys.
(7) But when the congregation is to be gathered together, ye shall blow, but ye shall not sound an alarm.
(8) And the sons of Aaron, the priests, shall blow with the trumpets; and they shall be to you for an ordinance for ever throughout your generations.
(9) And if ye go to war in your land against the enemy that oppresseth you, then ye shall blow an alarm with the trumpets;

and ye shall be remembered before the LORD your God, and ye shall be saved from your enemies.

(10) Also in the day of your gladness, and in your solemn days, and in the beginnings of your months, ye shall blow with the trumpets over your burnt offerings, and over the sacrifices of your peace offerings; that they may be to you for a memorial before your God: I am the LORD your God.

Joel 2:1

Blow ye the trumpet in Zion, and sound an alarm (רוּעַ) in my holy mountain: let all the inhabitants of the land tremble: for the day of the LORD cometh, for it is nigh at hand;

Psalms 81:3-4

(3) Blow up the trumpet in the new moon, in the time appointed, on our solemn feast day.

(4) For this was a statute for Israel, and a law of the God of Jacob.

Psalms 98:6

With trumpets and sound of cornet make a joyful noise before the LORD, the King.

Along with the Scriptures, it is good to make declarations of what is to happen in our lives as we hear the shofar. Say these out loud so that you can hear them being made as declarations before your King.

- May the sound of the Shofar be remembered before You Lord, as we battle the adversaries that oppress us.
- And may the sound of the shofar remind us that You have promised to give us victory over our enemies.
- May the sound of the shofar awaken us to the appointed seasons, and the call to spiritual warfare.
- And may the sound of the shofar shatter our complacency, and make us conscious of the corruption within us that still remains to be conquered
- May the sound of the shofar awaken us always to the enormity of our sins, and to the vastness of your mercy, to those who repent.

- And may the sound of the shofar break the bonds of enslavement to evil impulses, and cause us to always seek you for revival.
- May the sound of the shofar cause us to turn to You Lord, and come before You in repentance.
- And may the sound of the shofar cause us to say, "all that the Lord has spoken, that we will do."
- May the sound of the shofar cause us to renew our loyalty to You, the one true God, and Yeshua, Your Son.
- And may the sound of the shofar strengthen our determination to defy every false god, through the power of Your Spirit.
- May the sound of the shofar release the captives in jubilee, and proclaim liberty to those who would be set free.
- And may the sound of the shofar release gladness over our offerings, and be a memorial to You Lord, a way in which You are remembered.

Blessed are you Lord our God, King of the universe, who has given us life, sustained us, and brought us to this season. Amen.

Psalms 89:15
Blessed is the people that know the joyful sound: they shall walk, O LORD, in the light of thy countenance.

Psalms 98:6
With trumpets and sound of cornet make a joyful noise before the LORD, the King.

Blessed are You LORD our God, King of the universe, who has given us the way to salvation in Messiah Yeshua, Amen.

He is LORD, He is LORD, Yeshua Hamasheach He is LORD, every knee shall bow, every tongue confess, that Yeshua Hamasheach, HE IS LORD!

Exodus 15:11
Who is like unto thee, O LORD, among the gods? who is like thee, glorious in holiness, fearful in praises, doing wonders?

Psalms 106:1
Praise ye the LORD. O give thanks unto the LORD; for he is good: for his mercy endureth for ever.

Psalms 107:1
O give thanks unto the LORD, for he is good: for his mercy endureth for ever.

Psalms 118:1
O give thanks unto the LORD; for he is good: because his mercy endureth for ever.

Psalms 118:29
O give thanks unto the LORD; for he is good: for his mercy endureth for ever.

Psalms 136:1
O give thanks unto the LORD; for he is good: for his mercy endureth for ever.

LORD God, You are holy, and awesome is Your name, there is no God besides You. It is written. "The Lord of hosts is exalted through justice, and the holy God is sanctified through righteousness." Blessed are You O Lord, the holy King!

Revelation 4:8
Holy, Holy, Holy Is the Lord God of hosts. Who was, who is, and is to come

Our Father and our King, be merciful and answer us. Though we have no worthy deeds of our own, treat us charitably with loving kindness, for You have saved us.

The Lord of the Universe, who reigned before anything was created. When all was made by his will, He was acknowledged as King. And when all shall end, He still all alone shall reign.
He was, He is, and He shall be in glory.

And He is one, and there is no other, to compare or join Him. Without beginning, without end and to Him belongs dominion and power. And He is my G-d, my living G-d. To Him I flee in time of grief, and He is my miracle and my refuge, who answers the day I shall call.

To Him I commit my spirit, in the time of sleep and awakening, even if my spirit leaves, God is with me, I shall not fear.

We will sanctify Your name in this world just as it is sanctified in the highest heavens, as it is written by Your prophet: "And they call out to one another and say:
- 'Holy, holy, holy is Yahweh of hosts; the whole earth is full of his glory.' [Isaiah 6:3]

Those facing them praise Elohim saying:
- "Blessed be the Presence of Yahweh in his place." [Ezekiel 3:12]

And in Your Holy Words it is written, saying,
- "Yahweh reigns forever, Your Elohim, O Zion, throughout all generations. Hallelujah." [Psalms 146:10]

Throughout all generations we will declare Your greatness, and to all eternity we will proclaim your holiness. Your praise, O our Elohim, shall never depart from our mouth, for You are a great and holy Elohim and King. Blessed are You, O Yahweh, the holy Elohim. You are holy, and Your name is holy, and holy beings praise You daily. (Selah.) Blessed are You, O Yahweh, the holy Elohim.

Numbers 6:22-27
(22) And the LORD spake unto Moses, saying,
(23) Speak unto Aaron and unto his sons, saying, On this wise ye shall bless the children of Israel, saying unto them,
(24) The LORD bless thee, and keep thee:

(25) The LORD make his face shine upon thee, and be gracious unto thee:

(26) The LORD lift up his countenance upon thee, and give thee peace.

(27) And they shall put my name upon the children of Israel; and I will bless them.

יום כפר

YOM KIPPUR

Day of Covering
Day of Atonement

Yom Kippur is a day, known as the day of atonement. What does atonement mean? Does it mean all is forgiven, or does it mean something else? Atonement is a very essential theme in Scripture. As believers today, in order to understand the sacrifice that Messiah Yeshua made for us, we should take a look at how atonement was provided in the Scripture.

When we say that Jesus Christ, Yeshua HaMoshiach, provided atonement for us, what are we really saying? Atonement is such a big factor in Scripture that there was only one person who was even allowed to be involved in the process of coming before the Lord for the purpose of atonement. That person was the high priest, Aaron. While we know it is God that provides the atoning, He expected Aaron to follow His word meticulously.

The day of atonement was very important to the children of Israel. It was on this day, that judgment was being declared. As the high priest went before the Lord, would Yahweh atone for them for another year? In order to stand before a holy and righteous God, atonement was a necessity for coming back out from before the Lord alive.

To get a closer look at this day, we will again turn to Leviticus chapter 23, among other Scriptures. By now we should have an understanding of what a Sabbath is, what moedim are, and how they relate to us. Now we will continue looking forward to this day of atonement.

Leviticus 23:26-32
(26) And the LORD spake unto Moses, saying,
(27) Also on the tenth day of this seventh month there shall be a day of atonement: it shall be an holy convocation unto you; and ye shall afflict your souls, and offer an offering made by fire unto the LORD.
(28) And ye shall do no work in that same day: for it is a day of atonement, to make an atonement for you before the LORD your God.
(29) For whatsoever soul it be that shall not be afflicted in that same day, he shall be cut off from among his people.
(30) And whatsoever soul it be that doeth any work in that same day, the same soul will I destroy from among his people.

(31) Ye shall do no manner of work: it shall be a statute for ever throughout your generations in all your dwellings.
(32) It shall be unto you a sabbath of rest, and ye shall afflict your souls: in the ninth day of the month at even, from even unto even, shall ye celebrate your sabbath.

The first thing we will look at is the meaning of the day itself. The word "Yom" is Hebrew for the word "day." The word kippur is the word for atonement. In Scripture, this is literally called Yom HaKippurim or day of atonements. Why would atonement be plural? We will reveal this, as we continue later in this study.

The word for atonement is kippur. It is in the Strongs dictionary number
H3725.
כפר
Kippûr - kip-poor'
From H3722; expiation (only in plural): - atonement.

It is from the word kaphar which is in the Strongs dictionary, number H3722
כפר
kâphar
to cover, to expiate or condone, to placate or cancel: - appease, make atonement, cleanse, disannul, forgive, be merciful, pacify, pardon, to pitch, purge away, put off, make reconciliation

So far we see that definition of the word atonement means to cover, to pardon, to purge, or to make reconciliation. We can also get a good look at this word according to the Paleo Hebrew. Ancient Hebrew was in the form of pictographs. Letters were pictures. The pictures meant something. The meaning of the letter was the action that that letter performed. According to the ancient Hebrew lexicon of the Bible, the Paleo Hebrew for the word kippur would look like this,

ᚠᚥᚹ
ר פ כ (Paleo)
Cover : Lid : Atonement: A protective covering to go over something. Or the covering of a debt or wrong.

The pictures in the Paleo Hebrew reading from right to left are; a palm of the hand, a mouth and a head. The palm represents an open hand or something that has been shaped and formed by the hand into the will of another. The second letter is pay, it looks like a mouth. Pictograph has the meanings of speak and blow from the functions of the mouth as well the edge of something from the lips at the edge of the mouth. The last letter we see on the left is a resh, it looks like a head.

By this picture, we can see how atonement began or begins. A hand is taken and confession is made as the hand is laid over the head, thereby covering the head, and a person would receive atonement.

According to Leviticus 23 verse 27, a person is to afflict themselves on this day. What does this mean? Does this mean that on this day, we are literally supposed to beat ourselves? Does this mean that on this day, we are to inflict pain? No, let us keep looking to see what this day is about and how it was to be observed.

The Hebrew for the word afflict or deny is in the Strongs dictionary number H6031.

ע נ ה

'ânâh

looking down or browbeating; to depress literally or figuratively, abase self, afflict (self), answer, chasten self, deal hardly with, exercise force, humble (self), hurt, submit self, weaken

So now we know that to afflict means to humble, chasten, or to deal hardly with. Through Scripture this was synonymous with, but not limited to, fasting. So, what are we to afflict? Leviticus 23 verse 27 says you are to afflict your souls. This is in the Strongs dictionary number H5315, it is the word nephesh.

נ פ ש

nephesh

properly a breathing creature, used very widely in a literal, accommodated or figurative sense (bodily or mental): any, appetite,body, breath, desire, lust, man, me, mind, mortality, one, own, person, pleasure

The word nephesh is commonly translated as soul. We see that this means any appetite or desire. So, according to what we've just read, we are to deal harshly with our literal physical appetites, as well as our own desires, our own lusts, or personal pleasure. These things often get in the way of our pursuit of the Father. On this day, Yom Kippur, all the children of Israel were to focus on absolutely nothing but their relationship with the father and their need for atonement.

So other than fasting and focusing ourselves on spiritual things, what else was a person to do on Yom Kippur? Let us continue reading in Leviticus chapter 23.

Leviticus 23:28-29
(28) You shall do no manner of work in that same day; for it is Yom Kippur, to make atonement for you before the LORD your God.
(29) For whoever it is who shall not deny himself in that same day; shall be cut off from his people.

It's made clear in verse 28 that no type of work is to be done. No work at all. No manner of work. Verse 29 says, whoever it is that shall not deny himself will be cut off. What does it mean to be cut off? The Hebrew for this word cut off is in the Strongs dictionary, number H3772. It is the word Karat.

כרת
kârath
to cut (off, down or asunder); to destroy or consume; be chewed, fail, feller, hew down, lose, perish, utterly, want

So, we see that to cut off means to be destroyed. Isn't that what it means to be cut off from the Father? If our life, our sustenance, and everything we are is in our relationship with the Father, what would it mean if we were cut off from that? The Scripture continues,

Leviticus 23:30-31
(30) Whoever it is who does any manner of work in that same day, that person I will destroy from among his people.
(31) You shall do no manner of work: it is a statute forever throughout your generations in all your dwellings.

Not only will this person be cut off, but they will be destroyed. God said he would destroy this person from among His people. This word destroy is the Hebrew "abad" It is in the Strongs dictionary, number H6.

א ב ד
'âbad

to wander away, that is lose oneself, to perish (causatively, destroy): - break, destroy, not escape, fail, lose, perish, be undone, be void of, have no way to flee.

When a person separates himself from the things of God, and refuses to humble himself in the sight of God, that person will wander away from the covenants of God. He will end up broken, destroyed, undone, and have no place to flee. This is a picture of a person who has no atonement. This is to show us the necessity of atonement. Not just that, but it shows us that the only way to get atonement is the way the Father prescribed. The things we see on this day of atonement show us what the Messiah did for us and that when the King comes to judge, we will be covered.

Leviticus 23:31-32 continues with the observation for all Israel of Yom Kippur.
- (31) You shall do no manner of work:
- it is a statute forever
- throughout your generations
- in all your dwellings.
- (32) It shall be a Shabbat
- of solemn rest for you,
- and you shall deny yourselves.
- In the ninth day of the month at evening, from evening to evening,
- you shall keep your Shabbat."

Can you see the picture in Leviticus 23 verses 31 and 32? You shall do no manner of work. The emphasis is on you, you cannot do the work of atonement. It is a statute for ever, it shall last for ever. Through all generations, no matter where you live. It is a complete and total Sabbath rest. You shall deny yourself your earthly desires, your carnal nature. You shall seek the will of the Father, and that alone.

The Yom Kippur service is found in Leviticus 16. Before we look at the Yom Kippur service, let us understand the book that it is found in. The Hebrew word for the book of Leviticus is the word "Vayikra" which means "and he drew near." The plan for how the Father was to draw us near to Him is found in the book of Leviticus. This entire book in Scripture is all about drawing near to the presence of God.

God wanted men to build Him a sanctuary so that He could dwell with them. We see this in the book of Exodus. The problem was, God was still so Holy and separate from us and our sin that we could not approach the very place that He said He wanted to meet with us.

Exodus 40:34-35
(34) Then a cloud covered the tent of the congregation, and the glory of the LORD filled the tabernacle.
(35) And Moses was not able to enter into the tent of the congregation, because the cloud abode thereon, and the glory of the LORD filled the tabernacle.

The Father wanted the life of men to come into His very presence. Now that the glory of the Lord was in the tabernacle, even Moses could not approach it. The very man who spoke mouth-to-mouth with God on the top of the mountain could not go into the tabernacle. The Father was going to establish a way for His people to be in His presence. We have already seen the principle of substitution when God took the Levites as a substitution for (NOT REPLACEMENT OF) the firstborn.

Exodus 13:1-2
(1) And the LORD spake unto Moses, saying,
(2) Sanctify unto me all the firstborn, whatsoever openeth the womb among the children of Israel, both of man and of beast: it is mine.

Understand that what is really being said in Exodus chapter 13 is that the firstborn is to be in the service of Yahweh. In other words, the firstborn are the priests to the family of Israel. At the sin of the golden calf, it was the job of the firstborn to stand up for righteousness. They failed to do so, but the Levites stood up for righteousness. It was because of this that the Levites were taken to serve in the Temple and the tabernacle in the presence of God.

Numbers 3:11-12
(11) And the LORD spake unto Moses, saying,
(12) And I, behold, I have taken the Levites from among the children of Israel instead of all the firstborn that openeth the matrix among the children of Israel: therefore the Levites shall be mine;

In the stead of, not replaced, this is the Hebrew word tachat. It is in the Strongs dictionary number H8478.

תַּחַת
Tachath
From the same as H8430,
in lieu of, in (-stead), stead of

H8430
תֹּוהַ
to'-akh
to depress; humble

It's interesting to note that the word that is used to say in the stead of is from the word that means to humble. In choosing the Levites to serve Him, He was humbling all the firstborn, reminding them that they slacked in their responsibility.

Still, continuing on with the problem of a holy God wanting His people to be in His presence, we must look at how that is going to be done. Remember, the Father wants the life of His people to be with Him. He wants His life to be in His people. In order to have relationship and to be in communion with God, we must be able to approach Him.

In order to look at how we can approach God there is one very simple, very basic biblical understanding that we need. The life is in the blood!

Genesis 9:4&5-
But flesh with the life thereof, which is the blood thereof, shall ye not eat. And surely your blood of your lives will I require; at the hand of every beast will I require it, and at the hand of man; at the hand of every man's brother will I require the life of man.

Leviticus 17:11-
For the life of the flesh is in the blood: and I have given it to you upon the altar to make an atonement for your souls: for it is the blood that maketh an atonement for the soul.

Leviticus 17:14-
For it is the life of all flesh; the blood of it is for the life thereof: therefore I said unto the children of Israel, Ye shall eat the blood

of no manner of flesh: for the life of all flesh is the blood thereof: whosoever eateth it shall be cut off.

Deuteronomy 12:23-
Only be sure that thou eat not the blood: for the blood is the life; and thou mayest not eat the life with the flesh.

Why is it important to note that the life is in the blood? If we don't understand this concept, we will miss some of what the Messiah, Yeshua, was trying to tell us.

John 6:53 –
Then Jesus said unto them, Verily, verily, I say unto you, Except ye eat the flesh of the Son of man, and drink his blood, ye have no life in you.

John 6:54 –
Whoso eateth my flesh, and drinketh my blood, hath eternal life; and I will raise him up at the last day.

The life is in the blood. The lifeblood had a specific purpose; atonement. If we don't understand that the life is in the blood, how are we to understand how a person comes into the presence of Yahweh?

Taking a look back in Leviticus chapters 1 through 5, you see many different types of offerings and sacrifices. If it was a blood offering, a person was to lay their hands on the animal, confess their sins over the animal, slaughter the animal and catch the blood in a bowl. The blood was applied to the altar, along with the animal. The blood in the animal went up in smoke, literally into the face (presence) of the Father. This was the means for a persons life to go into the presence of Yahweh. The offerings and sacrifices were never about death, they were about life.

We read in Leviticus chapter 17, the purpose for the lifeblood was for atonement.

Leviticus 17:11- For the life of the flesh is in the blood:
- and I have given it to you upon the altar
- to make an atonement for your souls:
- for it is the blood that maketh an atonement for the soul.

It is life that makes atonement, not death. The life had to be brought near, not death. Yahweh is a God of life, not death. It is the life that He desires from His people.

Yeshua our Messiah said in Matthew 22:32
I am the God of Abraham, and the God of Isaac, and the God of Jacob God is not the God of the dead, but of the living.

The Father desires a close relationship with His people, for His people to worship Him, and to be in a close relationship with Him. This was accomplished by establishing a system of worship that allowed the worshipper to ascend into the presence of Yahweh. The Hebrew word for what we call a sacrifice or an offering in the book of Leviticus, is the word "Korban". It is in the Strongs dictionary number H7133.

קרבן
qorbân
From H7126; something brought near the altar, a sacrificial present: - oblation, that is offered, offering.

H7126
ק ר ב
qârab
A primitive root; to approach (causatively bring near) for whatever purpose: -(cause to) approach, (cause to) draw near, -go (near), be at hand, join, be near, offer, -present, produce, make ready, stand, take.

Even the name of the offerings that were brought, means *something brought near*. The idea was for a person to draw near into the presence of Yahweh. However, in order to approach, or to be brought near, there had to be atonement. Which brings us back to Leviticus 16.

The description of the Yom Kippur service is found in Leviticus 16.

Leviticus 16:1-34
(1) And the LORD spake unto Moses after the death of the two sons of Aaron, when they offered before the LORD, and died;
(2) And the LORD said unto Moses, Speak unto Aaron thy brother, that he come not at all times into the holy place within the vail before the mercy seat, which is upon the ark; that he die not: for I will appear in the cloud upon the mercy seat.

(3) Thus shall Aaron come into the holy place: with a young bullock for a sin offering, and a ram for a burnt offering.

(4) He shall put on the holy linen coat, and he shall have the linen breeches upon his
flesh, and shall be girded with a linen girdle, and with the linen mitre shall he be attired: these are holy garments; therefore shall he wash his flesh in water, and so put them on.

(5) And he shall take of the congregation of the children of Israel two kids of the goats for a sin offering, and one ram for a burnt offering.

(6) And Aaron shall offer his bullock of the sin offering, which is for himself, and make an atonement for himself, and for his house.

(7) And he shall take the two goats, and present them before the LORD at the door of the tabernacle of the congregation.

(8) And Aaron shall cast lots upon the two goats; one lot for the LORD, and the other lot for the scapegoat.

(9) And Aaron shall bring the goat upon which the LORD'S lot fell, and offer him for a sin offering.

(10) But the goat, on which the lot fell to be the scapegoat, shall be presented alive before the LORD, to make an atonement with him, and to let him go for a scapegoat into the wilderness.

(11) And Aaron shall bring the bullock of the sin offering, which is for himself, and shall make an atonement for himself, and for his house, and shall kill the bullock of the sin offering which is for himself:

(12) And he shall take a censer full of burning coals of fire from off the altar before the LORD, and his hands full of sweet incense beaten small, and bring it within the vail:

(13) And he shall put the incense upon the fire before the LORD, that the cloud of the incense may cover the mercy seat that is upon the testimony, that he die not:

(14) And he shall take of the blood of the bullock, and sprinkle it with his finger upon the mercy seat eastward; and before the mercy seat shall he sprinkle of the blood with his finger seven times.

(15) Then shall he kill the goat of the sin offering, that is for the people, and bring his blood within the vail, and do with that blood as he did with the blood of the bullock, and
sprinkle it upon the mercy seat, and before the mercy seat:

(16) And he shall make an atonement for the holy place, because of the uncleanness of the children of Israel, and because of their transgressions in all their sins: and so shall he do for the

tabernacle of the congregation, that remaineth among them in the midst of their uncleanness.

(17) And there shall be no man in the tabernacle of the congregation when he goeth in to make an atonement in the holy place, until he come out, and have made an atonement for himself, and for his household, and for all the congregation of Israel.

(18) And he shall go out unto the altar that is before the LORD, and make an atonement for it; and shall take of the blood of the bullock, and of the blood of the goat, and put it upon the horns of the altar round about.

(19) And he shall sprinkle of the blood upon it with his finger seven times, and cleanse it, and hallow it from the uncleanness of the children of Israel.

(20) And when he hath made an end of reconciling the holy place, and the tabernacle of the congregation, and the altar, he shall bring the live goat:

(21) And Aaron shall lay both his hands upon the head of the live goat, and confess over him all the iniquities of the children of Israel, and all their transgressions in all their sins, putting them upon the head of the goat, and shall send him away by the hand of a fit man into the wilderness:

(22) And the goat shall bear upon him all their iniquities unto a land not inhabited: and he shall let go the goat in the wilderness.

(23) And Aaron shall come into the tabernacle of the congregation, and shall put off the linen garments, which he put on when he went into the holy place, and shall leave them there:

(24) And he shall wash his flesh with water in the holy place, and put on his garments, and come forth, and offer his burnt offering, and the burnt offering of the people, and make an atonement for himself, and for the people.

(25) And the fat of the sin offering shall he burn upon the altar.

(26) And he that let go the goat for the scapegoat shall wash his clothes, and bathe his flesh in water, and afterward come into the camp.

(27) And the bullock for the sin offering, and the goat for the sin offering, whose blood was brought in to make atonement in the holy place, shall one carry forth without the camp; and they shall burn in the fire their skins, and their flesh, and their dung.

(28) And he that burneth them shall wash his clothes, and bathe his flesh in water, and afterward he shall come into the camp.

(29) And this shall be a statute for ever unto you: that in the seventh month, on the tenth day of the month, ye shall afflict

your souls, and do no work at all, whether it be one of your own country, or a stranger that sojourneth among you:

(30) For on that day shall the priest make an atonement for you, to cleanse you, that ye may be clean from all your sins before the LORD.

(31) It shall be a sabbath of rest unto you, and ye shall afflict your souls, by a statute for ever.

(32) And the priest, whom he shall anoint, and whom he shall consecrate to minister in the priest's office in his father's stead, shall make the atonement, and shall put on the linen clothes, even the holy garments:

(33) And he shall make an atonement for the holy sanctuary, and he shall make an atonement for the tabernacle of the congregation, and for the altar, and he shall make an atonement for the priests, and for all the people of the congregation.

(34) And this shall be an everlasting statute unto you, to make an atonement for the children of Israel for all their sins once a year. And he did as the LORD commanded Moses.

Yom Kippur Service (Leviticus 16)
- Aaron had to offer a sin offering and a burnt offering - He had to repent and be clean.
- He had to mikveh (Baptism) and put on the linen garments - the plain linen garments.
  - Yeshua emptied himself of his royal clothing and clothed himself with flesh.

Philippians 2:7-8
(7) but emptied himself, taking the form of a servant, being made in the likeness of men.
(8) And being found in human form, he humbled himself, becoming obedient to death, yes, the death of the cross.

Yom Kippur Service (Leviticus 16)
- Aaron took two goats
- Cast lots over them
- – for YHWH
- – for azazel
- the ram that was for azazel is what we call the scapegoat
- Azazel is a compound Hebrew word, "az" meaning goat, and "azal" meaning to go away.
- He offered the bull as a sin offering for himself
- Aaron could not offer the blood for the atonement of Israel if He himself had not been atoned for.

<u>Leviticus 4:3-5</u>
- (3) If the priest that is anointed do sin according to the sin of the people;
- *[This could better read as - if it is the anointed priest who sinned and brought guilt on the people]*
- then let him bring for his sin, which he hath sinned, a young bullock without blemish unto the LORD for a sin offering.
- (4) And he shall bring the bullock unto the door of the tabernacle of the congregation before the LORD; and shall lay his hand upon the bullock's head, and kill the bullock before the LORD.
- (5) And the priest that is anointed shall take of the bullock's blood, and bring it to the tabernacle of the congregation:

This is important to note. Yeshua is the only one who could provide a permanent atonement, because He was the only one who didn't need it.

1 John 3:3-5
- (3) And every man that hath this hope in him purifieth himself, even as he is pure.
- (4) Whosoever committeth sin transgresseth also the law: for sin is the transgression of the law.
- (5) And ye know that he was manifested to take away our sins; and in him is no sin.

- Aaron went in and offered incense.
- He took the blood of the bull (for himself) and sprinkled it on the mercy seat.
- He then took the ram that was for Yahweh.
- Then he offered the ram and sprinkled its blood on the mercy seat.
- He then made atonement through the blood for the altar and holy place.
- He then took the ram that was the scapegoat and confessed over it.
- Leviticus 16:21 -He shall put both of his hands on the goat's head and confess over it all the evils, sins, and rebellions of the people of Israel, and so transfer them to the goat's head. Then the goat is to be driven off into the desert by someone appointed to do it.

- Laying on hands and confession, put on the head of the goat what was confessed.
- Acts 8:18 - And when Simon saw that through laying on of the apostles' hands the Holy Ghost was given, he offered them money,
- 1Timothy 4:14 - Neglect not the gift that is in thee, which was given thee by prophecy, with the laying on of the hands of the presbytery.
- Hebrews 6:1-2   - Therefore, leaving behind the elementary teachings about Christ, let us continue to be carried along to maturity, not laying again a foundation of repentance from dead works, faith toward God,
  (2) instruction about baptisms, the laying on of hands, the resurrection of the dead, and
  eternal judgment.
- 1Timothy 5:22 - Lay hands suddenly on no man, neither be partaker of other men's sins: keep thyself pure.

- Aaron now does a mikveh (baptism) and offers on the altar the fat of the bull and ram.
- The one who took the ram into the wilderness will Mikveh.
- The remains of the bull and ram will be taken outside the camp and burned.
- The one who burns them will Mikveh, then return to the camp.

While it is not considered Scripture, the Mishnah gives an accurate historical account of many of the ceremonies and traditions of the people of Israel. The word Mishnah means repetition, so the Mishnah is a retelling of events, ceremonies and thoughts of the day. If we look in the Mishnah, we will find a portion given on Yom Kippur.

Mishnah Yoma – the ritual of Yom Kippur
(prior to this point, the High Priest has prepared himself by washing several times and clothing himself in linen before beginning the sacrifices of Yom Kippur)
- 3:8

He came over to his bullock. Now his bullock was set between the Porch and the Altar [two places in the Temple]. Its head was to the south and its face to the west. And the priest stands at the east, with his face to the west. And he puts his two hands on it and states the confession. And thus did he say: "O Lord, I have committed iniquity, transgressed, and sinned before you, I and my house. O Lord, forgive the iniquities, transgressions, and sins, which I have done by committing iniquity, transgression, and sin before you, I and my house. As it is written in the Torah of Moses, your servant For on this day shall atonement be made for you to clean you. From all your sins shall you be clean before the Lord (Lev. 16:30)." And they [those listening] respond to him: "Blessed is the name of glory of his kingdom forever and ever."

○ 3:9

He came to the east side of the courtyard, to the north of the altar, with the prefect at his right hand and the head of the court at his left. There were two goats. There was also a box with two lots.

○ 4:1

He shook the box and brought up the two lots. On one was written, "For the Lord," and on one was written, "For Azazel." The prefect was at his right, and the head of the court at his left. If the lot "for the Lord" came up on his right hand, the prefect says to him, "My lord, high priest, raise up your right hand." If the one "for the Lord" came up in his left hand, the head of the court says to him, "My lord, high priest, raise up your left hand." He put them on the two goats and says, "For the Lord, a sin offering." And they respond to him, "Blessed is the name of the glory of his kingdom forever and ever."

○ 4:2

He tied a crimson thread on the head of the goat which was to be sent forth, and set it up towards the way by which it would be sent out. And on that which was to be slaughtered he tied a crimson thread at the place at which the act of slaughter would be made [the throat].

And he came to his bullock a second time and put his two hands on it and made the confession. And thus did he say, "O Lord, I have committed iniquity, transgressed, and sinned before you, I and my house and the children of Aaron [the priests], your holy people. O Lord, forgive, I pray, the iniquities, transgressions, and sins which I have committed, transgressed, and sinned before you, I, my house, and the children of Aaron, your holy people. As it is written in the Torah of Moses, your servant For on this day shall atonement be made for you to clean you. From all your sins shall you be clean before the Lord (Lev. 16:30)." And they [those listening] respond to him: "Blessed is the name of the glory of his kingdom forever and ever."

- 6:2

He comes to the goat which is to be sent forth and lays his two hands on it and makes the confession. And thus did he say, "O Lord, your people, the house of Israel, has committed iniquity, transgressed, and sinned before you. Forgive, O Lord, I pray, the iniquities, transgressions, and sins, which your people, the house of Israel, have committed, transgressed, and sinned before you, . As it is written in the Torah of Moses, your servant For on this day shall atonement be made for you to clean you. From all your sins shall you be clean before the Lord (Lev. 16:30)."

And the priests and people standing in the courtyard, when they would hear the high priest pronounce the Name of God, would kneel and bow down and fall on their faces and say, "Blessed be the name of the glory of his kingdom forever and ever."

- 6:3

He gave the scapegoat over to the one who was to lead it out.

- 6:4

The eminent people of Jerusalem used to accompany him [the one who was to lead the goat] to the first booth. There were ten booths from Jerusalem to the ravine.

- 6:5

At each booth they would say to him, "Here is food, here is water." And they accompany him from one booth to the next, except for the man in the last booth among them, who does not go out with him to the ravine. But he stands from a distance and observes what he does.

- 6:6

Now what did he do? He divided the crimson thread. Half of it he tied to a rock and half of it he tied between its horns. He then pushed it over backwards, and it rolled down the ravine. And it did not reach halfway down the mountain before it broke into pieces. He came and sat himself down under the last booth until it got dark.

- 6:8

They said to the high priest, "The goat has reached the wilderness." Now how did they know that the goat had come to the wilderness? They made sentinel posts, and waved flags, so they might know that the goat had reached the wilderness.

- o Rabbi Ishmael says, "Now did they not have another sign? There was a crimson thread tied to the door of the sanctuary. When the goat had reached the wilderness, the thread would turn white, as it says, Though your sins be as scarlet, they shall be as white as snow."

Another book that gives an accurate historical account of things regarding temple rituals is called the Talmud. The word Talmud means instruction or learning. It is interesting to note, not just what happened, but also what did not happen. There were some interesting things regarding this day of Yom Kippur that were very unique to only the last 40 years that the second Temple stood. Remember the Temple was destroyed in about 70 CE, 40 years prior to this would be around 30 CE.

The following is quoted from the Talmud, Yoma 39A.

"Our Rabbis taught: Throughout the forty years that Simeon the Righteous ministered, the lot ['For the Lord'] would always come up in the right hand; from that time on, it would come up now in the right hand, now in the left. And [during the same time] the crimson-coloured strap would become white. From that time on it would at times become white, at others not. Also: Throughout those forty years the westernmost light was shining, from that time on, it was now shining, now failing;"

The following is quoted from the Talmud, Yoma 39A

"Our Rabbis taught: In the year in which Simeon the Righteous died, he foretold them that he would die. They said: Whence do you know that? He replied: On every Day of Atonement an old man, dressed in white, wrapped in white, would join me, entering [the Holy of Holies] and leaving [it] with me, but today I was joined by an old man, dressed in black, wrapped in black, who entered, but did not leave, with me. After the festival [of Sukkoth] he was sick for seven days and [then] died. His brethren [that year] the priests forbore to mention the Ineffable Name in pronouncing the [priestly] blessing. **Our**

226

Rabbis taught: During the last forty years before the destruction of the Temple the lot ['For the Lord'] did not come up in the right hand; nor did the crimson-coloured strap become white; nor did the westernmost light shine; and the doors of the Hekal would open by themselves, until R. Johanan b. Zakkai rebuked them, saying: Hekal, Hekal, why wilt thou be the alarmer thyself? I know about thee that thou wilt be destroyed, for Zechariah ben Ido has already prophesied concerning thee: Open thy doors, O Lebanon, that the fire may devour thy cedars."

There are some things that were different the last 40 years that the Temple stood.

- The ram for Yahweh now comes up in the left hand.
- The crimson cord would not turn white anymore.
- The westernmost light on the menorah would not shine.
- The doors to the Temple would open by themselves.

What we have seen, is how these were Messianic prophecies that Yeshua the Messiah fulfilled. The Temple was destroyed, not to tell the people that the sacrifices were wrong or bad, after all, Yahweh instituted the sacrificial system in the first place. But that they were putting their trust in the wrong thing, which was the offerings, and not in the one who provided the actual atonement. Our trust and our hope comes in Yeshua our Messiah through the Father. With the Temple gone, and the people still in need of atonement, where would they receive it? We truly are saved by grace through faith in Yeshua our Messiah. What we see in the ritual of Yom Kippur is the need for atonement, because God judges sin.

Romans 6:23
For the wages of sin is death; but the gift of God is eternal life through Jesus Christ our Lord.

As long as sin is still in the world, and still in the heart of man, we will still have people in need of atonement. Let us go back to Leviticus to continue looking at the pictures and shadows that were given to us in Scripture.

Leviticus 16:29-33
(29) And this shall be a statute for ever unto you: that in the seventh month, on the tenth day of the month, ye shall afflict

227

your souls, and do no work at all, whether it be one of your own country, or a stranger that sojourneth among you:

(30) For on that day shall the priest make an atonement for you, to cleanse you, that ye may be clean from all your sins before the LORD.

(31) It shall be a sabbath of rest unto you, and ye shall afflict your souls, by a statute for ever.

(32) And the priest, whom he shall anoint, and whom he shall consecrate to minister in the priest's office in his father's stead, shall make the atonement, and shall put on the linen clothes, even the holy garments:

(33) Then he shall make atonement for
[look at what atonement was made for. If we misunderstand atonement we won't understand any of this.]

- the Holy Sanctuary;
- and he shall make atonement for the Tent of Meeting
- and for the altar;
- and he shall make atonement for the Kohanim
- and for all the people of the assembly.

Do you remember what the word atonement means? The word atonement means to cover, it means to protect. The word atonement does not necessarily mean a forgiveness of sins. Look at verse 33, what was atonement made for? Was atonement made for the people alone? No, atonement was made for the holy sanctuary, the holy of holies. Atonement was made for the tent of meeting, for the altar, for the priests, and for the assembly. So, the question is, did the tent, the altar or the holy of holies, sin? No, but they were still in need of atonement.

The tabernacle was a holy place. There were two different types of sin offerings. We find this in the first couple of chapters in Leviticus. When the people brought a sin offering, they confessed their sins over the animal, then the animal was slaughtered and the blood was applied to the altar. While the tabernacle was a place of life and a place for meeting with God, it was also a place of death in that it involved confession of sin over the animals and then the life of the animal was to go up on the altar. In essence, the sins were put on the altar. This being the case, then there would still be a need for atonement of the altar, and all things associated with it.

Look at Leviticus 16:32 again, we will see a Messianic prophecy in this.

- o And the priest, who shall be anointed
- o (The Hebrew word for anointed is MASHACH) [- MOSHIACH means anointed one]
- o and who shall be consecrated
- o (TO ACCOMPLISH OR FULFILL)
- o to be priest in his father's stead
- o (FOR HIS FATHER) ,
- o shall make the atonement, and shall put on the linen garments, even the holy garments.
  [Remember, that Messiah took off his heavenly glory and splendor and put on common garments. In other words, the Messiah took off or emptied Himself of His glory and splendor and put on flesh, the same thing that all of the other priests of God wore.]

Leviticus 16:34
(34) And this shall be an everlasting statute unto you, to make an atonement for the children of Israel for all their sins once a year. And he did as the LORD commanded Moses.

We see an allusion to the Yom Kippur service in Hebrews chapter 9, specifically verse 12.

Hebrews 9:11-14
(11) But Christ being come an high priest of good things to come, by a greater and more perfect tabernacle, not made with hands, that is to say, not of this building;
(12) Neither by the blood of goats and calves, but by his own blood he entered in once into the holy place, having obtained eternal redemption for us.
(13) For if the blood of bulls and of goats, and the ashes of an heifer sprinkling the unclean, sanctifieth to the purifying of the flesh:
(14) How much more shall the blood of Christ, who through the eternal Spirit offered himself without spot to God, purge your conscience from dead works to serve the living God?

Hebrews chapter 9 verse 12 says that the blood of goats or calves, was used in the holy place. This was done only one day a year, on Yom Kippur. Then it says that He only had to enter once and He obtained eternal redemption and atonement for us. Remember, Aaron had to enter multiple times, once for himself and then again for others. Also remember, that when Aaron went into the holiest place he did not go in dressed in his royal high priestly garments. When Aaron entered the holy of holies he was dressed in white linen, just like all the other priests.

Philippians 2:5-11
(5) Let this mind be in you, which was also in Christ Jesus:
(6) Who, being in the form of God, thought it not robbery to be equal with God:
(7) But made himself of no reputation, and took upon him the form of a servant, and was made in the likeness of men:
(8) And being found in fashion as a man, he humbled himself, and became obedient unto death, even the death of the cross.
(9) Wherefore God also hath highly exalted him, and given him a name which is above every name:
(10) That at the name of Jesus every knee should bow, of things in heaven, and things in earth, and things under the earth;
(11) And that every tongue should confess that Jesus Christ is Lord, to the glory of God the Father.

Yeshua, our Messiah emptied Himself in order to provide atonement. He who had no sin, had to take on the form of flesh, to provide atonement for people with sin. His blood, His life, had to be applied to the altar before the Lord in order to provide atonement for His children. We are atoned for because of the life of the Messiah. We laid our hands on Him, and He laid His life down, giving it for the lives of many. He took on our sins, and by means of His blood on the altar before Yahweh, we have atonement.

Zechariah12:10
And I will pour upon the house of David, and upon the inhabitants of Jerusalem, the spirit of grace and of supplications: and they shall look upon me whom they have pierced, and they shall mourn for him, as one mourneth for his only son, and shall be in bitterness for him, as one that is in bitterness for his firstborn.

Zechariah 13:1
In that day there shall be a fountain opened to the house of David and to the inhabitants of Jerusalem for sin and for uncleanness.

Zechariah 13:6

And one shall say unto him, What are these wounds in thine hands? Then he shall answer, Those with which I was wounded in the house of my friends.

Romans 11:26-27

(26) and so all Israel will be saved, even as it has been written, "The Deliverer will come out of Zion, and He will turn away ungodliness from Jacob.

(27) And this is My covenant with them, when I take away their sins.“

Quoting - Isaiah 59:20, 21

(20) And the Redeemer shall come to Zion, and unto them that turn from transgression in Jacob, saith the LORD.

(21) As for me, this is my covenant with them, saith the LORD; My spirit that is upon thee, and my words which I have put in thy mouth, shall not depart out of thy mouth, nor out of the mouth of thy seed, nor out of the mouth of thy seed's seed, saith the LORD, from henceforth and for ever.

Psalms 85:1-2

(1) To the chief Musician, A Psalm for the sons of Korah. LORD, thou hast been favourable unto thy land: thou hast brought back the captivity of Jacob.

(2) Thou hast forgiven the iniquity of thy people, thou hast covered all their sin. Selah.

Jeremiah 31:33-34

(33) But this shall be the covenant that I will make with the house of Israel; After those days, saith the LORD, I will put my law in their inward parts, and write it in their hearts; and will be their God, and they shall be my people.

(34) And they shall teach no more every man his neighbour, and every man his brother, saying, Know the LORD: for they shall all know me, from the least of them unto the greatest of them, saith the LORD: for I will forgive their iniquity, and I will remember their sin no more.

When we are atoned for, we present our lives to the Father in faith that we are covered by the blood of the Messiah. Now that we have come to faith, we realize that we are made completely new. Everything of the old nature no longer exists, we are a new creation in Messiah Yeshua.

2 Corinthians 5:17-21

(17) Therefore if any man be in Christ, he is a new creature: old things are passed away; behold, all things are become new.
(18) And all things are of God, who hath reconciled us to himself by Jesus Christ, and hath given to us the ministry of reconciliation;
(19) To wit, that God was in Christ, reconciling the world unto himself, not imputing their trespasses unto them; and hath committed unto us the word of reconciliation.
(20) Now then we are ambassadors for Christ, as though God did beseech you by us: we pray you in Christ's stead, be ye reconciled to God.
(21) For he hath made him to be sin for us, who knew no sin; that we might be made the righteousness of God in him.

Now that we are a new creation, we have to learn how to produce good fruit. Atonement has been given, we have been covered, but that doesn't mean that we now have no sin in our life. We give our heart to the Father, but we are still learning how to walk righteously and upright before him.

Luke 6:43-49
For there is no good tree that brings forth rotten fruit; nor again a rotten tree that brings forth good fruit.
(44) For each tree is known by its own fruit. For people don't gather figs from thorns, nor do they gather grapes from a bramble bush.
(45) The good man out of the good treasure of his heart brings out that which is good, and the evil man out of the evil treasure of his heart brings out that which is evil, for out of the abundance of the heart, his mouth speaks.
(46) "Why do you call me, 'Lord, Lord,' and don't do the things which I say?
(47) Everyone who comes to me, and hears my words, and does them, I will show you who he is like.
(48) He is like a man building a house, who dug and went deep, and laid a foundation on the rock. When a flood arose, the stream broke against that house, and could not shake it, because it was founded on the rock.
(49) But he who hears, and doesn't do, is like a man who built a house on the earth without a foundation, against which the stream broke, and immediately it fell, and the ruin of that house was great."

Are we doing what Yeshua said? Our atonement came at a great price. We are given a new chance and are essentially born again. What we still need to understand however, is that now that we are born again, it doesn't mean that we are free to pursue the things and the ways of the world. We are free from the ways and things of this world to pursue the Father. Yeshua our Messiah was a great example that we are to follow.

Scripture says in first John chapter 3, that there was no sin in the Messiah. This had to be this way, because if there was any sin in Him, He could not have been our atonement. The Scriptures also say that if we are believers in Messiah that we should walk as He walked. We hold close to our heart the things that our Messiah held close to His heart.

1 John 2:1-6
(1) My little children, these things write I unto you, that ye sin not. And if any man sin, we have an advocate with the Father, Jesus Christ the righteous:
(2) And he is the propitiation for our sins: and not for ours only, but also for the sins of the whole world.
(3) And hereby we do know that we know him, if we keep his commandments.
(4) He that saith, I know him, and keepeth not his commandments, is a liar, and the truth is not in him.
(5) But whoso keepeth his word, in him verily is the love of God perfected: hereby know we that we are in him.
(6) He that saith he abideth in him ought himself also so to walk, even as he walked.

Yeshua our Messiah kept the word of His Father faithfully and blamelessly. If He was to be our atonement, without sin, it had to be this way. We know that everything that Messiah did, He did because the Father had told Him to do it. In order for Yeshua to be considered the Messiah, He had to keep His Father's word. In order for Him to be our atonement, He had to be without sin.

John 14:10
Believest thou not that I am in the Father, and the Father in me? the words that I speak unto you I speak not of myself: but the Father that dwelleth in me, he doeth the works.

John 15:14-15

(14) Ye are my friends, if ye do whatsoever I command you.
(15) Henceforth I call you not servants; for the servant knoweth not what his lord doeth: but I have called you friends; for all things that I have heard of my Father I have made known unto you.

Again, Yeshua our Messiah, the Son of the living God, faithfully kept his Father's word. We see in first John chapter 3 that there was no sin in Him. We also see the definition of sin. It says sin is transgression of the law or the Torah. If we would listen to the Father's voice, there would be no transgression of what He said. Messiah came to take away our sins. That means that all the transgressions of the Father's word are now taken away, cleaned and atoned for as we come to Yeshua our Messiah.

1 John 3:1-24
(1) Behold, what manner of love the Father hath bestowed upon us, that we should be called the sons of God: therefore the world knoweth us not, because it knew him not.
(2) Beloved, now are we the sons of God, and it doth not yet appear what we shall be: but we know that, when he shall appear, we shall be like him; for we shall see him as he is.
(3) And every man that hath this hope in him purifieth himself, even as he is pure.
(4) Whosoever committeth sin transgresseth also the law: for sin is the transgression of the law.
(5) And ye know that he was manifested to take away our sins; and in him is no sin.
(6) Whosoever abideth in him sinneth not: whosoever sinneth hath not seen him, neither known him.
(7) Little children, let no man deceive you: he that doeth righteousness is righteous, even as he is righteous.
(8) He that committeth sin is of the devil; for the devil sinneth from the beginning. For this purpose the Son of God was manifested, that he might destroy the works of the devil.
(9) Whosoever is born of God doth not commit sin; for his seed remaineth in him: and he cannot sin, because he is born of God.
(10) In this the children of God are manifest, and the children of the devil: whosoever doeth not righteousness is not of God, neither he that loveth not his brother.
(11) For this is the message that ye heard from the beginning, that we should love one another.

(12) Not as Cain, who was of that wicked one, and slew his brother. And wherefore slew he him? Because his own works were evil, and his brother's righteous.

(13) Marvel not, my brethren, if the world hate you.

(14) We know that we have passed from death unto life, because we love the brethren. He that loveth not his brother abideth in death.

(15) Whosoever hateth his brother is a murderer: and ye know that no murderer hath eternal life abiding in him.

(16) Hereby perceive we the love of God, because he laid down his life for us: and we ought to lay down our lives for the brethren.

(17) But whoso hath this world's good, and seeth his brother have need, and shutteth up his bowels of compassion from him, how dwelleth the love of God in him?

(18) My little children, let us not love in word, neither in tongue; but in deed and in truth.

(19) And hereby we know that we are of the truth, and shall assure our hearts before him.

(20) For if our heart condemn us, God is greater than our heart, and knoweth all things.

(21) Beloved, if our heart condemn us not, then have we confidence toward God.

(22) And whatsoever we ask, we receive of him, because we keep his commandments, and do those things that are pleasing in his sight.

(23) And this is his commandment, That we should believe on the name of his Son Jesus Christ, and love one another, as he gave us commandment.

(24) And he that keepeth his commandments dwelleth in him, and he in him. And hereby we know that he abideth in us, by the Spirit which he hath given us.

According to what we have just read, sin is violation of the Torah. We see that the Messiah had no sin. That means that He never once was in violation of the Torah. In other words, He faithfully kept every word that was given. It had to be this way for the Messiah, because if He would have directed people away from the word that was already given, He would nullify Himself as Messiah. We see this in Deuteronomy chapter 13.

Deuteronomy 13:1-5
(1) If there arise among you a prophet, or a dreamer of dreams, and giveth thee a sign or a wonder,

(2) And the sign or the wonder come to pass, whereof he spake unto thee, saying, Let us go after other gods, which thou hast not known, and let us serve them;

(3) Thou shalt not hearken unto the words of that prophet, or that dreamer of dreams: for the LORD your God proveth you, to know whether ye love the LORD your God with all your heart and with all your soul.

(4) Ye shall walk after the LORD your God, and fear him, and keep his commandments, and obey his voice, and ye shall serve him, and cleave unto him.

(5) And that prophet, or that dreamer of dreams, shall be put to death; because he hath spoken to turn you away from the LORD your God, which brought you out of the land of Egypt, and redeemed you out of the house of bondage, to thrust thee out of the way which the LORD thy God commanded thee to walk in. So shalt thou put the evil away from the midst of thee.

Matthew 5:17-19 (CJB)

(17) "Don't think that I came to destroy the Torah or the Prophets. I didn't come to destroy, but to fulfill.

(18) For most certainly, I tell you, until heaven and earth pass away, not even one smallest letter or one tiny pen stroke shall in any way pass away from the Torah, until all things are accomplished.

(19) Whoever, therefore, shall break one of these least mitzvot, and teach others to do so, shall be called least in the Kingdom of Heaven; but whoever shall do and teach them shall be called great in the Kingdom of Heaven.

Yeshua our Messiah fully kept the word of God. He kept the word in our stead for the times that we could not, and that includes the need for our atonement. He fully kept the covenant for us. The word of God will never go away. Messiah fully kept the word of God. It is because He upheld the word, that we can have faith, and rest in the assurance that we are partakers of the covenant with Him.

The following Scriptures are given in regards to the importance of the word and keeping it.

Matthew 24:35

Heaven and earth will disappear, but my words will never disappear."

Luke 21:33
Heaven and earth will disappear, but my words will never disappear."

Mark 8:38
If anyone is ashamed of me and my words in this adulterous and sinful generation, the Son of Man will be ashamed of him when he comes with the holy angels in his Father's glory."

John 8:45-47
(45) But it is because I speak the truth that you do not believe me.
(46) Can any of you prove me guilty of sin? If I am telling the truth, why don't you believe me?
(47) The one who belongs to God listens to the words of God. The reason you do not listen is because you do not belong to God."

John 12:44-50
(44) Then Jesus said loudly, "The one who believes in me does not believe in me but in the one who sent me.
(45) The one who sees me sees the one who sent me.
(46) I have come into the world as light, so that everyone who believes in me will not remain in the darkness.
(47) If anyone hears my words and does not keep them, I do not condemn him, for I did not come to condemn the world but to save it.
(48) The one who rejects me and does not receive my words has something to judge him: The word that I have spoken will judge him on the last day.

- John 5:45-46
(45) Do not think that I will accuse you to the Father: there is one that accuseth you, even Moses, in whom ye trust.
(46) For had ye believed Moses, ye would have believed me: for he wrote of me.

(John 12:49) For I have not spoken on my own authority. Instead, the Father who sent me has himself given me a commandment about what to say and how to speak.
(50) And I know that his commandment is eternal life. What I speak, therefore, I speak just as the Father has told me."

John 14:23

Jesus answered and said unto him, If a man love me, he will keep my words: and my Father will love him, and we will come unto him, and make our abode with him.

Matthew 7:21
Not every one that saith unto me, Lord, Lord, shall enter into the kingdom of heaven; but he that doeth the will of my Father which is in heaven.

1 John 2:1-29
(1) My little children, these things write I unto you, that ye sin not. And if any man sin, we have an advocate with the Father, Jesus Christ the righteous:
(2) And he is the propitiation for our sins: and not for ours only, but also for the sins of the whole world.
(3) And hereby we do know that we know him, if we keep his commandments.
(4) He that saith, I know him, and keepeth not his commandments, is a liar, and the truth is not in him.
(5) But whoso keepeth his word, in him verily is the love of God perfected: hereby know we that we are in him.
(6) He that saith he abideth in him ought himself also so to walk, even as he walked.
(7) Brethren, I write no new commandment unto you, but an old commandment which ye had from the beginning. The old commandment is the word which ye have heard from the beginning.
(8) Again, a new commandment I write unto you, which thing is true in him and in you: because the darkness is past, and the true light now shineth.
(9) He that saith he is in the light, and hateth his brother, is in darkness even until now.
(10) He that loveth his brother abideth in the light, and there is none occasion of stumbling in him.
(11) But he that hateth his brother is in darkness, and walketh in darkness, and knoweth not whither he goeth, because that darkness hath blinded his eyes.
(12) I write unto you, little children, because your sins are forgiven you for his name's sake.
(13) I write unto you, fathers, because ye have known him that is from the beginning. I write unto you, young men, because ye have overcome the wicked one. I write unto you, little children, because ye have known the Father.

(14) I have written unto you, fathers, because ye have known him that is from the beginning. I have written unto you, young men, because ye are strong, and the word of God abideth in you, and ye have overcome the wicked one.

(15) Love not the world, neither the things that are in the world. If any man love the world, the love of the Father is not in him.

(16) For all that is in the world, the lust of the flesh, and the lust of the eyes, and the pride of life, is not of the Father, but is of the world.

(17) And the world passeth away, and the lust thereof: but he that doeth the will of God abideth for ever.

(18) Little children, it is the last time: and as ye have heard that antichrist shall come, even now are there many antichrists; whereby we know that it is the last time.

(19) They went out from us, but they were not of us; for if they had been of us, they would no doubt have continued with us: but they went out, that they might be made manifest that they were not all of us.

(20) But ye have an unction from the Holy One, and ye know all things.

(21) I have not written unto you because ye know not the truth, but because ye know it, and that no lie is of the truth.

(22) Who is a liar but he that denieth that Jesus is the Christ? He is antichrist, that denieth the Father and the Son.

(23) Whosoever denieth the Son, the same hath not the Father: (but) he that acknowledgeth the Son hath the Father also.

(24) Let that therefore abide in you, which ye have heard from the beginning. If that which ye have heard from the beginning shall remain in you, ye also shall continue in the Son, and in the Father.

(25) And this is the promise that he hath promised us, even eternal life.

(26) These things have I written unto you concerning them that seduce you.

(27) But the anointing which ye have received of him abideth in you, and ye need not that any man teach you: but as the same anointing teacheth you of all things, and is truth, and is no lie, and even as it hath taught you, ye shall abide in him.

(28) And now, little children, abide in him; that, when he shall appear, we may have confidence, and not be ashamed before him at his coming.

(29) If ye know that he is righteous, ye know that every one that doeth righteousness is born of him.

1.John 3:22
- o and whatsoever we ask we receive of him,
- o because we keep his commandments
- o and do the things that are pleasing in his sight.

1 John 5:1-3
(1) Whosoever believeth that Jesus is the Christ is born of God: and every one that loveth him that begat loveth him also that is begotten of him.
(2) By this we know that we love the children of God, when we love God, and keep his commandments.
(3) For this is the love of God, that we keep his commandments: and his commandments are not grievous.

Deuteronomy 32:46-47
(46) And he said unto them, Set your hearts unto all the words which I testify among you this day, which ye shall command your children to observe to do, all the words of this law.
(47) For it is not a vain thing for you; because it is your life: and through this thing ye
shall prolong your days in the land, whither ye go over Jordan to possess it.

Romans 10:6-8
(6) But the righteousness which is of faith says this, "Don't say in your heart, 'Who will ascend into heaven?' (that is, to bring Messiah down);
(7) or, 'Who will descend into the abyss?' (that is, to bring Messiah up from the dead.)"
(8) But what does it say? "The word is near you, in your mouth, and in your heart;" that is, the word of faith, which we preach:

Deuteronomy 30:10-14
(10) If thou shalt hearken unto the voice of the LORD thy God, to keep his commandments and his statutes which are written in this book of the law, and if thou turn unto the LORD thy God with all thine heart, and with all thy soul.
(11) For this commandment which I command thee this day, it is not hidden from thee, neither is it far off.
(12) It is not in heaven, that thou shouldest say, Who shall go up for us to heaven, and bring it unto us, that we may hear it, and do it?
(13) Neither is it beyond the sea, that thou shouldest say, Who shall go over the sea for us, and bring it unto us, that we may hear it, and do it?
(14) But the word is very nigh unto thee,
- o in your mouth,

- and in your heart,
- that you may do it.

The following prayers and Scriptures are the suggested prayers and readings given for the day of Yom Kippur.

Mah Tovu –

How goodly your tents of Jacob your dwellings Israel, as for me in the multitude of your favor I will come into your house. I will prostrate myself in the sanctuary of your holiness in awe of you Adonai, I love your shelter, your house in the place of the tabernacle of your glory.

Leviticus 23:27-32

(27) Also on the tenth day of this seventh month there shall be a day of atonement: it shall be an holy convocation unto you; and ye shall afflict your souls, and offer an offering made by fire unto the LORD.

(28) And ye shall do no work in that same day: for it is a day of atonement, to make an atonement for you before the LORD your God.

(29) For whatsoever soul it be that shall not be afflicted in that same day, he shall be cut off from among his people.

(30) And whatsoever soul it be that doeth any work in that same day, the same soul will I destroy from among his people.

(31) Ye shall do no manner of work: it shall be a statute for ever throughout your generations in all your dwellings.

(32) It shall be unto you a sabbath of rest, and ye shall afflict your souls: in the ninth day of the month at even, from even unto even, shall ye celebrate your sabbath.

Leviticus 26:40-42

(40) If they shall confess their iniquity, and the iniquity of their fathers, with their trespass which they trespassed against me, and that also they have walked contrary unto me;

(41) And that I also have walked contrary unto them, and have brought them into the land of their enemies; if then their uncircumcised hearts be humbled, and they then accept of the punishment of their iniquity:

(42) Then will I remember my covenant with Jacob, and also my covenant with Isaac, and also my covenant with Abraham will I remember; and I will remember the land.

Isaiah 43:25-26
(25) I, yes I, am the one who blots out your offenses for my own sake; I will not remember your sins.
(26) Remind me when we're in court together — tell your side, make the case that you are right.

1 John 1:6-10
(6) If we say that we have fellowship with him, and walk in darkness, we lie, and do not the truth:
(7) But if we walk in the light, as he is in the light, we have fellowship one with another, and the blood of Jesus Christ his Son cleanseth us from all sin.
(8) If we say that we have no sin, we deceive ourselves, and the truth is not in us.
(9) If we confess our sins, he is faithful and just to forgive us our sins, and to cleanse us from all unrighteousness.
(10) If we say that we have not sinned, we make him a liar, and his word is not in us.

SHEMA part 1-
Deuteronomy 6:4-9
(4) Hear, O Israel: The LORD our God is one LORD:
(5) And thou shalt love the LORD thy God with all thine heart, and with all thy soul, and with all thy might.
(6) And these words, which I command thee this day, shall be in thine heart:
(7) And thou shalt teach them diligently unto thy children, and shalt talk of them when thou sittest in thine house, and when thou walkest by the way, and when thou liest down, and when thou risest up.
(8) And thou shalt bind them for a sign upon thine hand, and they shall be as frontlets between thine eyes.
(9) And thou shalt write them upon the posts of thy house, and on thy gates.

SHEMA part 2-
Deuteronomy 11:13-21
(13) And it shall come to pass, if ye shall hearken diligently unto my commandments which I command you this day, to love the LORD your God, and to serve him with all your heart and with all your soul,

(14) That I will give you the rain of your land in his due season, the first rain and the latter rain, that thou mayest gather in thy corn, and thy wine, and thine oil.

(15) And I will send grass in thy fields for thy cattle, that thou mayest eat and be full.

(16) Take heed to yourselves, that your heart be not deceived, and ye turn aside, and serve other gods, and worship them;

(17) And then the LORD'S wrath be kindled against you, and he shut up the heaven, that there be no rain, and that the land yield not her fruit; and lest ye perish quickly from off the good land which the LORD giveth you.

(18) Therefore shall ye lay up these my words in your heart and in your soul, and bind them for a sign upon your hand, that they may be as frontlets between your eyes.

(19) And ye shall teach them your children, speaking of them when thou sittest in thine house, and when thou walkest by the way, when thou liest down, and when thou risest up.

(20) And thou shalt write them upon the door posts of thine house, and upon thy gates:

(21) That your days may be multiplied, and the days of your children, in the land which the LORD sware unto your fathers to give them, as the days of heaven upon the earth.

SHEMA part 3 –
Numbers 15:37-41
(37) And the LORD spake unto Moses, saying,

(38) Speak unto the children of Israel, and bid them that they make them fringes in the borders of their garments throughout their generations, and that they put upon the fringe of the borders a ribband of blue:

(39) And it shall be unto you for a fringe, that ye may look upon it, and remember all the commandments of the LORD, and do them; and that ye seek not after your own heart and your own eyes, after which ye use to go a whoring:

(40) That ye may remember, and do all my commandments, and be holy unto your God.

(41) I am the LORD your God, which brought you out of the land of Egypt, to be your God: I am the LORD your God.

Mi Chamocha – Who Is Like You- Exodus 15:11
Who is like unto thee, O LORD, among the gods? who is like thee, glorious in holiness, fearful in praises, doing wonders?

Hodu – Give thanks-

Give thanks to the Lord for He is good for His mercy endures forever.

LIFT UP O GATES- Psalms 24:7-10
(7) Lift up your heads, O ye gates; and be ye lift up, ye everlasting doors; and the King of glory shall come in.
(8) Who is this King of glory? The LORD strong and mighty, the LORD mighty in battle.
(9) Lift up your heads, O ye gates; even lift them up, ye everlasting doors; and the King of glory shall come in.
(10) Who is this King of glory? The LORD of hosts, he is the King of glory. Selah.

Shemoneh Esrei—Amidah- the prayer of standing

My Lord, open my lips, that my mouth may declare your praise.

First Blessing- THE GOD OF HISTORY
Blessed are You, O Yahweh our Elohim and Elohim of our fathers, the Elohim of Abraham, the Elohim of Isaac and the Elohim of Jacob, the great, mighty and revered Elohim, the Most High Elohim who bestows loving kindnesses, the creator of all things, who remembers the good deeds of the patriarchs and in love will bring a redeemer to their children's children for his name's sake. O king, helper, savior and shield.
Blessed are You, O Yahweh, the shield of Abraham

Second Blessing- THE GOD OF NATURE
You, O Yahweh, are mighty forever, You revive the dead, You have the power to save. You sustain the living with loving kindnesses, You revive the dead with great mercy, You support the falling, heal the sick, set free the bound and keep faith with those who sleep in the dust. Who is like You, O doer of mighty acts? Who resembles You, a king who puts to death and restores to life, and causes salvation to flourish? And You are certain to revive the dead.
Blessed are You, O Yahweh, who revives the dead.

Third Blessing- SANCTIFICATION OF GOD
We will sanctify Your name in this world just as it is sanctified in the highest heavens, as it is written by Your prophet: "And they call out to one another and say:

- 'Holy, holy, holy is Yahweh of hosts; the whole earth is full of his glory.' [Isaiah 6:3]

Those facing them praise Elohim saying:

- "Blessed be the Presence of Yahweh in his place." [Ezekiel 3:12]

And in Your Holy Words it is written, saying,

- "Yahweh reigns forever, Your Elohim, O Zion, throughout all generations. Hallelujah." [Ps. 146:10]

Throughout all generations we will declare Your greatness, and to all eternity we will proclaim your holiness. Your praise, O our Elohim, shall never depart from our mouth, for You are a great and holy Elohim and King. Blessed are You, O Yahweh, the holy Elohim. You are holy, and Your name is holy, and holy beings praise You daily. (Selah.) Blessed are You, O Yahweh, the holy Elohim.

Fourth Blessing- PRAYER FOR UNDERSTANDING

You favor men with knowledge, and teach mortals understanding. O favor us with the knowledge, the understanding and the insight that come from You.

Blessed are You, O Yahweh, the gracious giver of knowledge.

Fifth Blessing- FOR REPENTANCE

Bring us back, O our Father, to Your Instruction; draw us near, O our King, to Your service; and cause us to return to You in perfect repentance.

Blessed are You, O Yahweh, who delights in repentance.

Sixth Blessing- FOR FORGIVENESS

Forgive us, O our Father, for we have sinned; pardon us, O our King, for we have transgressed; for You pardon and forgive.

Blessed are You, O Yahweh, who is merciful and always ready to forgive.

Seventh Blessing- FOR DELIVERANCE FROM AFFLICTION

Look upon our affliction and plead our cause, and redeem us speedily for Your name's sake, for You are a mighty redeemer.

Blessed are You, O Yahweh, the redeemer of Israel.

Eighth Blessing- FOR HEALING

Heal us, O Yahweh, and we will be healed; save us and we will be saved, for You are our praise. O grant a perfect healing to all our ailments, may it be Your will, Yahweh my Elohim, and the Elohim of my forefathers, that You quickly send a complete

recovery from heaven, spiritual healing and physical healing to all our loved ones who are in need of healing from You today, for You, almighty King, are a faithful and merciful healer.
Blessed are You, O Yahweh, the healer of the sick of his people Israel.

Ninth Blessing- FOR DELIVERANCE FROM WANT
Bless this year for us, O Yahweh our Elohim, together with all the varieties of its produce, for our welfare. Bestow a blessing upon the face of the earth. O satisfy us with Your goodness, and bless our year like the best of years.
Blessed are You, O Yahweh, who blesses the years.

Tenth Blessing- FOR GATHERING OF EXILES
Sound the great shofar for our freedom, raise the ensign to gather our exiles, and gather us from the four corners of the earth.
Blessed are You, O Yahweh, who gathers the dispersed of his people Israel.

Eleventh Blessing- FOR THE RIGHTEOUS REIGN OF GOD
Restore our judges as in former times, and our counselors as at the beginning; and remove from us sorrow and sighing. Reign over us, You alone, O Yahweh, with loving kindness and compassion, and clear us in judgment.
Blessed are You, O Yahweh, the King who loves righteousness and justice.

Twelfth Blessing –
FOR THE DESTRUCTION OF APOSTATES AND THE ENEMIES OF GOD
Let there be no hope for slanderers, and let all wickedness perish in an instant. May all Your enemies quickly be cut down, and may You soon in our day uproot, crush, cast down and humble the dominion of arrogance.
Blessed are You, O Yahweh, who smashes enemies and humbles the arrogant.

Thirteenth Blessing- FOR THE RIGHTEOUS AND PROSELYTES

May Your compassion be stirred, O Yahweh our Elohim, towards the righteous, the pious, the elders of Your people the house of Israel, the remnant of their scholars, towards proselytes, and towards us also. Grant a good reward to all who truly trust in Your name. Set our lot with them forever so that we may never be put to shame, for we have put our trust in You.

Blessed are You, O Yahweh, the support and stay of the righteous.

Fourteenth Blessing- FOR THE REBUILDING OF JERUSALEM
Return in mercy to Jerusalem Your city (Your people), and dwell in it as You have promised. Rebuild it soon in our day as an eternal structure, and quickly set up in it the throne of David.

Blessed are You, O Yahweh, who rebuilds Jerusalem.

Fifteenth Blessing - FOR THE MESSIANIC KING
Speedily cause the offspring of Your servant David to flourish, and let him be exalted by Your saving power, for we wait all day long for Your salvation.

Blessed are You, O Yahweh, who causes salvation to flourish.

Sixteenth Blessing- FOR THE ANSWERING OF PRAYER
Hear our voice, O Yahweh our Elohim; spare us and have pity on us. Accept our prayer in mercy and with favor, for You are a Elohim who hears prayers and supplications. O our King, do not turn us away from Your presence empty-handed, for You hear the prayers of Your people Israel with compassion.

Blessed are You, O Yahweh, who hears prayer.

Seventeenth Blessing- FOR RESTORATION OF TEMPLE SERVICE
Be pleased, O Yahweh our Elohim, with Your people Israel and with their prayers. Restore the service to the inner sanctuary of Your Temple, and receive in love and with favor both the fire-offerings of Israel and their prayers. May the worship of Your people Israel always be acceptable to You. And let our eyes behold Your return in mercy to Zion.

Blessed are You, O Yahweh, who restores his divine presence to Zion.

Eighteenth Blessing- THANKSGIVING FOR GOD'S UNFAILING MERCIES
We give thanks to You that You are Yahweh our Elohim and the Elohim of our fathers forever and ever. Through every generation

You have been the rock of our lives, the shield of our salvation. We will give You thanks and declare Your praise for our lives that are committed into Your hands, for our souls that are entrusted to You, for Your miracles that are daily with us, and for Your wonders and Your benefits that are with us at all times, evening, morning and noon. O beneficent one, Your mercies never fail; O merciful one, Your loving-kindnesses never cease. We have always put our hope in You. For all these acts may Your name be blessed and exalted continually, O our King, forever and ever. Let every living thing give thanks to You and praise Your name in truth, O Elohim, our salvation and our help. (Selah.)

Blessed are You, O Yahweh, whose Name is the Beneficent One, and to whom it is fitting to give thanks.

Nineteenth Blessing -FOR PEACE

My Elohim, guard my tongue from evil and my lips from speaking deceitfully. To those who curse me, let my soul be silent; and let my soul be like dust to everyone. Open my heart to Your Torah, then my soul will pursue Your commandments. As for all those who design evil against me, speedily nullify their counsel and disrupt their design. Act for Your Name's sake; act for Your right hand's sake; act for Your sanctity's sake; act for Your Torah's sake. That Your beloved ones may be given rest; let Your right hand save, and respond to me. May they be acceptable the words of my mouth and the thoughts of my heart, before You Yeshua, my rock and my redeemer. He Who makes peace in His heights may He make peace among us and upon all Israel. Grant peace, welfare, blessing, grace, lovingkindness and mercy to us and to all Israel your people. Bless us, O our Father, one and all, with the light of your countenance; for by the light of Your countenance you have given us, O Lord our God, a Torah of life, lovingkindness and salvation, blessing, mercy, life and peace. May it please you to bless your people Israel at all times and in every hour with your peace.

Blessed are you, O Lord, who blesses his people Israel with peace.. Amein.

Read Leviticus 16:1-34

Read Leviticus 23:26-32

Romans 3:21-26 (CJB)

248

(21) But now, quite apart from Torah, God's way of making people righteous in his sight has been made clear — although the Torah and the Prophets give their witness to it as well

(22) and it is a righteousness that comes from God, through the faithfulness of Yeshua the Messiah, to all who continue trusting. For it makes no difference whether one is a Jew or a Gentile,

(23) since all have sinned and come short of earning God's praise.

(24) By God's grace, without earning it, all are granted the status of being considered righteous before him, through the act redeeming us from our enslavement to sin that was accomplished by the Messiah Yeshua

(25) God put Yeshua forward as the kapparah for sin through his faithfulness in respect to his bloody sacrificial death. This vindicated God's righteousness; because, in his forbearance, he had passed over [with neither punishment nor remission] the sins people had committed in the past;

(26) and it vindicates his righteousness in the present age by showing that he is righteous himself and is also the one who makes people righteous on the ground of Yeshua's faithfulness.

The Redemption of Israel will be completed with Yeshua's return.

Read;
• Zechariah 12:10
• Zechariah 13:1
• Zechariah 13:6

Romans 11:26-27
(26) And so all Israel shall be saved: as it is written, There shall come out of Sion the Deliverer, and shall turn away ungodliness from Jacob:

(27) For this is my covenant unto them, when I shall take away their sins.

2 Corinthians 5:16-21
(16) Wherefore henceforth know we no man after the flesh: yea, though we have known Christ after the flesh, yet now henceforth know we him no more.

(17) Therefore if any man be in Christ, he is a new creature: old things are passed away; behold, all things are become new.

(18) And all things are of God, who hath reconciled us to himself by Jesus Christ, and hath given to us the ministry of reconciliation;

(19) To wit, that God was in Christ, reconciling the world unto himself, not imputing their trespasses unto them; and hath committed unto us the word of reconciliation.
(20) Now then we are ambassadors for Christ, as though God did beseech you by us: we pray you in Christ's stead, be ye reconciled to God.
(21) For he hath made him to be sin for us, who knew no sin; that we might be made the righteousness of God in him.

Hebrews 9:1-28
(1) Then verily the first covenant had also ordinances of divine service, and a worldly sanctuary.
(2) For there was a tabernacle made; the first, wherein was the candlestick, and the table, and the shewbread; which is called the sanctuary.
(3) And after the second veil, the tabernacle which is called the Holiest of all;
(4) Which had the golden censer, and the ark of the covenant overlaid round about with gold, wherein was the golden pot that had manna, and Aaron's rod that budded, and the tables of the covenant;
(5) And over it the cherubims of glory shadowing the mercyseat; of which we cannot now speak particularly.
(6) Now when these things were thus ordained, the priests went always into the first tabernacle, accomplishing the service of God.
(7) But into the second went the high priest alone once every year, not without blood, which he offered for himself, and for the errors of the people:
(8) The Holy Ghost this signifying, that the way into the holiest of all was not yet made manifest, while as the first tabernacle was yet standing:
(9) Which was a figure for the time then present, in which were offered both gifts and sacrifices, that could not make him that did the service perfect, as pertaining to the conscience;
(10) Which stood only in meats and drinks, and divers washings, and carnal ordinances, imposed on them until the time of reformation.
(11) But Christ being come an high priest of good things to come, by a greater and more perfect tabernacle, not made with hands, that is to say, not of this building;
(12) Neither by the blood of goats and calves, but by his own blood he entered in once into the holy place, having obtained eternal redemption for us.

(13) For if the blood of bulls and of goats, and the ashes of an heifer sprinkling the unclean, sanctifieth to the purifying of the flesh:

(14) How much more shall the blood of Christ, who through the eternal Spirit offered himself without spot to God, purge your conscience from dead works to serve the living God?

(15) And for this cause he is the mediator of the new testament, that by means of death, for the redemption of the transgressions that were under the first testament, they which are called might receive the promise of eternal inheritance.

(16) For where a testament is, there must also of necessity be the death of the testator.

(17) For a testament is of force after men are dead: otherwise it is of no strength at all while the testator liveth.

(18) Whereupon neither the first testament was dedicated without blood.

(19) For when Moses had spoken every precept to all the people according to the law, he took the blood of calves and of goats, with water, and scarlet wool, and hyssop, and sprinkled both the book, and all the people,

(20) Saying, This is the blood of the testament which God hath enjoined unto you.

(21) Moreover he sprinkled with blood both the tabernacle, and all the vessels of the ministry.

(22) And almost all things are by the law purged with blood; and without shedding of blood is no remission.

(23) It was therefore necessary that the patterns of things in the heavens should be purified with these; but the heavenly things themselves with better sacrifices than these.

(24) For Christ is not entered into the holy places made with hands, which are the figures of the true; but into heaven itself, now to appear in the presence of God for us:

(25) Nor yet that he should offer himself often, as the high priest entereth into the holy place every year with blood of others;

(26) For then must he often have suffered since the foundation of the world: but now once in the end of the world hath he appeared to put away sin by the sacrifice of himself.

(27) And as it is appointed unto men once to die, but after this the judgment:

(28) So Christ was once offered to bear the sins of many; and unto them that look for him shall he appear the second time without sin unto salvation.

Romans 3:21-26 (CJB)

251

(21) But now, quite apart from Torah, God's way of making people righteous in his sight has been made clear — although the Torah and the Prophets give their witness to it as well —

(22) and it is a righteousness that comes from God, through the faithfulness of Yeshua the Messiah, to all who continue trusting. For it makes no difference whether one is a Jew or a Gentile,

(23) since all have sinned and come short of earning God's praise.

(24) By God's grace, without earning it, all are granted the status of being considered righteous before him, through the act redeeming us from our enslavement to sin that was accomplished by the Messiah Yeshua.

(25) God put Yeshua forward as the kapparah for sin through his faithfulness in respect to his bloody sacrificial death. This vindicated God's righteousness; because, in his forbearance, he had passed over [with neither punishment nor remission] the sins people had committed in the past;

(26) and it vindicates his righteousness in the present age by showing that he is righteous himself and is also the one who makes people righteous on the ground of Yeshua's faithfulness.

Now, it is a good time to offer prayers of repentance and supplications.

The following prayer, is a traditional prayer called "al chet", or for the sin. It is a confession of sins that we may at times overlook. I encourage you to read these as a prayer from you to the Father. Feel free, of course, to add your own confessions.

For the sin which we have committed before You under duress or willingly.

And for the sin which we have committed before You by hard-heartedness.

For the sin which we have committed before You inadvertently.

And for the sin which we have committed before You with an utterance of the lips.

For the sin which we have committed before You with immorality.

And for the sin which we have committed before You openly or secretly.

For the sin which we have committed before You with knowledge and with deceit.

And for the sin which we have committed before You through speech.

For the sin which we have committed before You by deceiving a fellowman.

And for the sin which we have committed before You by improper thoughts.

For the sin which we have committed before You by a gathering of lewdness.

And for the sin which we have committed before You by verbal [insincere] confession.

For the sin which we have committed before You by disrespect for parents and teachers.

And for the sin which we have committed before You intentionally or unintentionally.

For the sin which we have committed before You by using coercion.

And for the sin which we have committed before You by desecrating the Divine Name.

For the sin which we have committed before You by impurity of speech.

And for the sin which we have committed before You by foolish talk.

For the sin which we have committed before You with the evil inclination.

And for the sin which we have committed before You knowingly or unknowingly.

For all these, God of pardon, pardon us, forgive us, atone for us.

For the sin which we have committed before You by false denial and lying.

And for the sin which we have committed before You by a bribe-taking or a bribe-giving hand.

For the sin which we have committed before You by scoffing.

And for the sin which we have committed before You by evil talk [about another].

For the sin which we have committed before You in business dealings.

And for the sin which we have committed before You by eating and drinking.

For the sin which we have committed before You by [taking or giving] interest and by usury.

And for the sin which we have committed before You by a haughty demeanor.

For the sin which we have committed before You by the prattle of our lips.

And for the sin which we have committed before You by a glance of the eye.

For the sin which we have committed before You with proud looks.

And for the sin which we have committed before You with impudence.

For all these, God of pardon, pardon us, forgive us, atone for us.

For the sin which we have committed before You by casting off the yoke [of Heaven].

And for the sin which we have committed before You in passing judgment.

For the sin which we have committed before You by scheming against a fellowman.

And for the sin which we have committed before You by a begrudging eye.

For the sin which we have committed before You by frivolity.

And for the sin which we have committed before You by obduracy.

For the sin which we have committed before You by running to do evil.

And for the sin which we have committed before You by tale-bearing.

For the sin which we have committed before You by swearing in vain.

And for the sin which we have committed before You by causeless hatred.

For the sin which we have committed before You by embezzlement.

And for the sin which we have committed before You by a confused heart.

For all these, God of pardon, pardon us, forgive us, atone for us.

And for the sins for which we are obligated to bring a burnt-offering.

And for the sins for which we are obligated to bring a sin-offering.

And for the sins for which we are obligated to bring a varying offering [according to one's means].

And for the sins for which we are obligated to bring a guilt-offering for a certain or doubtful trespass.

And for the sins for which we incur the penalty of lashing for rebelliousness.

And for the sins for which we incur the penalty of forty lashes.

And for the sins for which we incur the penalty of death by the hand of Heaven.

And for the sins for which we incur the penalty of excision and childlessness.

And for the sins for which we incur the penalty of the four forms of capital punishment executed by the Court: stoning, burning, decapitation and strangulation.

For [transgressing] positive and prohibitory mitzvot (commands), whether [the prohibitions] can be rectified by a specifically prescribed act or not, those of which we are aware and those of which we are not aware; those of which we are aware, we have already declared them before You and confessed them to You, and those of which we are not aware --- before You they are revealed and known, as it is stated:The hidden things belong to the Lord our God, but the revealed things are for us and for our children forever, that we may carry out all the words of this Torah. For You are the Pardoner of Israel and the Forgiver of the tribes of Yeshurun (upright ones) in every generation, and aside from You we have no King who forgives and pardons.

Holy (Revelation 4:8)
Holy, Holy, Holy
Is the Lord God of hosts
Who was, who is, and is to come

Our Father, our King
Our Father, our King, be merciful and answer us, though we have no worthy deeds. Treat us charitably, with lovingkindness, for You have saved us.

Barchee Nahfshe -Psalms 103:1-4
(1) [By David:] Bless Adonai, my soul! Everything in me, bless his holy name!
(2) Bless Adonai, my soul, and forget none of his benefits!
(3) He forgives all your offenses, he heals all your diseases,

256

(4) he redeems your life from the pit, he surrounds you with grace and compassion,

<u>Y'deed Nehfesh</u> – Lover of My Soul
   Lover of my soul, compassionate Father, draw your servant to your will. Then your servant shall run like a deer to bow before your majesty. To him, your friendship will be sweeter than the dripping of the honeycomb and any taste.
   Reveal Yourself, and spread upon me my beloved, the shelter of your peace. Illuminate the Earth with your glory, that we may rejoice and be glad with You. Come quickly, show love, for the appointed season has come, and show was grace as in days of old.

Additional readings for Yom Kippur:

- Morning Readings:
Leviticus 16:1-34
Numbers 29:7-11
Isaiah 57:14 to 58:14
Hebrews 5:1to 7:28

- Minchah/Afternoon readings:
Leviticus 18:1-30
Book of Jonah
Book of Micah
Hebrews 8:1 to 10:39
Revelation 19:11-16

<u>Aharonic Blessing</u>
Numbers 6:22-27
(22) And the LORD spake unto Moses, saying,
(23) Speak unto Aaron and unto his sons, saying, On this wise ye shall bless the children of Israel, saying unto them,
(24) The LORD bless thee, and keep thee:
(25) The LORD make his face shine upon thee, and be gracious unto thee:
(26) The LORD lift up his countenance upon thee, and give thee peace.
(27) And they shall put my name upon the children of Israel; and I will bless them.

סכות

Sukkot
The Feast
of Tabernacles

The feast of Tabernacles, also known as Sukkot, is the last of the feasts given in Leviticus chapter 23. What does this feast have to do with the Messiah? How does this feast relate to our lives today? What are the prophetic pictures that are given to us through the feast of Tabernacles?
What does it mean when we say the word tabernacle? What do we mean when we say that we are to tabernacle with God, and that he is to tabernacle us?

It's important to make a distinction between the feast of Tabernacles, in regards to what the tabernacle was that we were supposed to be in, and the tabernacle that was in the wilderness. The tabernacle that was in the wilderness is called the "Mishkan" or "Ohel" and even sometimes "Ohel moed". For the feast that we are to observe that is called the feast of Tabernacles, the word for tabernacle is the word "sukkah." So what is the difference?

Let's look at a couple of these words before we begin. The first use for this tabernacle is the word Mishkan. It is the word H4908 in the Strongs concordance.

H4908

מִשְׁכָּן

mishkân

mish-kawn'
From H7931; a *residence* (including a shepherd's *hut*, the *lair* of animals, figuratively the *grave*; also the *Temple*); specifically the *Tabernacle* (properly its wooden walls): - dwelleth, dwelling (place), habitation, tabernacle, tent.

It is from the word Shakan, which means to dwell.

H7931

שָׁכַן

shâkan

shaw-kan'
A primitive root (apparently akin (by transmutation) to H7901 through the idea of *lodging*; compare H5531 and H7925); to *reside* or permanently stay (literally or figuratively): - abide, continue, (cause to, make to) dwell (-er), have habitation, inhabit, lay, place, (cause to) remain, rest, set (up).

This is what is referred to when we talk about the Shekinah glory of God. We are talking about the dwelling presence of God. It is His presence that dwells with us, and among us, and even within us.

The next word that is used is the word "Ohel".
H168

אהל

'ôhel

o'-hel

From H166; a *tent* (as *clearly* conspicuous from a distance): - covering, (dwelling) (place), home, tabernacle, tent.

The word "Ohel" means a tent or a covering, a home. So Ohel moed would mean the tent of meeting. In Scripture where you see the phrase "the tent of meeting" it is this phrase Ohel moed. We see many times in Scripture were Moses went to the tent of meeting. The tent of meeting is where the people gathered. That is the place where God resided.

Where the people reside? That is the word sukkah. It is the singular for the word Sukkot. Sukkot means Tabernacles. A sukkah is a booth, a Pavilion, which can also be called a tabernacle or a tent. So, a Sukkah does not have to specifically be a tent.

The Hebrew for the word sukkah is in the Strongs concordance. It's the Hebrew word H5521

סכה

sûkkâh

Feminine of H5520 סך

a hut or lair: - booth, cottage, covert, pavilion, tabernacle, tent.

So now that we have the plain definition, let's look at what the feast is and how it is supposed to be celebrated, along with what it means to the children of God. To begin our journey we will again look at Leviticus chapter 23.

Leviticus 23:33-44 KJV
(33) And the LORD spake unto Moses, saying,

261

(34) Speak unto the children of Israel, saying, The fifteenth day of this seventh month shall be the feast of tabernacles for seven days unto the LORD.

(35) On the first day shall be an holy convocation: ye shall do no servile work therein.

(36) Seven days ye shall offer an offering made by fire unto the LORD: on the eighth day shall be an holy convocation unto you; and ye shall offer an offering made by fire unto the LORD: it is a solemn assembly; and ye shall do no servile work therein.

(37) These are the feasts of the LORD, which ye shall proclaim to be holy convocations, to offer an offering made by fire unto the LORD, a burnt offering, and a meat offering, a sacrifice, and drink offerings, every thing upon his day:

(38) Beside the sabbaths of the LORD, and beside your gifts, and beside all your vows, and beside all your freewill offerings, which ye give unto the LORD.

(39) Also in the fifteenth day of the seventh month, when ye have gathered in the fruit of the land, ye shall keep a feast unto the LORD seven days: on the first day shall be a sabbath, and on the eighth day shall be a sabbath.

(40) And ye shall take you on the first day the boughs of goodly trees, branches of palm trees, and the boughs of thick trees, and willows of the brook; and ye shall rejoice before the LORD your God seven days.

(41) And ye shall keep it a feast unto the LORD seven days in the year. It shall be a statute for ever in your generations: ye shall celebrate it in the seventh month.

(42) Ye shall dwell in booths seven days; all that are Israelites born shall dwell in booths:

(43) That your generations may know that I made the children of Israel to dwell in booths, when I brought them out of the land of Egypt: I am the LORD your God.

(44) And Moses declared unto the children of Israel the feasts of the LORD.

According to the Scriptures that we have just read, this was a feast that was kept unto the Lord. The people of Israel were to dwell in the sukkahs, otherwise known as booths or tabernacles, for a seven day time frame. Do we have an explanation as to why the children of Israel were to dwell in booths? Yes we do. We can look at verses 42 and 43 in Leviticus chapter 23 for the answer.

(42 CJB) You are to live in sukkot for seven days; every citizen of Isra'el is to live in a sukkah,
(43 CJB) so that [for the purpose of]
- generation after generation of you will know
- that I made the people of Isra'el live
- in Sukkot
- when I brought them out of the land of Egypt;
- I am Adonai your God.' "

According to the Scriptures, the people of Israel were to live in a sukkah for seven days. The purpose of this was so that generation after generation would know that God himself caused the people of Israel to live. Not just to live, but to live in temporary dwellings. He redeemed them and brought them out of the land of Egypt and out of the yoke of their bondage.

The Father ends this explanation very simply by saying, "I am Adonai your God." We see in Scripture more than once, where God says ,"I am Adonai your God." Why does He need to tell us this? There are times in our lives when we think that we know better than God does. Or worse yet, we feel that because we don't understand an aspect of the word, that it relieves us of our responsibility to heed it.

There are some things in Scripture that the Father gave us that we will not understand. When He gives us these things, He simply tells us, "I am your God." Do we accept this in faith, or do we say that because I don't understand, I don't have to do it?

We should accept the word that we are given in faith. When the children of Israel came out of Egypt, they had to dwell in temporary dwelling places. We need to understand the whole concept that this place that we are in is not our home. We are on a journey. Are we willing to follow the Father and listen to Him, even when we don't understand?

The emphasis here for Sukkot is that YHWH caused us to dwell. In our temporary dwelling in this life, or in the wilderness, He will also dwell with us. This is an important concept to us as believers today. We need to learn how to dwell with our Heavenly Father and with each other. In any relationship we encounter in this life, there is a period of time that we learn how to dwell with each other in that relationship. We are learning about each other and how we respond to one another. You could even say that we are learning our boundaries with each other.

This cultivates our relationship, and in this process we decide within ourselves how far we will allow this relationship to go. Will we receive from one another? Will we seek each other out for council or comfort? Will we invite each other into our homes? Or, will we remain casual acquaintances that rarely speak to one another? Will we limit our relationship to a casual "Hello, how's the weather?", or will it be more?

Is learning to dwell with one another so important? Learning to dwell with one another was the first thing that the Father _brought_ the children of Israel to when they came out of Egypt. Scripture says "they journeyrd from Rameses and went to Succot." This is a picture for us today. The very first thing we have to learn after our redemption is how to dwell with the Father and how to dwell with our fellow man. We see this in Exodus chapter twelve.

Exodus 12:36-37
(36) and Adonai had made the Egyptians so favorably disposed toward the people that they had let them have whatever they requested. Thus they plundered the Egyptians.
(37) The people of Isra'el traveled from Ra`amses to Sukkot, some six hundred thousand men on foot, not counting children.

As soon as they came out of Egypt, they went to a place called Sukkot. This was a reminder to the children of Israel that this was only temporary. Sukkot was a place that the children of Israel had to come to in order to learn how to dwell with one

264

another before they went into the wilderness. In the wilderness, the children of Israel were going to learn how to rely on God and how to rely on each other. It was in the wilderness that God was going to reveal Himself. It was during their times in the wilderness, that the glory of God was the strongest. What we know from Scripture, is that God desires for His children to be in unity. That's when the spirit of God flows in the midst of the camp.

Even the prophets spoke of us learning how to dwell together in unity . Scripture talks about restoring the fallen tabernacle of David. What does that mean, and how does that happen? We see that it starts with dwelling in unity and restoration. God desires restoration and reconciliation with all of His children. The first thing we need after repentance, is to learn how to dwell with one another. Another way to put it is, we need to learn how to play nice, even when we are in the middle of the wilderness experience.

We see James speaking of this at the Jerusalem council in the book of Acts, chapter 15.

Acts 15:13-17 KJV
(13)   And after they had held their peace, James answered, saying, Men and brethren, hearken unto me:
(14)   Simeon hath declared how God at the first did visit the Gentiles, to take out of them a people for his name.
(15) And to this agree the words of the prophets; as it is written,
(16) After this I will return, and will build again the tabernacle of David, which is fallen down; and I will build again the ruins thereof, and I will set it up:
(17) That the residue of men might seek after the Lord, and all the Gentiles, upon whom my name is called, saith the Lord, who doeth all these things.

Acts 15 is quoting from Amos chapter 9.
Amos 9:11

In that day will I raise up the tabernacle of David that is fallen, and close up the breaches thereof; and I will raise up his ruins, and I will build it as in the days of old:

Did you notice the word tabernacle or some translations say "tent" of David? This is not the word that is used in Scripture to say the Tabernacle of the LORD. Look at it again.

Amos 9:11
- In that day will I raise up the
- Tabernacle [סֻכַּת – Sukkat David – Sukkah of David]
- of David that is fallen, and close up the breaches thereof; and I will raise up his ruins, and I will build it as in the days of old:

So, the restoration is going to be the sukkah of David, or the dwelling place of David. Our Messiah is called the son of David. Some of the rabbis believe that this is a prophecy regarding the house of David. This refers to a time when the house of David will rule again. What we see here, is that when this happens, there will be people coming from all over and they will be brought into this restoration and reconciliation process.

It is interesting to note that the feast of Tabernacles is an agricultural feast. It is celebrated at a time when the harvest is finished. The labor had been done, and everyone had already gone out and gathered all of their crops. The harvest was gathered and they were now bringing in the sheaves of the harvest.

Another word for the feast of Sukkot is the feast of ingathering. When all the work is finished and the people bring in the fruits of all of their labor, there is an ingathering to one common place, the mountain of the Lord, and the Temple of God.

Look at Leviticus 23 verse 39, the feast was celebrated after all the fruit of the land had been gathered in.

Leviticus 23:39 KJV
- Also in the fifteenth day of the seventh month,
- when ye have gathered in the fruit of the land,

266

- ye shall keep a feast unto the LORD seven days:
- on the first day shall be a sabbath,
- and on the eighth day shall be a sabbath.

The gathering in of the harvest, or of the fruit of the land, is a representation of all of the people of the land (the Earth).

Luke 10:2 KJV
Therefore said he unto them, The harvest truly is great, but the labourers are few: pray ye therefore the Lord of the harvest, that he would send forth labourers into his harvest.

Matthew 13:24-30 KJV
(24) Another parable put he forth unto them, saying, The kingdom of heaven is likened unto a man which sowed good seed in his field:
(25) But while men slept, his enemy came and sowed tares among the wheat, and went his way.
(26) But when the blade was sprung up, and brought forth fruit, then appeared the tares also.
(27) So the servants of the householder came and said unto him, Sir, didst not thou sow good seed in thy field? from whence then hath it tares?
(28) He said unto them, An enemy hath done this. The servants said unto him, Wilt thou then that we go and gather them up?
(29) But he said, Nay; lest while ye gather up the tares, ye root up also the wheat with them.
(30) Let both grow together until the harvest: and in the time of harvest I will say to the reapers, Gather ye together first the tares, and bind them in bundles to burn them: but gather the wheat into my barn.

Revelation 14:15-16 KJV
(15) And another angel came out of the temple, crying with a loud voice to him that sat on the cloud, Thrust in thy sickle, and reap: for the time is come for thee to reap; for the harvest of the earth is ripe.

(16) And he that sat on the cloud thrust in his sickle on the earth; and the earth was reaped.

When the harvesting is done and everything else is finished, we are to be in the presence of the Lord. We are to rejoice and to praise Him in the feast that He has prepared for us. How do we see this in the Scripture? We've already seen that Sukkot is the ingathering feast. We know that in the end times people from every tribe tongue and nation will stand before the Lord. They will either be gathered into his people or cast out.

Today, in Israel, people take what is called a lulav and they rejoice before the Lord while holding this lulav. Which would lead to the question, what is a lulav? Is this just a tradition, or do we see it in Scripture?
We do see it in Scripture, in Leviticus 23:40. It is a symbol that we are to worship the Father with our whole being, with all that we are. Let us look at Leviticus 23 verse 40 to see the application of the lulav and how it is a picture of men.

Leviticus 23:40 KJV
- And ye shall take you on the first day
- the boughs of goodly trees,
- branches of palm trees,
- and the boughs of thick trees,
- and willows of the brook;
- and ye shall rejoice before the LORD your God
- seven days.

As we break down this verse, we see something that we don't see every day. We are told to take hold of specific things and to come into the presence of God to rejoice with these things. Have we ever seen anything like this today? This whole idea may seem simple or antiquated, even archaic to us today. The question for us today is, does God change?

Malachi 3:6 KJV
For I am the LORD, I change not; therefore ye sons of Jacob are not consumed.

Hebrews 13:8 KJV
Jesus Christ the same yesterday, and to day, and for ever.

The question should more be, is there something we can learn or gain from this experience, other than the fact that it was said to do it? Let us look again at Leviticus 23:40.

- And ye shall take you on the first day
- the boughs (fruit) of goodly (hadar) trees,
- branches of palm (tamar) trees,
- and the boughs (anaf- cover, twig) of thick (intwined) trees, (myrtle)
- and willows (arav) of the brook;
- and ye shall rejoice before the LORD your God
- seven days.

We are told in Scripture to take these four things and rejoice before the Lord. What does rejoice mean? Rejoice is the Hebrew word Samach.

H8055 שָׂמַח śâmach
to brighten up, make gleesome: - cheer up, be (make) glad, have joy, be merry, (cause to, make to) rejoice

As you come before the Lord with these four things, it will cause you to have joy, be merry, and cause you to be joyous in the sight of the Lord. What are these four things specifically and how do they relate to us?

The four Species according to Leviticus 23:40.

- The fruit of Hadar trees (Citron or Etrog)
- A branch of a palm tree
- A twig from a myrtle tree
- And willows from the brook

Upon closer examination of these four items we will see that they all relate to us.

- The palm looks like a backbone.
- The myrtle leaves look like eyes.

269

- The willow leaves look like a mouth.
- And, the etrog looks like the heart

The lesson from these four items is a reminder to us that we are supposed to thank God and worship Him with our whole body. Even more so as One Body of Messiah.

The traditional teaching within Judaism regarding the four species is; Just as there are four kinds of plants, so there are four kinds of people.
- The willow has no taste and cannot be smelled. It is like the one who learns no Torah and who does no good deeds.
- The myrtle branch can be smelled, but has no taste. This is like the one who knows a little Torah (some of the word), but who still does many good deeds.
- The palm branch has a taste, but no smell. This is like the one who knows much Torah, but who does not do good deeds.
- The etrog can be both tasted and smelled. This is like the one who both knows much Torah (the Word of YHWH) and does good deeds.

According to the traditional teaching, the etrog and lulav help us remember that we should both learn about what is right by studying the Word of God, and work hard to find opportunities to help others. Real community is found when all are bound together and brought under one roof."

As we have mentioned, each of the four species relates to a particular part of man through which he is to serve God. We will take a little deeper look at these items and their relationship to man.

ETROG—refers to the heart, the place of understanding and wisdom.
- It is shaped like a heart.
- It has a thick, dense skin.
- It bruises very easily so it requires much care to keep it unmarred.

- Inside it has many seeds, each of which has the ability to produce fruit.
- The etrog tree cannot be grafted with any other fruit tree.
- Great care is taken to protect the trees and their fruit.
- Many etrog growers trim the thorny leaves on the tree to prevent them from scarring the fruit.
- Winds can cause the leaves to brush against the fruit — enough to scratch them.

Each of the four relates to a particular part of man through which he is to serve
God.

Much can be said just by listing out the characteristics of the etrog. At times we feel our heart has a thick skin around it and that we can protect our heart ourselves. However, in reality our heart can be bruised very easily and much care is required to keep it from being hurt or marred. There are many seeds inside of our heart, seeds of doubt or seeds of faith, seeds of victory or seeds of defeat, seeds of the word of God or seeds of the speech of men. Many different types of seeds are there and each seed has the ability to produce fruit.

We must take great care to keep our heart guarded. At times, we need to guard our heart from ourselves. How many times have we said things that in the end come back to hurt us? The etrog is guarded even from the tree it grows on. There are thorns on the tree that can press against the fruit and cause blemishes in the fruit. Even when the wind blows, if there are thorns around the fruit, it will push the thorns into the fruit. Even the process of watering can cause damage. Each tree has to be hand watered so as not to damage the fruit or the tree.

- LULAV—refers to the backbone, or uprightness. We are to be upright in all our ways before the Lord. We are to stand in the righteousness of God.
- MYRTLE—corresponds to the eyes, or enlightenment. We should worship the Father even with our eyes. Be careful of what you set your gaze upon.
- WILLOW (aravah) —represents the lips, or the service of the lips (which is prayer). Out of the mouth the heart speaks. We should be ones to glorify God with our lips

and let them be a revealing of outpouring to the Father from our hearts. Remember, out of the mouth you will speak life or death, blessing or cursing, choose your words wisely.

Proverbs 18:20-21 KJV
(20) A man's belly shall be satisfied with the fruit of his mouth; and with the increase of his lips shall he be filled.
(21) Death and life are in the power of the tongue: and they that love it shall eat the fruit thereof.

Something else that is interesting concerning the four species is that they each have a special relationship with water. If we look at this it will again reveal something a little deeper.

- The citron (etrog) and willow depend on constant supplies of water. They need a continual supply of water to live and flourish. The ideal place to find them is by a stream or river.
- The date palm is a native to hot, wet oasis. It is a sign of water in the desert. Though it may seem dry all around, there is an oasis in the midst of it.
- The myrtle can survive many months without water and in drought type scenarios.

What is the lesson to be learned here? Like the willow, citron, and date palm, our lives depend on water. Not just any water, but living water, fresh, life giving water. Like the myrtle, at times we need to survive long months of dryness. Are there times in our life when we feel we are in a dry place? The four species help us to focus on a fervent plea for rain, for living water, for the life giving water that can come only from the Father.

In the landscapes they evoke, these four plants recall Israel's passage from the dry desert to the fertile (if watered by rain) land of Israel. This time is celebrated during the seasonal passage from dry to wet.

Why a Citron (Etrog)? The word Etrog is Aramaic, which means "delightful." The English equivalent of this word, Citron, is derived from the Greek word "Kedros". The word Kedros in Greek is the same as "Hadar" in Hebrew, which means Citrus.

The word "Kedros" was Latinized as Cedrus. Cedrus then evolved into Citrus. Citrus then evolved into Citron. In Second Temple times (the time that Yeshua would have been there), the Etrog was the only known Citrus fruit. Since it was the only known citrus fruit, it was the only choice for the Sukkot ritual of Leviticus 23:40.

According to the Rabbis, the word הדר hadar can also be rendered as הדיר hadir, meaning a sheep pen. Why would an etrog tree be related to a sheep pen? Just as a sheep pen has both old and young animals, an etrog tree has fruit that continues to grow through all seasons, this is quite unique. This allows for a single etrog tree to have fruit in multiple stages of growth. Doesn't this testify to the body of believers today? We all are sheep, we are all to be in the pen of the Good Shepherd, but we are all in different stages of growth. This fact is reminiscent of the trees by the river of life coming from the throne of God.

Revelation 22:1-2 KJV
(1) And he shewed me a pure river of water of life, clear as crystal, proceeding out of the throne of God and of the Lamb.
(2) In the midst of the street of it, and on either side of the river, was there the tree of life, which bare twelve manner of fruits, and yielded her fruit every month: and the leaves of the tree were for the healing of the nations.

We do see places in Scripture where trees are associated with people.

Psalms 1:1-3 KJV
(1) Blessed is the man that walketh not in the counsel of the ungodly, nor standeth in the way of sinners, nor sitteth in the seat of the scornful.
(2) But his delight is in the law of the LORD; and in his law doth he meditate day and night.
(3) And he shall be like a tree planted by the rivers of water, that bringeth forth his fruit in his season; his leaf also shall not wither; and whatsoever he doeth shall prosper.

Another interesting fact that has been mentioned before is the tree that the Etrogim (plural of etrog) grows on has thorns, so the fruit must be constantly monitored and tended to ensure that the thorns do not cause marks on the fruit. The fruit must be protected even from the tree that it grows on. Have you heard before that trees in scripture often represent people? What can we learn from this?

The tree requires much water in order to produce good fruit. We need the living water in our lives and a constant supply of the Spirit of YHWH to wash us and make us clean. The tree and the fruit require a good amount of sunlight in order to produce good fruit. Yeshua said that He is the light of the world in John 8:12. We need the light of the world to shine over us in order to produce good fruit. Many trees are also watered manually to avoid moving irrigation equipment through the groves. We are all individual and need to be watered individually. We are all at different stages of growth in our walk with the Father. We need just the right amount of water at the right time and delivered the proper way in order to grow properly and produce good fruit. Moses says in Deuteronomy 32 how the word of the Lord should be to us.

Deuteronomy 32:1-2 KJV
(1) Give ear, O ye heavens, and I will speak; and hear, O earth, the words of my mouth.

(2) My doctrine shall drop as the rain, my speech shall distil as the dew, as the small rain upon the tender herb, and as the showers upon the grass:

The etrog used in the mitzvah (command or good deed) of the four species must be largely unblemished, with the fewest black specks or other flaws. It represents to us a heart that has been cleansed and presented to the Father. Extra special care is needed to cut around the leaves and thorns that may scratch the fruit. There are times in our lives when we need a good pruning to get rid of all the things that don't need to be there.

It is also important to protect the fruit-bearing trees from any dust and carbon, which may get caught in thestomata of the fruit during growth, and may later appear as a black dot. We should protect ourselves from dots, spots, blemishes and any imperfections in our hearts.

Man is made from the dust of the earth. We are carbon based life forms. We should be careful not to allow the teachings and traditions of men into our hearts that should be kept pure unto the Father. If we do, it will become spots to us.

2 Peter 2:12-20 KJV
(12) But these, as natural brute beasts, made to be taken and destroyed, speak evil of the things that they understand not; and shall utterly perish in their own corruption;
(13) And shall receive the reward of unrighteousness, as they that count it pleasure to riot in the day time. **Spots they are and blemishes**, sporting themselves with their own deceivings while they feast with you;
(14) Having eyes full of adultery, and that cannot cease from sin; beguiling unstable souls: an heart they have exercised with covetous practices; cursed children:
(15) Which have forsaken the right way, and are gone astray, following the way of Balaam the son of Bosor, who loved the wages of unrighteousness;
(16) But was rebuked for his iniquity: the dumb ass speaking with man's voice forbad the madness of the prophet.

(17) These are wells without water, clouds that are carried with a tempest; to whom the mist of darkness is reserved for ever.

(18) For when they speak great swelling words of vanity, they allure through the lusts of the flesh, through much wantonness, those that were clean escaped from them who live in error.

(19) While they promise them liberty, they themselves are the servants of corruption: for of whom a man is overcome, of the same is he brought in bondage.

(20) For if after they have escaped the pollutions of the world through the knowledge of the Lord and Saviour Jesus Christ, they are again entangled therein, and overcome, the latter end is worse with them than the beginning.

Jude 1:8-25 KJV

(8) Likewise also these filthy dreamers defile the flesh, despise dominion, and speak evil of dignities.

(9) Yet Michael the archangel, when contending with the devil he disputed about the body of Moses, durst not bring against him a railing accusation, but said, The Lord rebuke thee.

(10) But these speak evil of those things which they know not: but what they know naturally, as brute beasts, in those things they corrupt themselves.

(11) Woe unto them! for they have gone in the way of Cain, and ran greedily after the error of Balaam for reward, and perished in the gainsaying of Core.

(12) **These are spots in your feasts** of charity, when they feast with you, feeding themselves without fear: clouds they are without water, carried about of winds; trees whose fruit withereth, without fruit, twice dead, plucked up by the roots;

(13) Raging waves of the sea, foaming out their own shame; wandering stars, to whom is reserved the blackness of darkness for ever.

(14) And Enoch also, the seventh from Adam, prophesied of these, saying, Behold, the Lord cometh with ten thousands of his saints,

(15) To execute judgment upon all, and to convince all that are ungodly among them of all their ungodly deeds which they have

ungodly committed, and of all their hard speeches which ungodly sinners have spoken against him.

(16) These are murmurers, complainers, walking after their own lusts; and their mouth speaketh great swelling words, having men's persons in admiration because of advantage.

(17) But, beloved, remember ye the words which were spoken before of the apostles of our Lord Jesus Christ;

(18) How that they told you there should be mockers in the last time, who should walk after their own ungodly lusts.

(19) These be they who separate themselves, sensual, having not the Spirit.

(20) But ye, beloved, building up yourselves on your most holy faith, praying in the Holy Ghost,

(21) Keep yourselves in the love of God, looking for the mercy of our Lord Jesus Christ unto eternal life.

(22) And of some have compassion, making a difference:

(23) And others save with fear, pulling them out of the fire; hating even the garment spotted by the flesh.

(24) Now unto him that is able to keep you from falling, and to present you faultless before the presence of his glory with exceeding joy,

(25) To the only wise God our Saviour, be glory and majesty, dominion and power, both now and ever. Amen.

We now return to the relationship of each of the four species with water. We will now look at the willow. The willow only flourishes near abundant water. Not just any water, but abundant and clean water. It is so dependent on water, that if a spring dries up, the willows nearby will wither.

The willow then represents our dependence on water and our prayer and hope for rain at the right time. The willow resembles a mouth. We see again in Deuteronomy 32 when Moses says "may my teaching fall like rain." The teaching from our mouths should be life and living water to those around us. Life and living water are synonyms for Torah (the teaching and instruction of God) in Jewish communities.

The words from our mouths as priests of the Most High God, should be wholesome and should be the word of God!

Malachi 2:4-7 KJV
(4) And ye shall know that I have sent this commandment unto you, that my covenant might be with Levi, saith the LORD of hosts.
(5) My covenant was with him of life and peace; and I gave them to him for the fear wherewith he feared me, and was afraid before my name.
(6) **The law of truth was in his mouth**, and **iniquity was not found in his lips**: he walked with me in peace and equity, and did turn many away from iniquity.
(7) For the priest's lips should keep knowledge, and they should seek the law at his mouth: for he is the messenger of the LORD of hosts.

Exodus 13:9 CJB
"Moreover, it *(observation of unleavened bread)* will serve you as a sign on your hand and as a reminder between your eyes, so that Adonai's Torah may be on your lips; because with a strong hand Adonai brought you out of Egypt.

Joshua 1:8 CJB
Yes, keep this book of the Torah on your lips, and meditate on it day and night, so that you will take care to act according to everything written in it. Then your undertakings will prosper, and you will succeed.

Now we get to the lulav and its relationship with water. The lulav is from the palm tree. It is a sign of water, or an oasis in the desert. When things are dry, can we tap into the water of life and emerge victorious? Will we arise from the dryness of life and see that we have a source of living water, even in times when it cannot be seen?

Additionally, the lulav's sword-like shape may be the source of the tree's association with victory. In the ancient near east, the victor in a court case would emerge carrying a palm frond. The Hasmoneans used the palm to symbolize their triumph over the Syrian-Greeks. It even appears on ancient (and modern Israeli) coins.

We now come to the myrtle, and we will examine its relationship with water. The myrtle is able to withstand very dry conditions, even fire! Its fragrant leaves remain green and upright without water long after cutting. It came to symbolize immortality and prosperity because it was resistant to decay and corruption. In this we see that even in trying or difficult times, when we feel we are "in the fire", that we must hold on to the living water that sustains us (even in the dry season).

Remember that the myrtle looks like an eye? What does scripture say about our eyes?
Matthew 6:21-23
(21) For where your wealth is, there your heart will be also.
(22) 'The eye is the lamp of the body.' So if you have a 'good eye' [that is, if you are generous] your whole body will be full of light;
(23) but if you have an 'evil eye' [if you are stingy] your whole body will be full of darkness. If, then, the light in you is darkness, how great is that darkness!

If we take all of the four species mentioned in Leviticus 23:40 we see that altogether they symbolize;
- The whole man
- The entire community
- Unity of the body
- Unity of the community

It is important that when the ingathering happens that we stand together as one body of Messiah and not as many factions of a disconnected body.

Ephesians 4:16
Under his control, the whole body is being fitted and held together by the support of every joint, with each part working to fulfill its function; this is how the body grows and builds itself up in love.

So, when we see the ingathering and become one body, we shall remember to be joyful before the LORD and rejoice before Him all as One.

Psalms 104:33
I will sing unto the LORD as long as I live: I will sing praise to my God while I have my being.

Psalms 150:6
Let every thing that hath breath praise the LORD. Praise ye the LORD.

The celebration of Sukkot.

The celebration of Sukkot was seven days, plus one for a total of eight days. Why would it be listed as seven days plus one? Seven means something special in Scripture. Seven means a perfection or a completion. A time of seven days and the work of the ingathering is complete. Eight means a new beginning, a new time, a new season.

On the eighth day there was a special water pouring out ceremony. We don't explicitly see in Scripture that on the eighth day there was to be a water libation but it was done. It was a tradition that was followed by the priesthood in the temple. We do see this time in Scripture as John chapter 7 tells a story concerning Yeshua and the feast of tabernacles.

John 7:37-38 KJV
(37) In the last day, that great day of the feast, Jesus stood and cried, saying, If any man thirst, let him come unto me, and drink.
(38) He that believeth on me, as the scripture hath said, out of his belly shall flow rivers of living water.

What is the last day? What is the great day of the feast? Is this just for that specific day or is Yeshua speaking prophetically toward the literal last day, that great day? In this case, He is at the temple during the feast of tabernacles, as we saw earlier in John chapter 7.

What was it that Yeshua said on this last great day (the eighth day, the new beginning)? Come to Him and He will give you rivers of living water. The river of LIFE.
The river of life flows from the throne of God through His holy temple and to the world through the hearts of men.

Ezekiel 47:1
Then he brought me back to the entrance of the house (temple), and I saw water flowing eastward from under the threshold of the house, for the house faced east. The water flowed down from under the right side of the house, south of the altar.

Revelation 22:1
Next the angel showed me the river of the water of life, sparkling like crystal, flowing from the throne of God and of the Lamb.

Revelation 21:1-4 KJV
(1) And I saw a new heaven and a new earth: for the first heaven and the first earth were passed away; and there was no more sea.
(2) And I John saw the holy city, new Jerusalem, coming down from God out of heaven, prepared as a bride adorned for her husband.
(3) And I heard a great voice out of heaven saying, Behold, the tabernacle of God is with men, and he will dwell with them, and they shall be his people, and God himself shall be with them, and be their God.
(4) And God shall wipe away all tears from their eyes; and there shall be no more death, neither sorrow, nor crying, neither shall there be any more pain: for the former things are passed away.

Why would Yeshua choose this day, the last great day, to cry out about living water? The water libation ceremony in the temple was being conducted at this time and they were praying that YHWH would send the rain (water, dew, life) at their appropriate time. There were many things that were going on during this feast of ingathering that made this the perfect time for such a statement from the Messiah.

During the feast of Sukkot; many offerings were brought. We read that seventy bulls were brought as offerings. An increase of offerings showed an increase of the desire of the people to be in the presence of God. There were additional lights that were lit in the temple. The lights from the temple could be seen anywhere around Jerusalem. You did not have to guess where the temple was, you could find it by the radiant light emanating from it so that all could see it. The temple was illuminated by four gold lampstands. The lampstands were stationed in the Court of Women (one of the areas on the temple mount) and each lampstand had on it four golden bowls.

There was a water pouring out ceremony at the altar. For the ceremony a gold vessel of water was filled from the pool of Siloam and was then taken to the altar. Another gold vessel was filled with wine. Both of these vessels would be poured out together. The water and the wine would flow down a conduit and would flow to the Kidron brook.

During this process the priest would be praying for YHWH to provide the people with water, rain and life at the appropriately needed time. The water and wine flowing is a picture of the water and the blood that would be shed by our Messiah Yeshua.

John 19:33-34
(33) But when they came to Jesus, and saw that he was dead already, they brake not his legs:
(34) But one of the soldiers with a spear pierced his side, and forthwith came there out blood and water.

I will say again that this ceremony was a tradition. But it should also be said that Yeshua chose to reveal Himself to the people during this tradition. Look at John 7:37 and 38 again.

John 7:37-38
- (37) In the last day,
- that great day of the feast,
- Jesus stood and cried, saying,
- If any man thirst, let him come unto me, and drink.
- (38) He that believeth on me, as the scripture hath said, out of his belly shall flow rivers of living water.

This is a picture of the last great day after all has been gathered and after the wheat and tares are separated. We will all come and feast with our Lord and Savior at the great wedding supper of the Lamb. It will be a new beginning for all mankind and we will be forever dwelling with our King.

Revelation 19:5-9 KJV

(5) And a voice came out of the throne, saying, Praise our God, all ye his servants, and ye that fear him, both small and great.

(6) And I heard as it were the voice of a great multitude, and as the voice of many waters, and as the voice of mighty thunderings, saying, Alleluia: for the Lord God omnipotent reigneth.

(7) Let us be glad and rejoice, and give honour to him: for the marriage of the Lamb is come, and his wife hath made herself ready.

(8) And to her was granted that she should be arrayed in fine linen, clean and white: for the fine linen is the righteousness of saints.

(9) And he saith unto me, Write, Blessed are they which are called unto the marriage supper of the Lamb. And he saith unto me, These are the true sayings of God.

In the process of the feasts we see our walk with the Father. We have seen that we are betrothed to Yeshua our Messiah. We are the bride, He is the Bridegroom. What we didn't see was how these were revealed to us in the feasts and appointed times of the LORD. When Yeshua came and spoke of the wedding feasts and coming for the bride, it was not a new concept. It was known that we are betrothed to Him.

This is just a further revealing of how these Scriptures that we may not have seen applies to us and how they prophetically speak to us.

Matthew 22:1-14 KJV

(1) And Jesus answered and spake unto them again by parables, and said,

(2) The kingdom of heaven is like unto a certain king, which made a marriage for his son,

(3) And sent forth his servants to call them that were bidden to the wedding: and they would not come.

(4) Again, he sent forth other servants, saying, Tell them which are bidden, Behold, I have prepared my dinner: my oxen and my fatlings are killed, and all things are ready: come unto the marriage.

(5) But they made light of it, and went their ways, one to his farm, another to his merchandise:

(6) And the remnant took his servants, and entreated them spitefully, and slew them.

(7) But when the king heard thereof, he was wroth: and he sent forth his armies, and destroyed those murderers, and burned up their city.

(8) Then saith he to his servants, The wedding is ready, but they which were bidden were not worthy.

(9) Go ye therefore into the highways, and as many as ye shall find, bid to the marriage.

(10) So those servants went out into the highways, and gathered together all as many as they found, both bad and good: and the wedding was furnished with guests.

(11) And when the king came in to see the guests, he saw there a man which had not on a wedding garment:

(12) And he saith unto him, Friend, how camest thou in hither not having a wedding garment? And he was speechless.

(13) Then said the king to the servants, Bind him hand and foot, and take him away, and cast him into outer darkness; there shall be weeping and gnashing of teeth.

(14) For many are called, but few are chosen.

Matthew 25:1-13 KJV

(1) Then shall the kingdom of heaven be likened unto ten virgins, which took their lamps, and went forth to meet the bridegroom.

(2) And five of them were wise, and five were foolish.

(3) They that were foolish took their lamps, and took no oil with them:

(4) But the wise took oil in their vessels with their lamps.

(5) While the bridegroom tarried, they all slumbered and slept.

(6) And at midnight there was a cry made, Behold, the bridegroom cometh; go ye out to meet him.

(7) Then all those virgins arose, and trimmed their lamps.

(8) And the foolish said unto the wise, Give us of your oil; for our lamps are gone out.

(9) But the wise answered, saying, Not so; lest there be not enough for us and you: but go ye rather to them that sell, and buy for yourselves.

(10) And while they went to buy, the bridegroom came; and they that were ready went in with him to the marriage: and the door was shut.

(11) Afterward came also the other virgins, saying, Lord, Lord, open to us.

(12) But he answered and said, Verily I say unto you, I know you not.

(13) Watch therefore, for ye know neither the day nor the hour wherein the Son of man cometh.

John 2:1-2 KJV

(1) And the third day there was a marriage in Cana of Galilee; and the mother of Jesus was there:

(2) And both Jesus was called, and his disciples, to the marriage.

Yeshua and His disciples are the ones called to the Marriage!
Are you a disciple?
Will you be called to the great wedding feast?
Even so, LORD come!
Come Yeshua, to a bride prepared for her groom.

To review the fall moedim in Leviticus 23;
-YOM TERUAH
-YOM KIPPUR
-SUKKOT

YOM TERUAH
• THE TRUMPET SHOUTS
• TO AWAKEN THE SAINTS
• TO CALL ALL TO REPENTANCE

YOM KIPPUR
• Atonement / Judgment – is the blood applied?

SUKKOT
• A NEW BEGINNING
• YHWH WILL DWELL IN THE MIDST OF THE CAMP WITH HIS PEOPLE
• Time to dwell with the Father for eternity starting with this wedding feast of the Lamb!

As we have gone through this journey of exploring the appointed times, Moedim, I hope that we are awakened to the relevance of these times in our lives. There are some things in Scripture that may be difficult to comprehend. Sometimes we may struggle to see how certain aspects of Scripture apply to us as believers. That doesn't mean that the Word of YHWH doesn't apply to us. It does however mean that we may not understand certain areas of Scripture. We are told by Paul that all Scripture is good for us to seek for understanding.

2 Timothy 3:16-17
(16) All scripture *is* given by inspiration of God, and *is* profitable for doctrine, for reproof, for correction, for instruction in righteousness:
(17) That the man of God may be perfect, thoroughly furnished unto all good works.

By looking into the appointed times and seasons, along with the understanding of how they were given, we see another aspect of our LORD and Savior that we may not have seen or understood before. We can see how these times were, and still are, prophetic in nature. We can see and understand how these times reveal our Messiah. We can also see what Yeshua, our Messiah, came to do for us by looking into these appointed times.

The LORD will reveal Himself to those who are looking for Him. He has chosen to use His Word to do so. The Word works together with the Ruach HaKodesh (Holy Spirit) to reveal the Father to His people. As we walk in the Word we will grow in our understanding of it. Sometimes we just have to do something in order to understand it. We have heard the expression that hindsight is 20/20. So it is with the moedim of the LORD. As we walk in them we come to understand them. As we seek to observe them in faith, we will realize how they enrich our lives and our service to our loving, heavenly Father who just wants to be in relationship with His people.

To recap, the moedim of the LORD are,
- Shabbat
- Passover
- Unleavened bread
- Firstfruits
- Shavuot
- Yom Teruah
- Yom Kippur
- Sukkot

A recap of the moedim by their meaning would be,
• ENTER HIS REST – A DECISION OF COVENANT
• BY THE BLOOD YOU HAVE BEEN SAVED, REDEEMED AND CALLED OUT
• NOW EAT ONLY A SINLESS LIFE
• TO BE A PART OF THE GATHERING OF THE FIRSTFRUITS
• WHERE YHWH GIVES HIS WORD AND SPIRIT- NOW GO HARVEST

•WE ARE NOW EQUIPPED TO AWAKEN THE SAINTS AND CALL ALL TO REPENTANCE
• SO WE ALL CAN HAVE ATONEMENT
• WHERE WE ENTER IN FOR THE GREAT WEDDING FEAST, TO DWELL WITH YHWH FOR EVER ON THAT LAST GREAT DAY.

Revelation 22:17-21

(17) And the Spirit and the bride say, Come. And let him that heareth say, Come. And let him that is athirst come. And whosoever will, let him take the water of life freely.

(18) For I testify unto every man that heareth the words of the prophecy of this book, If any man shall add unto these things, God shall add unto him the plagues that are written in this book:

(19) And if any man shall take away from the words of the book of this prophecy, God shall take away his part out of the book of life, and out of the holy city, and *from* the things which are written in this book.

(20) He which testifieth these things saith, Surely I come quickly. Amen. Even so, come, Lord Jesus.

(21) The grace of our Lord Jesus Christ *be* with you all. Amen.

Bo Yeshua,
Come Yeshua

Amen.

BIBLIOGRAPHY

Complete Jewish Bible (CJB)

Scripture quotations are taken from the *Complete Jewish Bible*, copyright 1998 by David H. Stern. Published by Jewish New Testament Publications, Inc. www.messianicjewish.net/jntp. Distributed by Messianic Jewish Resources. www.messianicjewish.net. All rights reserved. Used by permission.

King James Bible (KJV)

Quotes are from the 1769 King James Version of the Holy Bible (also known as the Authorized Version)

Jewish Publication Society (JPS)

The Holy Scriptures (Old Testament) by the Jewish Publication Society (1917)

The Hebrew Names Version (HNV)

The Hebrew Names Version of the World English Bible (WEB) and is in public domain

Young's Literal Translation (YLT)

Young's Literal Translation of the Holy Bible by J.N. Young, 1862, 1898 (Author of the Young's Analytical Concordance)

Revised Version (RV)

1885 Revised Version

Dictionary

Noah Webster's 1828 Dictionary of American English

Concordance

Strong's Hebrew and Greek Dictionaries, Strong's exhaustive concordance by James Strong, S.T.D., LL.D., 1890

Check out other books by

Dr. David E. Jones

Famine!

Walking In Blessing In A Time Of Famine

ISBN – 978-0-9841613-0-0

Look it up on Amazon.com or
Barnesandnoble.com

Ruach Ministries International

P.O. Box 6370

Brandon FL 33508

To learn more about the Hebraic Heritage of the Christian Faith, or for more teachings and resources write us. Or you can visit our website

www.ruachonline.com

or email me

djones@ruachonline.com

Numbers 6:24-26 HNV

'The LORD bless you, and keep you. (25) The LORD make his face to shine on you, and be gracious to you. (26) The LORD lift up his face toward you, and give you shalom.'

LaVergne, TN USA
03 April 2011
222600LV00002B/1/P